# THE LINCOLN ENIGMA

## Gettysburg Civil War Institute Books

Published by Oxford University Press
Edited by Gabor S. Boritt

*Why the Confederacy Lost*

*Lincoln, the War President: The Gettysburg Lectures*

*Lincoln's Generals*

*War Comes Again: Comparative Vistas
on the Civil War and World War II*

*Why the Civil War Came*

*The Gettysburg Nobody Knows*

*Jefferson Davis's Generals*

*The Lincoln Enigma*

## Other books by Gabor S. Boritt

*Lincoln and the Economics of the American Dream*

*The Lincoln Image: Abraham Lincoln and the Popular Print*
(with Harold Holzer and Mark E. Neely, Jr.)

*The Confederate Image*
(with Mark E. Neely, Jr. and Harold Holzer)

*The Historian's Lincoln: Pseudohistory, Psychohistory, and History*
(with Norman O. Forness)

*The Historian's Lincoln, Rebuttals:
What the University Press Would Not Print*

*Of the People, By the People, For the People
and Other Quotations from Abraham Lincoln*
(with Jakob B. Boritt, Deborah R. Huso, and Peter C. Vermilyea)

# THE LINCOLN ENIGMA

## The Changing Faces of an American Icon

EDITED BY
**Gabor Boritt**

ESSAYS BY

Gabor Boritt
Douglas L. Wilson
Jean H. Baker
Gerald J. Prokopowicz
David Herbert Donald
Allen C. Guelzo
William C. Harris
Robert V. Bruce
Gabor Boritt and Harold Holzer

OXFORD
UNIVERSITY PRESS

# OXFORD
UNIVERSITY PRESS

Oxford  New York
Auckland  Bangkok  Buenos Aires
Cape Town  Chennai  Dar es Salaam  Delhi  Hong Kong  Istanbul
Karachi  Kolkata  Kuala Lumpur  Madrid  Melbourne  Mexico City  Mumbai
Nairobi  São Paulo  Shanghai  Singapore  Taipei  Tokyo  Toronto

and an associated company in Berlin

First published by Oxford University Press, Inc., 2001
198 Madison Avenue, New York, New York 10016
First issued as an Oxford University Press paperback, 2002

Oxford is a registered trademark of Oxford University Press

Library of Congress Cataloging-in-Publication Data

The Lincoln enigma / edited by Gabor Boritt
p.  cm.
Includes bibliographical references and index.
ISBN 0-19-514458-9 (cloth)    ISBN 0-19-515626-9 (pbk.)
1. Lincoln, Abraham, 1809–1865.   2. Lincoln, Abraham, 1809–1865—Influence.
3. Presidents—United States—Biography.   I. Boritt, G. S., 1940–
E457.8 L.737    2001
973.7'092—dc21
[B]    00-051647

1  3  5  7  9  8  6  4  2

Printed in the United States of America
on acid-free paper

FOR
TINA, LINDA, MARTI,
DIANE AND DAN
WITH THANKS

B. BORITT '00

MARRIED WITH CHILDREN Mixed media by Beowulf Boritt

Who was he? This enigma? People ask persistent questions and answers take both boldness and great care. Were Mary and Abraham happily married? Or did they live in barely bearable discord? Was he straight or gay? Racist or emancipator? On the verge of madness? Military genius or daydreamer about field command? Defender of the Constitution or almost a dictator? Maker of peace or demanding unconditional surrender? What did he believe? Was there life after death? Modern historians speak in this book and in the end so do modern artists: Picasso and company.

# Contents

By late June it is usually warm,
even hot in Gettysburg.
In the night at our farm,
the fireflies glow in the dark,
fleeting specks illuminating the woods and
turning Marsh Creek into a pageant.
In the daytime along the side of the road,
orange tiger lilies proclaim their eternal message.
My heart overflows;
it is time to see old friends again,
time to make new ones.
it is the time for the Gettysburg Civil War Institute.

*Gabor Boritt*

# Introduction

As the new millennium dawned at the Green Parrot in Key West, the Rocking Jakes played loud and the crowd roared and swayed. A watering place for locals, its New Year's patrons were happy. Key West is the southernmost town in the United States. Next to the pinball machine, "Revenge from Mars," above the jukebox, close to the pictures of the Beatles and Muhammed Ali, hung a large portrait of Abraham Lincoln. Nobody looked at him, no more than at other parts of the decor. Lincoln was safe and forgotten—an American security blanket.

At the Ebenezer Baptist Church in Atlanta, where the Rev. Dr. Martin Luther King, Jr., had preached, the mood, as always, was prayerfully solemn.

The millennium dawns at Key West. Photo: Jake Boritt

So it was in many black churches across the country on this Emancipation Day or Jubilee Day. The celebrations "represent the real Fourth of July or Independence Day for African Americans," explained an NAACP leader. "The first one, July 4, 1776, did not apply to us."[1]

In Gettysburg the revelers congregated in the town square. The cold made breaths steam, but nothing could dampen the palpable happiness. Locals mixed with visitors, some from lands faraway. Pickpockets worked the crowd. Close to midnight a beautiful young woman wandered out of the hotel in the square, her white wedding dress cut low, bare arms raised, champagne in hand. She danced. Then the spectacular fireworks started heralding the new millennium.

In one corner of the square named after him stood Abe Lincoln, barely on the curb, an arm on the back of a tourist. Nearly six foot four, an exact life-size bronze, his face based on a life mask (a plaster cast taken by sculptor Clark Mills in 1865), his hands based on a plaster cast also made from life in 1860, his black suit a perfect copy of the one he wore to Ford's Theatre, his hat, too, authentic, down to the label inside it, his boots sized to the outline of his feet drawn by a Pennsylvania shoemaker in 1864. Seward Johnson's sculpture stood there as the twentieth century ended with fireworks and noise, readily ignored by all, for he was so much part of the place.

At the local college's beautiful modern library, in the spacious dark of the apse, slept an exhibit of Sam Fink's 15 watercolors, each containing Lincoln and a dazzling calligraphy of the 272 words of the Address. Dark of the night now. But the students would return, the lights would come on; and the exhibit, "The Gettysburg Address is Alive and Well," would stay up through the year 2000. As the new millennium dawned, Lincoln was alive and well.

A few weeks earlier, Ohio State University's women's rugby team, visiting the nation's capital for a game, wished to be noticed; so a dozen members went to the Lincoln Memorial and posed topless. A *Washington Post* photographer caught the action. In the brouhaha that followed someone observed that the Memorial should be remembered for "Martin Luther King, Jr., not for the breasts of the Ohio State women's rugby team."[2] But the women athletes, with a $600 yearly budget, wanted more equality, and turned to Lincoln.

Gays wanting the same did the same by trying to recruit him posthumously. Larry Kramer, playwright and gay activist firebrand, claimed to have discovered the diary and letters of Joshua Speed, Lincoln's intimate friend, which proved that they had a long affair, not a long friendship. Almost certainly this is a hoax, but it has accomplished its purpose: having the country, indeed the world, contemplate the possibility that its greatest son was gay. As

2000 dawned the Memorial got its play, too, with some 1,000 gay people holding a mock marriage ceremony around it. And the first notable Lincoln book of the new century, Jan Morris's *Lincoln: A Foreigner's Quest* from Simon & Schuster appears to suggest a gay young man. Its author used to be a man.

David Herbert Donald, the author of the Lincoln Prize–winning, best-selling biography, *Lincoln* (1995), found during his book tour the question, "was Lincoln gay," the most commonly asked. I myself have been queried about his sexual orientation, from as far away as ABC of Australia. In fact it is possible to find evidence that to twenty-first-century readers might suggest homoerotic behavior. Historian Robert H. Wiebe has argued that Lincoln found security in a male dominated political world, that he harbored a deep emotional attachment to male fraternity. He was a "man's man." Of course male bonding is not the same as homosexuality. As a young man Lincoln had shared for years the bed of his closest friend, Speed, and later riding the circuit as a lawyer he shared the beds of countless others—as did most everyone else. Anyone familiar with the ways of poor societies would find nothing unusual about such practices.

But Lincoln's male bonding went beyond what circumstances dictated. If we believe a Union officer's recollections about the scuttlebutt that went around in the company that guarded the president at Washington's Soldiers' Home, the summer White House where he spent a large portion of his time, we have this:

> Captain [David V.] Derickson, in particular, advanced so far in the President's confidence and esteem that, in Mrs. Lincoln's absence, he frequently spent the night at his cottage, sleeping in the same bed with him, and—it is said—making use of His excellency's night-shirts! Thus began an intimacy which continued unbroken until the following spring. . . .

In November 1862, Lincoln wrote that "Captain Derrickson [*sic*] . . . and his Company are very agreeable to me; and while it is deemed proper for any guard to remain, none would be more satisfactory to me than Cpt. D and his company."[3] So it was to be, the Company remained the presidential guard until the end of the war, but its Captain was appointed provost marshal in Pennsylvania the following spring.

Where does this leave us? Pretty much where Wiebe put us. Lincoln strongly bonded with men but what may suggest homosexuality in our time most likely did not so much as occur to most people in his time. There is no evidence that it did to Lincoln. In history, context is all-important and the first

*Gay Icon* by Jeff Crosby. The artwork first appeared in Salon.com, at *http:// www.salon.com*. An online version remains in the Salon archives. Reprinted with permission.

duty of the historian is to understand the past in the terms understood by those who lived that past.*

Yes, Lincoln is alive and mostly well, and, once again, lots of people want a piece of him. But not everyone. A professor took a taxi through the black neighborhood of a big midwestern city, and carried on an amiable conversation with the driver. But then he was asked what he did for a living? Teach Abraham Lincoln. The white driver stopped on the spot and ordered his passenger to "get the hell out." Look around you. See how you'll do. On the other side of the spectrum, Minister Louis Farrakhan thinks Lincoln was one awful racist honky and a sworn enemy of blacks. An *Ebony* magazine editor proposed that much in 1968 and expanded the ahistorical hobby horse into a 650-page book in 2000.

But at Tiannamen Square when a lone student stood before a column of tanks, the other students supporting him had Lincoln's words on their lips: "of the people, by the people, for the people." Uncomfortably enough, when the president of China, Jiang Zemin, came calling on the United States, he, too,

---

* I am indebted to Matthew Pinsker for sharing his discovery of the Derickson material that, for the first time, puts the president in bed with someone other than his wife.

cited Lincoln. So did Pope John Paul II during his visit. When General Colin Powell declined to run for the presidency of the United States, he pointed with reverence to only one name. Earlier, in Tehran, before the revolution was stolen, Lincoln's words appeared in blood red on the city's walls. And the Republic of Togo saw fit to greet the new millennium with a stamp of the American hero.

Harry Hahn, a 67-year-old Lincoln presenter—one of a group of several dozen Lincoln look-and-dress-alikes who perform around the country—met his maker as Mr. Lincoln before elementary school students in Gettysburg, in February 2000. About the same time, as Cuba and the United States sparred over the fate of a young boy, Elián González, back home in his small town his best friend waited for him: Lincoln Anthony. On the lighter side, "The Stinkin' Lincolns," a five-man rock band dressed up as Abes, continued to perform. The armed bandit known to the Maryland police as "Dishonest Abe" robbed nine stores "disguised" as the president, before being captured. And according to my latest search engine scouring the World Wide Web, *Abe Lincoln's Air Force* is at last flying. About time.

Folksinger Ray Owen sings his tune:

Lincoln—the man, the car, the tunnel
My how in time your name has grown
Lincoln—the diner, the penny, the highway
And that building with the great big beautiful dome[4]

The whole country rides Abraham Lincoln, as the epilogue to this book helps illustrate visually. Scholars do, too. And well they should. The story stays alive, and though some would stuff him and mount him, he won't let us. It is a cliché by now yet still true that history is a never-ending conversation between the past and the present, and among Lincoln scholars the goal still is—some will call it anachronistic—to find the truth. So it is good that our cab stops and we are forced to get out and take stock.

Chapter 1, "The Voyage to Linconia," looks at the most discussed serious Lincoln subject among both young people and African Americans who talk about such matters. For a century and more Lincoln was "The Great Emancipator," the American saint, but during the last generation some, perhaps many, came to think of him as just another "honky." He had issued the Emancipation Proclamation but also used the "n" word and proposed a constitutional amendment to colonize black people abroad, perhaps in Africa. "Did He Dream of a Lily-White America?"

The problem of slavery and its corollary, race, grew into the paramount issue of the nineteenth century and it helped lead to the Civil War. Lincoln, in turn, came to believe that the nation's survival depended on emancipation. He had always hated slavery, but white prejudice seemed irremediable. He must have shared some of it himself: this was the mid-nineteenth century. On a few occasions he could not avoid being goaded into admitting that, while he opposed slavery, he did not favor civil rights for blacks and had a dim view of the future of race relations. If it were impossible for blacks to be free, equal, and prosperous in the United States, the government should help make it possible elsewhere. For the sake of whites as well as blacks, Lincoln came to support black colonization.

He managed to avoid directly confronting the utter improbability of transporting four and a half million working people abroad, 15 percent of the population. The mental processes that allowed the down-to-earth president to advocate such a road can be understood via modern psychoanalytic theory, but common sense itself provides an explanation. The country had to embrace black freedom to survive physically and spiritually. The white majority opposed emancipation unless accompanied by colonization. Lincoln went along, refusing to see, for a time, that colonization was a "lullaby." Chapter 1 quotes Shakespeare's *King Lear:* "I have no way, therefore want no eyes."

Chapter 1 also shows that Lincoln's colonization policy was aimed not at blacks but whites. But if he used a chimera to advance emancipation, barely below the surface he frequently betrayed his disbelief in the scheme. Once emancipation was in place, he quickly abandoned the notion. Instead he turned to making black people into soldiers and citizens. That, in any case, was what the vast majority of African Americans desired by then, inspired in part by the president. Starting to advocate limited black franchise for Louisiana by the spring of 1864, Lincoln explained "they would probably help, in some trying time to come, to keep the jewel of liberty within the family of freedom."[5]

Colonization came to nothing and chapter 2 takes a step back to "Young Man Lincoln." In it Douglas L. Wilson points to questions all young people face: "Who am I?," "Who do I want to be?," perhaps even "What is my destiny?" From early on Lincoln was a person with a "wish and will to be different." He also hoped to accomplish "great" things, to do good that would be remembered. Doubts beset him, however, about his own powers and about his destiny. Suffering at times from depression and raised in fatalism, he saw "dark forces within him [self] that he could not control, that could, in fact, take control of *him* and draw him under."

Through a deep reading of evidence, Wilson finds a Lincoln who may have even worried about his own sanity. Back in the 1820s, a fortune-favored friend of his Indiana youth, Matthew Gentry, had gone suddenly raving mad. Young man Lincoln had snuck out at night to listen to his friend's moaning. In the 1840s, he returned to the scene, found Gentry, and wrote a poem about him. Its first stanza:

> But here is an object more of dread
>> Than ought the grave contain—
> A human form with reason fled,
>> While wretched life remains.

Lincoln himself survived and triumphed. And in the White House he reminded another old friend, Kentucky's Joshua Speed, of his youthful anxieties and longings, and explained how meaningful it was to do good with the Emancipation Proclamation. "We frequently hear," Wilson concludes, "that true champions . . . take no counsel of their fears. These are, indeed, heroic qualities and well beyond the capabilities of most of us. In this light, it seems important to recognize that Abraham Lincoln, our greatest national hero, was apparently not such a person."

In chapter 3, Jean H. Baker turns to marriage, one of the most controversial subjects of turn of the century Lincoln scholarship. Even as feminist historians reshape the scholarly landscape, the discussion of the Lincoln marriage grows more heated and more complex. Nor does it stay within the confines of academe. In the mid-1980s novelist Gore Vidal promoted his best-selling novel *Lincoln* by appearing to suggest on various talk shows and the like that Lincoln had syphilis, had infected his wife, and caused the early death of three of his four children. In 1998, during the Clinton soap opera, a story of unfaithful presidents ran through the media and listed Lincoln among them. Lack of evidence mattered not. If in the nineteenth century, and well beyond, the Lincoln marriage was idealized—for Americans wanted a happy family in their White House—in our time, in an Age of Divorce and changing sexual mores, people still want their Lincoln on their side. He remains the attractive fellow.

Much of the scholarly discussion of the Lincoln marriage inevitably relies on at times conflicting reminiscences. "Mary and Abraham: A Marriage" goes beyond that and anchors the subject in the sociological literature of the nineteenth century American courtship, wedding, and marriage. "Marriage is a noose," Baker begins ironically, and the reader quickly realizes that, for once, the largely male domain of Lincoln scholarship is leavened by a woman's viewpoint. Instead of a hellcat preying on her husband, Baker finds a very interesting woman who was very important to Lincoln's success in life. Their marriage followed the route of so many other middle-class marriages of the time, with its separate spheres for men and women. It had its rough times, but its bonds, coming from "sex, parenting, and politics," proved strong. "Mary, Mary *we* are elected," said Lincoln, as he rushed home with the news of the presidential election in 1860.

Then they were in the White House, the war came and did not go well for the Union. Lincoln agonized about the lack of military success. "If I had gone up there, I could have whipped them myself," he exclaimed after the Battle of Gettysburg. The commander in chief had fervently hoped that the great battle would at last end the bloody war. Instead, the defeated Robert E. Lee skillfully disengaged his Army of Northern Virginia, retreated to the Potomac, stood his ground, and finally escaped back to Virginia. "My dear general," Lincoln wrote to George Gordon Meade, his commander in the field, "I do not believe you appreciate the magnitude of the misfortune involved in Lee's escape. He was within your easy grasp, and to have closed upon him would . . . have ended the war. As it is, the war will be prolonged indefinitely. If you could not safely attack Lee last Monday [in Pennsylvania], how can you possibly do so South of the river. . . . Your golden opportunity is gone, and I am distressed immeasurably because of it."[6] Lincoln never sent the letter, but the aftermath of Gettysburg left him in tears.

In chapter 4 Gerald J. Prokopowicz takes quite seriously Lincoln's notion of taking field command. After all, he spoke in a like vein at other times, too, and even acted on his words in a modest way. Also, social norms of the day expected the war leader to show his own physical courage. But what might have happened had Lincoln taken to the field? How would he have done? The would-have-beens of history are many, and few are the historians with the courage—or foolhardiness—to take them on. Prokopowicz faces the challenge squarely and ventures forth with an original assessment.

Chapter 5 by David Herbert Donald compares the commanders in chief of the United States and the Confederate States. The constitutions of the two republics defined the war powers of the president with identical language and the similarities in how Lincoln and Davis conceived of their jobs as general-in-chief is "striking." Their strategic plans amounted to "mirror images." Both got involved in detailed military planning and kept control of the selection of generals. Both considered taking the field of battle. Both received scathing denunciations, and the reader will be hard put to identify from a sample list which was aimed at whom.

But the contrasts turned out to be more important than the similarities. Donald notes but does not emphasize differences in personalities: one quick to take offense; the other conciliatory. Instead he focuses on the different ways the two presidents understood their war powers. Lincoln defended the United States by going well beyond "any express constitutional authorization or any legislation of Congress," his actions ranging from the suspension of the writ of *habeas corpus* to emancipation. Davis purposefully contrasted himself to such actions of the administration in Washington and allowed his road to be "negatively defined by the steps Lincoln took." Refusing to use his war powers

broadly, Davis failed to curb sufficiently "the dissent and disloyalty that signally contributed to the collapse of the Confederacy." Donald does not follow
David Potter's famed 1959 Gettysburg lecture, which proposed that had the
warring republics exchanged presidents, "the Confederacy might have won its
independence."[7] But it is clear who was the better commander in chief.

Chapter 6 focuses sharply on questions of liberty, war, and the Constitution.
Many appear to believe that to save the American Union, Lincoln sacrificed the
fundamental law of the land. Some decry this destruction of liberty by a would-
be dictator. Others praise what they see as the justified subordination of a cum-
bersome, perhaps antiquated document to the noble ideas of the Declaration of
Independence and a commitment to equality. Both sides see a "closet revolutionary" and, Allen C. Guelzo argues, both are wrong. Did Lincoln "regard the Constitution as a wax nose, to be reshaped according to his own egalitarian idealism," or did he yield to his supposed desire to be a dictator, Guelzo asks.

His rousing "No!" shows a thinker who, from an early age on, displayed a
deep regard for the Constitution, whether pertaining to technical language or
original intent. As for Jefferson's Declaration, it "was the central statement of
Lincoln's political idealism." It buttressed his hatred of slavery, but it did not
take away from his reverence for the fundamental law. Rather than seeing a conflict between the two, Lincoln saw them as complementary. When war forced
him toward extra-Constitutional remedies, he limited these to military necessity
and sought careful legal advice. Most strikingly, in the middle of the horror of
civil war, he ran for reelection and, at least at times, expected to lose. Said he afterwards, "The election was a necessity. We cannot have free government without elections; and if the rebellion could force us to forego, or postpone a national
election, it might fairly claim to have conquered and ruined us. . . ."[8]

In chapter 7 William C. Harris challenges the past generation's orthodoxy
about the kind of peace Lincoln looked for at the end of the war. The fortunate
initials of his most popular general, U.S. Grant, victor at Fort Donelson and, it
seemed, ever after, metamorphosed into "Unconditional Surrender" Grant,
and by 1864 many assigned the general in chief's sobriquet to the president as
a policy. Historians, too, in recent decades have spoken about how winning the
election that year created a mandate to demand the unconditional surrender of
the Confederacy. Harris argues, however, that Lincoln never intended to impose such harsh, radical terms on the defeated foe.

He was reelected on a platform of Union and Emancipation, and that is what
he hoped to achieve in peace, using a lenient reconstruction plan for the post-war
South that relied on Southern Unionists. Unconditional surrender might create anarchy and would derail "a Union of hearts and hands as well as of States." And so
in February of 1865, at the Hampton Roads, Virginia, meeting with Confederate

peace commissioners, Lincoln reaffirmed his generosity, going so far as to favor substantial monetary compensation for slave owners. (His cabinet would have none of it.) In the waning days of the war, meeting with his generals on the *River Queen* at City Point, Virginia, in essence Lincoln told Grant, Sherman, and Admiral David Dixon Porter to "let 'em up easy." After hundreds of thousands of deaths, he seemed almost childishly anxious to prevent one last battle. "Must more blood be shed!" he was remembered to say, "can not this last bloody battle be avoided?" He wanted the Confederate army to go home and take up a life of peace. He desired no punishment, even for the leaders. Northern soldiers sang about hanging Jeff Davis on "a sour apple tree"; Lincoln hoped he would escape, "unbeknownst to me." The president worked hard for the Thirteenth Amendment to create Constitutional support for the Emancipation Proclamation. "A King's cure for all," he called it. Together with it he also wanted a return to loyalty to the United States by all. He wanted no more. He wanted peace.

Lincoln believed his cause to be just, but the cost was horrifying. "War, at best, is terrible," he said in 1864, "and this war of ours . . . is one of the most terrible. . . . It has carried mourning to almost every home, until it can almost be said that the 'heavens are hung in black.'"[9] The war planted death all around him. But as Robert V. Bruce shows in chapter 8, death was Lincoln's old, lifelong acquaintance. Throughout the nineteenth century and earlier, too—well before the Civil War—death held an intimate part in the life of Americans. This was ever so much more true of Abraham Lincoln. "The Riddle of Death" played a central role in his thoughts.

On the eve of his presidency, in an autobiography, Lincoln wrote in a matter-of-fact way that "in his tenth year he was kicked by a horse, and apparently killed for a time." He used humor at times to deal with death. But in that same year his mother's aunt and uncle had died of the "milk sickness" (brucellosis), and then his mother died, too, all within a matter of days. A brother he never knew died before Lincoln was born. His other sibling, sister Sarah, died in childbirth when he was 18 and she barely older. When his sweetheart, Ann Rutledge, died, we know that Lincoln fell into a deep depression in response. Lincoln and death were intimate, indeed.

If in the frontier society of his youth the end of life was looked upon as a release from toil and hardship, his own reaction displayed uncommon emotion. His favorite poems, songs, and dramas focused on the subject. In 1846, the future author of the Gettysburg Address could write that "I would give all I am worth, and go into debt," to be able to author an indifferent poem by little known Scottish poet William Knox. Its message: life is short, "A flash of lightning, a break of the wave." If around Lincoln peaceful pictures of heaven eased the pain for most people, his lawyerlike mind rejected such visions. And yet, the prospect of oblivion terrified him. So he turned to another defense: to have life after death one needed to survive in the memory of people. "If Lincoln did not believe that those who died for the Union would afterward live in a blissful Valhalla," Bruce writes, he could at least believe that, as he said at Gettysburg, they would live in everlasting memory." As for himself, he helped save the Union, and, as he told his friend Speed, with the Emancipation Proclamation "my fondest hopes will be realized."

In an epilogue to this book, Harold Holzer and I look at how Lincoln lives in modern art. "Modern" is a controversial term, and chapter 9 begins somewhat arbitrarily, at the great trauma of the twentieth century (comparable to a degree to the Civil War): the Depression and World War II. "Lincoln in 'Modern' Art" moves all the way to the dawn of the new millennium. "Art," too, is a controversial term, perhaps undefinable. This chapter focuses on painters and sculptors, but it takes note of folk art, commercial art, postage stamps, caricature, film, televison, and the World Wide Web. In the process it turns up a treasure trove of Lincoln art—an American icon throbbing with life. As Holzer and I quote Picasso's words about Lincoln, here is "real American elegance."

One of the works included in the modern art portfolio is *Lincoln and Ravens*, part of *The Columbus Suit* created by Carl Beam as the country moved toward the 1992 quincentenary of the European discovery of America (see photo on p. 191). Beam, who continues to work on the theme, was raised on a reservation with an Ojibway mother and a European-American father. Not surprisingly, his work speaks of both the great achievements and the great tragedies of the "discovery." His *Lincoln and Ravens*, a photo emulsion steel engraving, hangs as the centerpiece of a permanent exhibition at Gettysburg College, in a large room where the faculty meets and where distinguished visitors at times speak. The work testifies that Lincoln, as a central symbol of America, carries on his shoulders the glory of this nation—and sometimes also the burden of its sins.[10]

In Native American history, Lincoln is not a heroic figure. He is best known for his action in the aftermath of the Minnesota Sioux uprising of 1862. The Sioux had been "treatied" out of their lands, cheated and starved. One functionary announced that "if they are hungry let them eat grass or their own dung." Instead they revolted and killed some 350 of the enemy—men, women, and children—the largest number of casualties ever inflicted by Indians on whites in U.S. history. Some might find it easy to say that the whites got what they deserved.

The massacres (that is what they were to whites) took place as General Robert E. Lee invaded the North. The Indian uprising seemed to threaten the very existence of the United States. Already engaged in a lethal struggle with the slaveholding empire of the Confederacy at its front, the Minnesota Sioux attacked from the back. People whose sons and husbands fought in the Union army, away from home, were near revolt. Lincoln knew little about the Indians but sent west General John Pope of Second Bull Run fame (or lack thereof), where he put down the uprising harshly and followed it with military trials. Three hundred and three men received death sentences. Lincoln demanded full records of the cases and, also, the names of the real culprits. Pope responded by darkly threatening "indiscriminate" massacres by the populace if leniency were shown. The junior senator from Minnesota loudly seconded the opinion. Lincoln hoped to return the cases west for review, but was told that only he could exercise the pardon. He then went laboriously through the records, reducing the death list to 39. All but one died in the largest public execution in the history of the United States. More important to the majority at the time, Lincoln cheated the gallows of 264 Indians. He performed by far the largest act of executive clemency in American history. The outraged senator from Minnesota knew that there was no hope for the country "except in the death of the President and a new administration." The Sioux continued to die and suffer.

And we have Beam's *Lincoln and Ravens*. In Native American cultures the raven carries heavy symbolism. In various Indian religions it stands for both death and myth. The raven is "as capable of massive blunders as he is of glorious exploits."[11] But Beam also illustrates the complex way multiculturalism sometimes works and the cliché that truth is in the eye of the beholder. For Lincoln's admirers can find in Beam a heroic image, the chiseled face, the manly beauty, the symbol of freedom, unity, and of the American Dream of the right to rise. Reaching deeper, the black ravens might remind the viewer of the ending of slavery. Lincoln the Emancipator. Some will conjure up Edgar Allan Poe's lines—"Nevermore!"—and the horrors of slavery and of a brother's war.

Great Emancipator—Saver of Indian Lives—Indian Executioner. The United States at the end of the second millennium is perhaps the greatest of nations, the most prosperous in the history of humankind, powerful, ever more free, tolerant. Lincoln is her most fitting symbol. Beam's Lincoln allows for all that and also reminds us of the underside of American history and so tries to point to an even better future. As we enter the new millennium and note heartily that Lincoln is alive and well in American culture, we can also point to a future that beckons: *Lincoln and Ravens*.

*Autumn 2000*                                              *Gabor Boritt*
*Farm by the Ford*
*Gettysburg*

# Acknowledgments

For the first time since the establishment of the Civil War Institute, in the summer of 2000 a full session focused on Abraham Lincoln. As the millennium dawned, it seemed "altogether fitting and proper" to do this. More important, the renaissance of Lincoln studies during the 1990s demanded that we take a good look at the field and provide a platform for such grand old voices as those of Robert V. Bruce and David Herbert Donald, and also for the important new voices that emerged more recently. My thanks go to all the participants, both speakers and students, who played their vital parts well in the creation of *The Lincoln Enigma*.

Not all the chapters of this book were aired at this CWI session, though all had been delivered at Gettysburg College under its auspices. Bruce first gave "The Riddle of Death" as the R. Gerald McMurtry Lecture at the Lincoln Museum, Fort Wayne, Indiana, then revised it for the CWI. Gerald J. Prokopowicz in turn gave an earlier version of his thoughts on military fantasies at the Lincoln Forum. I am indebted to both institutions for permitting the second coming of these lectures at the CWI.

The Civil War Institute would be a very different place, much less of a place, without its good-natured staff. It deserves credit for creativity, backbreaking hard work, the long, long hours, competence, cheer, and friendship. Tina Grim leads this staff, the general commanding. Linda Marshall always has a good word and a smile, whatever calamity might await us. Diane Brennan is the effective frontline. Marti Shaw, my secretary for seven years, returned from retirement to help see this manuscript through publication. And friend to us all, Dan DePalma volunteers so much of his time that he earns his honored place in the group. This book is dedicated to them.

Student assistants, all Gettysburg College undergraduates, make the CWI offices a lively place and their help deserves recognition. At the 2000 session one and all excelled: Lindsay Boehme, Andrew Dangel, Kevin Luy, Kristine Meier, Amber Moulton, Theresa Obyle, Tim Parry, Jared Peatman, and

Kathryn Porch. In addition, Charles Dittrich, though a distinguished graduate of the College, returned to provide invaluable help. That Tim Parry has also volunteered his help with research during the school year, and specifically for this book, must be emphasized. Most important, Jared, my official research assistant, has become my reliable right hand—his contributions ranging from checking the accuracy of quotations to creative suggestions for improvements. I shudder to think that Tim and Jared will graduate with the class of 2002. But then, above all, I am a teacher.

David Thomas, now Gettysburg College, Class of 2004, served as a high school student intern at the CWI office, and contributed to the making of this book at an important moment.

Peter Vermilyea once again enriched the 2000 session for the CWI's high school student scholarship holders. William Hanna, in turn, with the assistance of Dennis Smyth, led the work for the teachers who had earned scholarships. All thirty of these students and teachers attended the CWI through the generosity of other participants. Many thanks go to the donors of these scholarships.

At Oxford University Press the association with Peter Ginna, my editor, continues happily. In addition Ruth Mannes and Rudy Faust have provided able support. The title of this book became *The Lincoln Enigma* through the good advice of the Oxford staff. The 300-some students of the 2000 CWI session voted overwhelmingly for this title and the 30 students of my Gilder Lehrman Institute Lincoln Seminar did so unanimously. My thanks to all the participants.

Then, as always, my thanks go to my family though now increasingly scattered. My wife, Liz, is always there with love and makes sure I do not get swallowed up in my work. Norse, busy with his lively career as a stage designer in New York, continues to take time to create the Pennsylvania Dutch dedication designs of the book. Jake, a budding documentary film maker, held many challenging conversations with me. He made me a better person and a better historian. College student Daniel, now in Africa working to save the cheetah, cheers our family always. Thanks to all.

The final words will take these acknowledgments far away from Gettysburg. In the autumn of 2000 I had the pleasure of delivering the Frank and Virginia Williams Lecture at Louisiana State University at Shreveport. The International Lincoln Center for American Studies had been just established there and a campaign of sort was started against it. Letters denounced the tyrant Lincoln, "a man that condoned slavery . . . and the ill-treatment of women." One person wrote about "the coming race war." "An International Abraham Lincoln Center?" asked another. "To honor the mass murderer who slew 300,000 southern men, women and children? That precursor of Lenin, Hitler, and Stalin? Are you out of your mind?" And there was praise for the black journalist who labored mightily to turn the legend of the Great Emancipator into the legend of the Racist-in-Chief. It was curious and instructive to see protestors figuratively waving the Confederate flag in one hand and black activist Lerone Bennett, Jr.'s *Forged Into Glory* in the other. One hundred thirty-five years after the assassination, some "southern patriots" found it possible to hand out posters of Lincoln with the legend: *Wanted Dead or Alive.*

Of course the majority of Americans think differently. Friendly people came to Shreveport, too, from different parts of Louisiana, the South, the globe. One group flew in from Lincoln, Argentina. Enthusiasm prevailed. My favorite moment came when rap artist David Wells sang about "The Greatest." He was funny and also pretty harsh:

> You ask who's the greatest of the presidents,
> The finest of all White House residents

The rap beat pulsated through the auditorium.

> No Massachusetts playboy like JFK
> No liberal Texas shyster like LBJ

> No drunken Andy Johnson, no Tennessee tailor,
> No witless Jimmy Carter, no peanut farmer failure.

> You can have your demagogue, your Arkansas faker,
> I'll just take the Confederacy's undertaker.

The conclusion filled the hall:

> But look me in the eye and I will tell you without blinking,
> This Southerner prefers Abraham Lincoln.

I tell the story of my Louisiana visit in part because I have been lecturing and publishing about Lincoln and the Civil War for many years and the protestors reminded me to thank, at last, the broad public: for listening, for reading, for remaining loyal—from Maine to Florida, from New York to California, from England to India.

*Autumn, 2000*                                          *Gabor Boritt*
*Farm by the Ford*
*Gettysburg*

## CHAPTER I

# Did He Dream of a Lily-White America?
# The Voyage to Linconia

## Gabor Boritt

*"We are opposed to emancipating negro slaves, unless on some plan of colonization. . . ."*

Tammany meeting, 1862

*"Now, if you could give a start to white people, you would open a wide door for many to be made free."*

Lincoln on colonization to a black deputation, 1862

*"Sir, that alarm [about emancipation] would spread to every man of my constituents who loves his country and his race if the public mind was not lulled and put to sleep with the word 'colonization.'"*

Congressman Charles Biddle of Pennsylvania, 1862[1]

The men sitting around in the room must have felt uneasy—however memorable the occasion. August, 1862. For the first time in the history of the great Republic, the prejudiced Republic, a group of black people was being entertained in the White House by the president of the United States. Lincoln's patronizing tone would have revolted a Frederick Douglass, and many African

American leaders, had any of them been invited; the chief practical thrust of Lincoln's message would have divided them. The president spoke of colonization.

The guests did not know that their host had made up his mind weeks earlier to issue an emancipation proclamation. Almost no one knew. What they heard instead seemed to be a plea for help to recruit some black folks to colonize outside of the United States. Lincoln was blunt. "Whether it is right or wrong I need not discuss," he was reported to have said, but the fact remained that both blacks and whites suffered from one another's presence in the country. Whites were killing each other in a bloody war because of slavery. As for African Americans: "Your race are suffering . . . the greatest wrong inflicted on any people." It would be best if the races separated, and the president wanted some black volunteers to start colonization. There were a lot more whites than blacks in the country, so it was clear who should go.[2]

This was not the first time Lincoln had endorsed the idea that could create a lily-white America. In 1852, in a eulogy for Henry Clay, Lincoln's "beau ideal of a statesman," the Illinois politician praised Clay's desire to end slavery and restore the freed people to "their long lost fatherland."[3] Lincoln also addressed the Illinois Colonization Society in the fifties, became one of its nominal leaders, and mentioned the issue a few times during his campaigns against Illinois Senator Stephen A. Douglas.

Colonization was not the only subject related to slavery and race that he addressed in the 1850s. He began his fight against Illinois Senator Stephen Douglas in the great 1858 contest by announcing: "Let us discard all this quibbling about this man and the other man—this race and that race and the other race being inferior, and therefore they must be placed in an inferior position. . . ." "Who shall say, 'I am the superior, and you are the inferior?'"[4] Before long, however, he ended up uttering these words:

> I am not, nor ever have been in favor of bringing about in any way the social and political equality of the white and black races . . . I am not nor ever have been in favor of making voters or jurors of negroes, nor of qualifying them to hold office, nor to intermarry with white people; and I will say in addition to this that there is a physical difference be-

tween the white and black races which I believe will for ever forbid the two races living together on terms of social and political equality. And inasmuch as they cannot so live, while they do remain together there must be the position of superior and inferior, and I as much as any other man am in favor of having the superior assigned to the white race. . . . [5]

In our iconoclastic and at times cynical political age, these may well be Lincoln's most often quoted words among young people, and they sound very harsh to twenty-first-century ears. Should one doubt the ugliness of the words, let her or him substitute in the above paragraph any ethnic group for blacks: I am not, nor ever have been in favor of bringing about in any way the social and political equality of the white and Irish (Jewish, Italian, Hispanic, German, Chinese, whatever) races. How did Lincoln, who, according to historian Douglas Wilson, carried the "compulsion" to help the downtrodden;[6] how did the politician who as a young man dared denounce slavery in the Illinois legislature in a minority of six (from among the 81 members); how did the decent human being who, in the eyes of many, later earned the sobriquet "Great Emancipator"; how did he end up saying what he did? Can our twenty-first-century ears and sensibilities be placated?

Lincoln's words do become understandable as coming from a great anti-slavery champion of the political world if placed in their 1850s context. He spoke in response to the predictable baiting of Senator Douglas of Illinois. "Do you desire to turn this beautiful State into a free negro colony?" Douglas asked during the Great Debates of 1858, and the crowd roared "No, no." When slaves would be freed "the free negro" would "flow in"—"never" roared the crowd—"and cover our prairies."

If you desire negro citizenship—if you desire them to come into the State and stay with white men—if you desire to let them vote on an equality with yourselves—if you desire to make them eligible for office—to have them serve on juries and judge of your rights—then go with Mr. Lincoln. . . . ["Never, never"] I believe that this government was made on the white basis. ["Good"] I believe it was made by white men for the benefit of white men and their posterity forever. . . . But Mr. Lincoln . . . reads the Declaration of Independence that all men are created free and equal. . . . I do not question Mr. Lincoln's conscientious belief that the negro was made his equal, and hence is his brother. ["Laughter"] But, for my own part, I do not regard the negro as my equal, and I positively deny that he is my brother, or any kin to me whatever."

The Douglas crowd replied again with a defiant "never." "Hit him again," people cried and they cheered. The Little Giant also appealed to class prejudice while condemning interracial intercourse (social with sexual overtones) by claiming to have seen Frederick Douglass with a "beautiful young lady" in a "magnificent" carriage, while the white owner, presumably the father, served as the driver.[7]

This was what Lincoln had replied to, and he still lost the election in an antebellum Illinois where black people could not vote, could not serve on juries, could not bear arms, could not marry whites, in fact could not legally come into the state. Not many whites wished things to be different. Even for many antislavery Republicans, the party's chief tenet, excluding slaves from the territories, meant excluding black people. What was in Lincoln's heart can be debated and presumably he did not say what ran opposite to his beliefs. But when under hard pressure he conceded publicly that he sought no social and political equality, he conceded nothing that was practically feasible in the 1850s.

More than this, his comments on the subject of slavery and race fit Lincoln's style of argumentation that he also used in the courtroom. There he would often concede all points to the opposition, more than what a jury required, giving the impression of a highly reasonable adversary. He would concede all, except the central point. In the 1850s his central point was the "monstrous injustice" of slavery and the absolute need to make, over the long run, "all" of the "house divided" free.[8]

It is worth digressing to note that if Lincoln's comments opposed to racial equality were forced out of him by politics, on his own he told black jokes, occasionally using the "n" word, and attended minstrel shows. He also told what our time would describe as sexist jokes, and pilloried the dominant immigrant groups of his time, making fun of Irish Paddy and the Dutch (German) farmer. Latter-day attacks on Lincoln on these grounds are about as useful to historical understanding as attacking a central figure of the scientific revolution, Isaac Newton, for believing in astrology or for not knowing the laws of physics that any child learns in school in the twenty-first century.

When in the 1850s Douglas raised the race issue, he raised a red herring—but for good political reasons. As the anti-slavery crusade entered mainstream America, Lincoln rose to be one of its leaders. His opponents then attempted to shift the political argument from slavery, an issue on which they feared they may not win, to that of race, an issue on which they thought they could not lose. The Democrats, led by Douglas, argued at times in crude language, that Lincoln and the Republicans did not merely wish to stop the expansion of slavery, but wished to bring about the social and political equality of black people. Lincoln replied in kind, using the polite form of a vulgar word, "fudge," to say no, and also tried to poke fun of his nemesis. "It was a false logic that assumed that because a man did not want a negro woman for a *slave,* he must needs want her for a *wife.*"[9] He avowed that he desired no civil rights for black people, only the right to the fruit of their own labor. Had he not done so, we would never have heard of Abraham Lincoln. America's most effective antislavery champion would have disappeared from history. For such was antebellum Illinois, such was the United States.

While keeping alive the antislavery fight in Illinois by disavowing a desire for racial equality, Lincoln also invoked in a vague way colonization. The concession that he sought no social and political equality for blacks, and his newfound colonizationism served the same cause. But while Lincoln would have been hard-put to defend well the justice of his first position, colonization could be given a better foundation. Indeed, to the extent the idea penetrated his thought, it was buttressed by a to-the-bone egalitarianism, his democratic faith that "all men are created equal."

In the conflict between egalitarianism and racism, he leaned to the noble idea. Lincoln knew that "he who would *be* no slave, must consent to *have* no slave." On occasion, as he did in early 1860 New England, he even dared to lay out a non-racial "central idea" for America.

I am not ashamed to confess that twenty-five years ago I was a hired laborer, mauling rails, at work on a flat-boat—just what might happen to any poor man's son! I want every man to have a chance—and I believe a black man is entitled to it—in which he *can* better his condition—

when he may look forward and hope to be a hired laborer this year and the next, work for himself afterward, and finally to hire men to work for him! That is the true system.[10]

It was very hurtful for whites to have a permanent underclass; much more so for blacks to be that class. And if it were not possible for blacks to be free, equal, and prosperous in the United States, it should be made possible elsewhere. Colonization carried the promise that the country had denied African Americans throughout her history.

The notion that blacks and whites should separate had something of a history in the country. The first colonizer, Paul Cuffe, an African-American ship owner, sent 38 black people to Africa in 1815. Cuffe died soon after, and with it, for a time, his dream amongst his people. The grandeur of black liberation attempts should not be conflated with the white movement that followed, and which for some simply meant getting rid of blacks. But Cuffe's dream soon helped give birth to the American Colonization Society. This preeminently ineffectual organization of whites found few black takers. Still, talk of black emigration never died out in the country, and the movement revived in the 1850s. Congress passed the Fugitive Slave Law to help recapture escaped people, and the Supreme Court handed down the Dred Scott decision, decreeing that blacks could not be citizens. Racism waxed, the future looked bleak.

Lincoln alluded to the Fugitive Law in a private letter to his old friend Joshua Speed of Kentucky: "I hate to see the poor creatures hunted down, and caught, and carried back to their stripes, and unrewarded toils; but I bite my lip and keep quiet." He would say nothing publicly. When he denounced the Dred Scott decision he ignored the citizenship issue and focused on the pro-slavery aspect of the Court's work. But in general terms he did dare to use strong public language to describe the state of the Union for the African American:

One after another they have closed the heavy iron doors upon him, and now they have him, as it were, bolted in with a lock of a hundred keys, which can never be unlocked without the concurrence of every key; the keys in the hands of a hundred different men, and they scattered to a hundred different and distant places. . . .

His accusation rang loud: "You have taken the negro out of the catalogue of man. . . ." He added at another time: "are you quite sure the demon which you have roused *will not turn and rend you?*"[11]

If the 1850s saw the prominent Frederick Douglass reject colonization, other African-American intellectuals endorsed it. The "pioneer black nationalists," to quote historian George M. Fredrickson, "put forth a prophetic view of black redemption."[12] Martin R. Delany, physician, novelist, destined to be the highest ranking black officer in the Union Army, placed himself at the forefront of these hopes. Henry Highland Garnet established the African Civilization Society. By 1859 the Haytian Emigration Bureau published its own newspaper and captured the interest of free people. Though neither Delany nor Garnet thought mass migration possible, others, too, praised what seemed a beautiful dream. Even Douglass wavered at moments. One of Lincoln's black neighbors in Springfield, Illinois, Samuel S. Ball, visited Liberia and published a report praising the country as a potential home for African Americans. Lincoln may have read Ball's pamphlet. (However, he also knew that Ball kept his wife and six children in Springfield, and by 1858 a meeting of local blacks firmly rejected colonization and appealed to Jefferson's Declaration instead.) Among antislavery whites none spoke as eloquently and as effectively as Harriet Beecher Stowe's best-seller, *Uncle Tom's Cabin*. In its soaring conclusion, the reader glimpsed black freedom in Africa. Lincoln, too, turned to colonization at moments in the 1850s, driven to it by politics, but his love of equality, his dream of a better future for whites and blacks also played a role.[13]

Then the war came, Lincoln was president. He took up colonization. He carried on long and earnest private discussions with his cabinet, diplomats, border state politicians, and colonizing entrepreneurs. Supportive Congressional Republicans ranged from conservatives like Francis P. Blair, Jr., to radicals like Benjamin Wade. They passed colonization measures under the president's discreet prodding. In public, too, Lincoln staunchly championed the idea. At the end of 1862 the president went so far as to ask for a constitutional amendment to facilitate the design. Indeed a few hundred volunteers shipped off to an isle close to Haiti.

Lincoln's fundamental rationale for colonization remained noble, as far as nobility was possible on behalf of such a proposal. He continued to argue that the unequal relationship of whites and blacks in the United States harmed them both. For the blacks this relationship was "the greatest wrong inflicted on any people" anywhere. He was pessimistic about a change (and for a century after him the all-too-small achievements in race relations vindicated his judgment). The solution to the problem was federally aided emigration of the oppressed people. He was too just a man to claim much morality for this solution, and enough of a pragmatist and a politician not to concede its inequity. "Whether it is right or wrong I need not discuss," he said, and then took the ground of expediency that almost amounted to "absolute necessity." Not until 1864 did his secretary and confidant, John Hay, note that the Tycoon had "sloughed off" all these notions.[14]

After the seriousness and sincerity of Lincoln's colonizing intent is recognized, so must be an ever-present element of deep contradiction barely below the surface. From the start, the inaccuracy of the scholarly practice of referring to the president's projects as "deportations" should be clear. He was no latter-day Assyrian, much less a predecessor of Stalin or Hitler. Lincoln used the term occasionally, but in one of its unmistakable nineteenth-century connotations, that of voluntary emigration. He evidently managed to avoid the thought that black people might not want to leave the place of their birth until well into the Civil War. Even then, to quote the diary of Secretary of the Navy Gideon Welles, he "objected unequivocally to compulsion." He did give passing thought to granting freedom to the slaves on the condition that they colonize, but rejected this option. His policy, as he said, was support for black emigration "so far as individuals may desire." When Attorney General Edward Bates ventured that such a stance was tantamount to a policy of no colonization, the president brushed him aside.[15]

Contradiction and ambivalence were the hallmarks of Lincoln's support of colonization. On the one hand, he lauded the restoration of "a captive people to their long lost fatherland," and on the other, he affirmed, even in the heat of the Great Debates, that there was "room enough for us all to be free," black and white. In the message to Congress, a month before the Emancipation Proclamation, in which he proposed constitutional amendments authorizing, among other things, the appropriation of money for colonization, he also brusquely dismissed as a "mere catch argument" the notion that free blacks would injure the whites if they remained in the country. He took pains to point to communities that had large populations of such folk and that nonetheless thrived. Indeed, he devoted approximately 15 printed lines to his colonization amendment and the argument for it and 50 lines to his view that no harm would come if the freedmen stayed in the United States.[16]

By virtue of his office, Lincoln could, and did, become the leading proponent of black emigration. Yet when, in response, Congress placed the small sum of $600,000 at his disposal, he spent only $38,000 of it during the two years it was available to him. He appointed an inept commissioner of emigration, James Mitchell, and the new officer, by provoking the ire of the successive secretaries of the interior, only weakened the governmental effort. He appointed an agent, Senator Samuel C. Pomeroy of Kansas, a man rumored to be a shady character and who lived up to his reputation. Most important, the obvious choice as colonists, the multitudes of displaced slaves—the "contrabands"—were not tapped. Indeed, it is difficult to escape the conclusion that Lincoln's colonization policy, while addressed to black people, was meant for white ears.[17]

The chief executive's most publicized attempt on behalf of his much advertised policy was the one-sided interview with a black delegation in August 1862—just before he issued the Preliminary Emancipation Proclamation. (A pamphlet by his commissioner of emigration immediately advertised this meeting as "one of the most important chapters in the history of the country.")[18] The black delegation, with four of the five members newly freed slaves, did not come from the leadership of the Washington community, much less of the country, and Lincoln used a condescending tone that he would never use with a Frederick Douglass, but that fit how most whites thought a president should address black people.

To the White House visitors, who by their mere presence as guests further fractured existing racial barriers, Lincoln advocated the separation of races. But then he remarked that in America the races were "attached . . . at all events." He passingly confessed doubts about the likelihood of successful colonization, but brushed aside the moral dilemma of inviting men to partake in dubious ventures by noting that the government, too, might lose money in the process. Also there was the supposed grandeur of the undertaking.[19]

In the end, his message boiled down to a plea for colonists. The plea seemed to carry conviction, yet in a revealing moment Lincoln appeared to suggest that what was really needed was a "start" to a black movement out of the country rather than a sustained movement, "a successful commencement" to appease white people so that emancipation might follow. The comment was clearly unwitting, yet the way he scaled down his request from a 100 to 50 to 25 souls, all in the same breath, resembled nothing as much as Lincoln's Biblical namesake, Abraham, bargaining with the Lord God about saving Sodom if only 50, 40, even ten righteous men could be found there. One cannot escape the feeling that by 1862, even as the colonization hype crested, Lincoln began to allow himself a glimpse of the fact that the idea of large-scale emigration was about as realistic as Abraham's hope of saving Sodom. His last words to the black delegation of 1862 were "no hurry at all."[20]

Lincoln's ambivalence toward colonization also gained expression through uncharacteristic sloppiness in his thought. He was extremely interested in population growth and the promotion of immigration. Seeking economic development (as it was understood at the time) was indeed a central motif of the first and longer part of his career. He paid no attention, however, to the effect that the loss of four and a half million working men and women might have on the country. To the opponents of colonization who hammered away at this point, even in the cabinet, he gave no hearing. He simply hoped that it would be "not against our interest" to transfer the black people to another clime, and investigated no further. The one potential economic benefit of these projects, the planting of commercial outposts, making Central America, to cite Frank Blair, "our India, but under happier auspices," clashed with the president's antipathy not only toward imperialism but even geographical expansionism.[21]

In the very state paper that recommended amending the Constitution to sanction federal financing of colonization, Lincoln also devoted much space to the glorious prospects awaiting the United States. He made meticulous projections into the twentieth century about rapidly growing population levels and densities. But neither his figures (which included immigration statistics) nor his discussion of them took any account of possible territorial gains via colonization or of the proposed loss of the 14 percent of the total American population of 31 million in

1860. In a man of Lincoln's carefulness, this was more than a mere oversight. It indicates further an unconscious avoidance of the realities of colonization. Indeed, this same state paper, his second annual message to Congress, saw fit to contrast the United States with the unhappy condition of a Europe that was "compelled" to send part of her native born peoples away. It is not surprising to see the Presidential Proclamation of Thanksgiving in 1864 expressing gratitude for the large augmentation of the free American population "by emancipation and by immigration."[22]

Lincoln's precision of thought was one of his trademarks. He was fond of statistics, was willing to estimate the value of slaves at two billion dollars (and later less), was willing to offer various states and the Confederacy huge sums for compensated emancipation. When it came to colonization, however, he failed to think in terms of "dollars and cents" even vis-à-vis so relatively simple a factor as transportation. At the beginning of his antislavery crusade, he indulged himself in "a moment's reflection" on the subject, and this convinced him that over the short run there were "not surplus shipping and surplus money enough in the world" to do the job. (The issue was made real for Lincoln, since his neighbor, Ball, wanted the Illinois legislature to appropriate money for colonization.) In 1859 Lincoln warned Kansas that if it allowed slavery to come in but later changed its mind, "all the rest" of the state's property "would not pay" for sending black Kansans to Liberia. Yet he did not develop this line of thought at all. He continued to preach colonization and could defend its feasibility by pointing to the example of the children of Israel leaving Egypt. Had Lincoln reflected on the matter with just a little greater intensity, had he become a little more specific, the colonization bubble would have burst instantly.[23]

He could avoid applying his rigorous mind to the problem in part because statesmen from Thomas Jefferson to Henry Clay had lent a semblance of credibility to the policy and in part because the immediate issue before him was at first slavery expansion and later emancipation. And the ready-made concept of colonization was eminently serviceable. It permitted Lincoln to pursue his fight against slavery without having to break his head against the specifics of the problem of the freedmen in American society, a problem that perplexed him. The colonization idea also had immense political value because it eased the fears of the Northern white masses about blacks who would "swarm forth" from the South after emancipation "and cover the whole land" (to repeat Lincoln's angrily mocking mime of the black-hater). One did not have to be a master politician to recognize this factor, and if the president could somehow have overlooked it, the elder Francis Blair and the second secretary of interior, John P. Usher, for example, took care to remind him of it.[24]

Lincoln did not directly discuss political motives for talking colonization. Perhaps early in the war he thought the policy would help end the bloodbath by appealing to the poorer white masses in the South. The Union-saving properties of colonization were certainly touted by the younger Blair: "The very prejudice of race which now makes the non-slaveholders give their aid to hold slaves in bondage will induce them to unite in a policy which will rid them of the presence of negroes."

In that context, before Lincoln is readily condemned for a willingness to make peace early without ending slavery—he believed the institution would die over the long run if stopped from expanding—we should remember that the war cost 1.5 million casualties in a nation of 31 million. In a nation of 275 million that the United States is at the dawn of the millennium, that figure translates into over 13 million people. Lincoln did not like war, though he fought a most terrible one to save the nation and what he understood it to stand for.

The colonization propaganda, however, did not help with the Confederates. Historian Vorenberg suggests that even in the North, emancipation "may have seemed to Lincoln so radical a policy" that without colonization "it could result only in the demise of the Republican party in Congress and in the northern state legislatures."[25] The death of the party during the Civil War was likely to mean an end to the United States and the expansion of slavery. Not surprisingly then, Lincoln accompanied his early steps toward emancipation with vigorous exercises about colonization.

All in all, Lincoln's record suggests that he employed the idea of colonization to allay his own uncertainties, and more importantly the fears of the vast majority of whites, concerning the eventual place of the free black people in the United States. One part of his mind told him that America's future depended on the destruction of slavery, the other spoke of fears about the results of such a course. Taking into the equation a vague concept of colonization permitted him to go with a lighter heart and broader public support to the heavy task at hand: helping to set black people free.

During the first part of the nineteenth century, the most notable historic function of colonization was to furnish for many whites the illusion of a future lily-white America. For some whites the policy also provided an outlet for antislavery humanitarian activity, and for some African Americans the dream of a free homeland. In contrast, the Civil War president transformed colonization into an effective road to emancipation. He provided thereby an illustration of an immense capacity to bend various, often conflicting, forces to his own ends—and to the nation's good.[26]

The popular theory that God had created a natural limit to slavery, that it could not expand north or west in the United States, Lincoln called "a palliation—a lullaby."[27] It probably was that, for both its authors and the antislavery portion of the nation that accepted it as truth. The same must be said of Lincoln's colonization proposals. They were a lullaby for the antiblack majority of the political spectrum.

This state of things was indeed at least partially recognized by some, supporters as well as opponents of colonization. The latter included not only radical abolitionists but also foes of emancipation. One suspects that Senator Charles Sumner's later thought crossed the minds of many: colonization, he said, was advanced "perhaps to divert attention from the great question of Equal Rights." And he added: "it is vain to say that this is the country of the 'white man.' It is the country of Man." The president's schemes received derisive notice in the diary of another radical, Salmon P. Chase: "How much better would be a manly protest against prejudice against color!—and a wise effort to give freemen homes in America!" On the opposite side of the fence, however, Pennsylvania Representative Charles J. Biddle declared that the people would not stand, for a moment, talk of emancipation were it not for—and he used Lincoln's very expression—the pernicious "lullaby" of colonization. The whole idea, he concluded, was "political economy run mad." If justice was on the side of Sumner and Chase, the majority leaned to Biddle's persuasion. Lincoln's actions and words indicate that he sensed this. Therefore, he stood in the middle and thus provided more effective leadership than did the senator from Massachusetts or the presidential aspirant in his cabinet. But Lincoln, Sumner, and Chase were all heading in the same direction.[28]

When Lincoln proclaimed emancipation, and colonization should have become the next point on the agenda, he did very little to that end. That little attested before his own conscience to his past good faith. And that little he abandoned after minor failures caused by the involvement of swindlers. Lincoln was not a man to be diverted from great causes by little failures. Colonization, however, was never a great cause to him, never, to cite the words of historian Winthrop Jordan, "the compelling fantasy" it may have been for many of his countrymen.[29] Once emancipation was a *fait accompli*, the lullaby had served its purpose. If the Preliminary Emancipation Proclamation still emphasized colonization, Lincoln judged that the final Proclamation could ignore the matter entirely.

Lincoln had held his breath after his Preliminary Proclamation as the country may have come as close to a military coup as U.S. history has seen. Not far from Washington the adored commander of the largest of armies, George McClellan, pondered what to do about what he saw as Lincoln turning the war into an abolition war. The commander in chief fired him, for military reasons, too, and the general went quietly. (In 1864 he ran against the president and emancipation, and in favor of peace.) The American political tradition held.

Problems did not disappear after January 1, 1863, but the North was changing slowly, and emancipation provoked no great white revolt. As late as 1864 a general might have to be courtmartialed for saying that the Lincoln government's policy was "to prolong the war, to free the slaves." "I say God damn the government." But facing no massive resistance, Lincoln abandoned not only the idea of colonization but even the one established colony near Haiti that badly needed help—this in contrast with his interest in free labor experiments at home. Indeed, after 1862 never again did he mention colonization in public. For one who had professed to be a believer, he discarded the idea with almost indecent haste. Thus he left an even deeper mark on the nation than heretofore noted. It was under his tutelage, and with the mighty help of African Americans who chose to stay and fight, that the illusion of long generations of white Americans about a future white America came largely to an end through a process of first being loudly encouraged and then instantly crushed.[30]

As Lincoln said it might, the whole colonization effort came to little more than "nothing." And as the preeminent African-American historian Benjamin Quarles has concluded, the one man "most responsible" for this was the Civil War president, for he helped give black people "the feeling that they could make their way in America, that this country was ready to take its first big steps. . . ."[31]

As the colonization talk reached a fever pitch in 1862, a name was suggested for a new black homeland: Linconia.[32] But the voyage to that colony was destined to come to naught—instead the United States would be Linconia. *Why* the Civil War president had talked up the fantasy voyage is easy enough to understand: it quieted his fears and aided the indispensable white acceptance of emancipation. More difficult to understand is *how* the pragmatic, down-to-earth Lincoln could believe in an unrealistic design that by 1860, to use the words of historian James M. McPherson, had proved to be a "miserable failure."[33]

The answer appears to lie in the defense mechanism that psychologists call avoidance. Lincoln was something of an anomaly. He was an extraordinarily honest man, whereas his craft, politics, more than most others required the periodic stretching of the truth. On more than one occasion he overcame this contradiction through the use of avoidance. Faced with seemingly insoluble realities, people often avoid confronting them. In the case of the "American Dilemma," to borrow Gunnar Myrdal's later classic words, Lincoln, like others, refused for a time to see what at some level of consciousness he knew: that colonization was a highly unrealistic solution. He needed that policy to pursue his antislavery crusade. He did not allow himself to see that it was a chimera. No elaborate psychoanalytic theories are required to explain this mental process. Shakespeare explained matters well enough in *King Lear,* a play Lincoln loved well: "I have no way, and therefore want no eyes." "Honest Abe" found it difficult to lie, but by blocking out even from his own awareness unwanted information, he forged ahead. This is how honest people lie. So long as he did not know the truth, he was not obliged to tell it.

The end to slavery that he so deeply desired, and that seemed so faraway through much of his life, grew possible as the war changed the United States. Then he could embrace "a new birth of freedom" into the center of his being. Long before, as a very ambitious young man, he had announced that "towering genius" in America could reach great renown by either "emancipating slaves, or enslaving freemen." Twenty-five years later he confided that his stature in history would depend on his decree of freedom. As he signed the Proclamation on January 1, 1863, he explained: "If my name ever goes into history it will be for this act." He was also remembered to have described emancipation as "the great event of the nineteenth century." Humble man, this Lincoln? He underscored the depth of his conviction early in 1863 by inviting the painter Edward Dalton Marchant to live in the White House for four months. The artist created the presidential portrait with broken chains. In 1864 Lincoln invited another painter, Francis Carpenter, for six months, to paint *The First Reading of the Emancipation Proclamation*. It depicted the moment the president told his Cabinet that he would go ahead with emancipation—and needed no advice about the substance of his decision. The hero going it almost alone. Somehow Carpenter was led to carefully arrange to Lincoln's right that majority of the Cabinet that was weary of the decision. And to his old and intimate friend, Speed, Lincoln recalled the time when they were both young, and Lincoln despaired about leaving a mark on the world. Now, he knew, he would be remembered.[34]

Some people said then, and do still, that the Emancipation Proclamation freed no one. (Nor did the Declaration of Independence.) Lincoln understood that he would be attacked from such quarters, too, and given his deep committment to freedom few acts measure better the depth of Lincoln's greatness and his self-denial than his careful politics combined with the mundane wording of the Proclamation. The man whose very being was tied to this act, who said "if slavery is not wrong, nothing is wrong,"[35] who had the ability to craft the Gettysburg Address and the Second Inaugural, chose to use boring legalese language, among other reasons, because he judged the antiblack majorities required it.

Colonization talk also seemed part of the requirement. But Lincoln's refusal to face the facts on that issue for a long time raises questions about the price America had to pay for this detour from reality. The benefit of the venture, the catalysis of emancipation, was immense. Ending abruptly the dreams of a lily-white America was good medicine for the country. When the government brought back from the isle off

Haiti the survivors of its token colony, nearly all the men signed up to be soldiers in blue.

But harm, too, stemmed from Lincoln's delusion, however inescapably, the curtailed ability to confront realistically (in the president's case until the very last years of his life, if fully then) the problems for blacks in post-emancipation America. Whatever the price the nation had to pay, it probably included little fanning of hatred. Colonization, judged a careful student of the subject, "was not an issue that aroused the emotions racists customarily appealed to."[36] Of course, African Americans worried about such possible results. Douglass, for one, felt deeply insulted by the policy. And one shudders to think of the ways that relieved the frustrations of those who had put a deep faith in the false promises of black emigration.

Did Lincoln ever became conscious of the deception to which he had subjected himself, and also the American people, on the issue of colonization? Very probably not. Even as he sent Congress his proposal for amending the Constitution to pay for colonization, he grumbled angrily about another matter to his friend, Senator Orville H. Browning: "Why will men believe a lie, an absurd lie, that could not [be] impose[d] upon a child, and cling to it and repeat it in defiance of all evidence to the contrary?" He might have known some of the reasons why this could occur, his understanding of the human condition being profound. "We have been mistaken all our lives," he said in his 1862 interview, "if we do not know whites as well as blacks look to their self-interest."[37] A recognition of this fact was central to his thinking. Thus, perhaps he might have known that when people felt that their interest demanded and could sense no other open way, they might, to use the language of the twenty-first century, avoid the perception of reality; in short, allow themselves to be fooled or even fool themselves. Not all the people all the time, but, in this case, enough people, from presidents down, for a time long enough to make colonization a giant and, at least during Lincoln's presidency, a mostly beneficial feature on the mental landscape of America.

＊＊＊

Colonization was dead and Lincoln did not mourn. He did not march backwards. Was the colonization detour necessary? Was the denial of equal rights that continued through the war necessary? Did Lincoln move forward fast enough? Many reformers thought not, but their job was relatively easy: agitate, tell the truth. The politician had to bring people along. None put matters better than Frederick Douglass. In 1865 as African Americans mourned Lincoln, murdered by a black-hating Confederate sympathizer, Douglass called back to life "emphatically the black man's President." This carried much truth, especially if one compared Lincoln with his predecessors. By 1876, however, the venerable black orator gave a more nuanced evaluation. Lincoln was "preeminently the white man's President . . . an American of the Americans." To black people, "Father Abraham" was only a stepfather. Lincoln had grown into the American saint first among many of the slaves (even while among whites he was still only a controversial president who might not get reelected, or perhaps should be shot). But by 1876 Douglass was willing to take away from his people parts of the image of the patron saint. Perhaps he was pointing toward black self-reliance. Douglass understood his own time, the war years as well as 1876; he understood history. Lincoln, he said, held white prejudices, but they served as "one element of his wonderful success in organizing the loyal American people for the tremendous conflict before them. . . . Viewed from genuine abolition ground, Mr. Lincoln seemed tardy, cold, dull, and indifferent; but measuring him by the sentiment of his country, a sentiment he was bound as a statesman to consult, he was swift, zealous, radical, and determined." Earlier Douglass mused that Lincoln was "the first American President who . . . rose above the prejudice of his times."[38]

Little more needs to be said. The tall, often humble son of a slave state, who lived most of his life in an Illinois that denied African Americans many of their most basic rights, spoke of the American future in 1863: "And then, there will be some black men who can remember that, with silent tongue, and clenched teeth, and a steady eye, and well-poised bayonet, they have helped mankind on to this great consummation; while, I fear, there will be some white ones, unable to forget that, with malignant heart, and deceitful speech, they have strove to hinder it." The politician who had been goaded into announcing in 1858 that he did not favor "bringing about in any way the . . . political equality" of the races, began to push in 1864 for limited suffrage for black people: "They would probably help, in some trying time to come, to keep the jewel of liberty within the family of freedom." The man who in 1858 had disclaimed wanting to bring about "in any way" the "social" equality of black people, invited them to the White House for the New Year's Day reception, 1865. Emancipation Day. African Americans came in large numbers. They would have to wait for a new century to be invited again by a president.[39]

In April of 1865 the first Union troops to march into Richmond, the ruined, burning capital of the Confederacy, were African Americans. "Double quick, march," ordered the Colonel of the 29th Connecticut, and the men "charged through the main street to the capitol and halted in the square. . . ." A day later Lincoln came, too, holding the future and his twelve-year-old son Tad by the hand. Like the troops before, the president was greeted by a joyous crowd of black people. "Glory to God! glory! glory! glory!" At one point an old man with tears in his eyes stopped before the president, raised his hat, bowed, and called for God to bless him. In reply, an eyewitness reported, Lincoln "removed his own hat and bowed in silence."[40]

## CHAPTER 2

# Young Man Lincoln

### Douglas L. Wilson

To do for Abraham Lincoln what Erik Erikson did for Martin Luther in his famous book *Young Man Luther* may appear to be the goal of this essay, but its aim is more modest. Erikson was a professional psychologist with his own theory of human development, a theory that focused his observations and prompted his insights into Martin Luther's young manhood. While I am not a psychologist and come at my subject from a different direction, I share Erikson's belief that we gain a better understanding of the mature person by studying the events of his childhood and youth.

The subject before us is unusually familiar. Though we know the names of many notable Americans and something of what they are famous for, most of us know relatively little about their personal lives, especially their early lives. Abraham Lincoln is a notable exception. Since his assassination in 1865, most Americans have become acquainted with at least a brief version of his life, and it goes like this: Abraham Lincoln was born to poor and uneducated parents, grew up on a primitive farm in the middle of nowhere, had very little schooling and was mostly self-educated, worked as a storekeeper and postmaster in a small village and studied in the evenings by firelight, pulled himself up by his own bootstraps, became a lawyer (and even more remarkably, an honest one), earned distinction as a politician and debater opposed to slavery, and finally was elected to the presidency of the United

States, where he distinguished himself by freeing the slaves and saving the Union.

There are admittedly many embellishments to this basic story, some of which are largely folklore or fiction, but the brief outline of his life just rehearsed is what is commonly believed and is, happily enough, substantially true. What is not in this outline, nor in the embellishments, nor even in most biographies, if truth be told, is an adequate treatment of the struggles and difficulties of Lincoln's formative years. I should make it clear that I am not talking about hardships. As the story outline indicates, there were plenty of those. Neither am I talking about failures. It has become commonplace to talk about Lincoln's persistence in the face of many failures, but this has been overdone and ultimately gives, I think, the wrong impression. Lincoln certainly knew failure, but his life could not, by any reasonable measure, be characterized as a series of failures. The struggles and difficulties I refer to in his formative years, which is to say his youth and young manhood, were severe, but they were, for the most part, not unusual. They are, in fact, reasonably familiar to every maturing person. They centered upon such basic questions as identity ("Who am I?"), vocation ("What am I going to do?"), and coming to terms with the opposite sex ("Who am I going to marry?"). I have written about these things in my book *Honor's Voice*, but here I would like to explore the first of these further—the question of identity—and, without attempting to follow or imitate Erikson, to try to say some more about it.

I want to begin by addressing what I believe is one of the most formidable barriers to historical understanding, and that is what might be called the hindering effect of hindsight. Kierkegaard memorably observed that life must be lived forward but can only be understood backward. Thus our historical understanding is necessarily retrospective, but it tends to be impaired because we know too much; we know how it all comes out. We naturally think of this as an advantage, and it is, but it is also a serious liability. This is because we see the events of the past in terms that are free of the uncertainty experienced at the time and thus tend to leave a very important ingredient out of the historical equation. Sometimes this is offset by the situation itself, such as when Lincoln, in his Farewell Address to his friends and neighbors of Springfield, called attention to the enormous difficulty and uncertainty in which he found himself. "I now leave, not knowing when, or whether ever, I may return, with a task before me greater than that which rested upon Washington."[1] Granted that we still know how it all comes out—that Lincoln will succeed in his task but, tragically, will not return to Springfield alive—yet it is hard to read that famous speech without feeling something of the tremendous weight of anxiety that Lincoln himself felt at the time.

In the case of other phases of his life, particularly his early years, we are not so fortunate. Here we have no *direct* evidence or testimony, for if Lincoln kept a journal of his inner thoughts and feelings at the time, such as that kept by John Adams, for example, it has not come down to us. Almost all we know about Lincoln during these years, in addition to the meager details in his autobiographical statements, is what the people who knew him then said or wrote many years later. Understandably, this testimony offers few clues to what was going on in Lincoln's mind at the time, but since we know that he grew up, got married, and made a successful career for himself as a lawyer and politician, and became the greatest hero in American history, we are tempted to conclude that all must have been well. But I believe this was not the case, and I would like, in the balance of my remarks, to try to explain why.

This year we have been reminded over and over that the coming of the new year brings with it a new century, about which most of us presumably have reason to be hopeful. If you will cast your mind back 60 years to the end of 1939, and think about the state of the Western world at that time, you will recall that Adolf Hitler was on the move and menacing all of Western Europe. Having successfully launched his offensive, it seemed likely that he intended to invade and conquer the British isles. Particularly for the English, it was an ominous time. Here is what the British poet W. H. Auden wrote in a New Year's poem for January 1, 1940:

> Tonight a scrambling decade ends,
> And strangers, enemies and friends
> Stand once more puzzled underneath
> The signpost on the barren heath
> Where the rough mountain track divides
> To silent valleys on all sides,

Endeavoring to decipher what
Is written on it but cannot,
Nor guess in what direction lies
The overhanging precipice.[2]

From our perspective at the end of the twentieth century, we can read Auden's chilling lines with equanimity, for we know the outcome of the international crisis that Auden could only contemplate at the time with apocalyptic fear and dread. In much the same way, when we read about the young Lincoln, we tend to see his youthful experience in the light of his ultimate triumph. We endure his struggles without apprehension, thus discounting and underestimating them, simply because we know how it all turns out. But when Lincoln was coming up as a young man in his twenties and early thirties, his sense of his own situation was probably much more like Auden's in "New Year Letter": not able to glimpse the future and filled with apprehensions of failure, misadventure, and even doom.

What reasons do we have for thinking this was the case, and what does this have to do with the question of identity? Let me start with the latter. Like every other human being in the act of growing up, Abraham Lincoln had to confront the question of who he was. It is, of course, a complex question that presents itself in different forms. One familiar form of the question has to do with what appears as the given, the irreducible conditions of our existence. We ask ourselves not just "Who am I?" but "Who am I *inherently, in essence?*" Given all the roles we must learn to play, "Who or what is the *real* me?" In the case of something that is perceived as a given, there is presumably little we can do about this aspect of our being except to know something about it, try to accept it, and find a way to live with it. This contrasts with another familiar form of the question, one that *does* afford a measure of choice, "Who do I want to be?" Now granted that these are, for the most part, private and intensely personal matters, still, by studying his autobiographical statements and what his friends and neighbors reported years later, I believe we can catch glimpses of the young Lincoln in the grip of such questions as these.

So much has been made of Lincoln's honesty that one might be tempted to assume that this must have been an intrinsic part of his makeup, that he was inherently honed in on the truth. But this does not seem to have been the case. His honesty is actually a complex subject, for although he seems to have been a notably honest man, there were undeniably circumstances and situations in which he felt free to mislead and dissemble. As a way of simplifying the matter for our purposes, let me propose that the phenomenon we think of as his honesty was probably more an aspect of his independence. He had the physical assets and strength of character that permitted him to tell things as he saw them, and not as he was expected or pressured to by his peers. For this reason, he became sought after as a judge of horse races in New Salem, and this was apparently where he first earned the nickname Honest Abe. There is much that might be said on this subject in another context, but here it will suffice to say that complete honesty—the inherent disinclination or inability to misrepresent—does not seem to have been an inborn quality of Abraham Lincoln.

One of the things that *does* seem to have been part of his nature, and that he had to learn to cope with and accept, was that he was unusually tenderhearted.[3] We see this in several reports of his childhood that depict him as concerned about cruelty to animals. When his playmates would turn helpless terrapins on their backs and torture them, which was apparently a favorite pastime, the young future president would protest against it. He wrote an essay on the subject as a school exercise that was remembered years afterward. This instinctive sympathetic reaction seems to have been recognized by his stepbrother as a vulnerable spot in Lincoln's makeup, for he is reported as having taunted Lincoln as he was preaching a mock sermon by bashing a terrapin against a tree. At another point in his Indiana childhood, Lincoln went to considerable trouble to carry home a drunken man he found passed out on the road to keep him from freezing to death.

Other stories that relate to his early life tell about his inability to ignore the difficulties of other creatures in trouble without offering assistance, animals and human beings alike. One story that Lincoln told to one of his girlfriends, Mary Owens, involved a pig buried in mire that Lincoln took pity on and rescued, even though he was dressed up in his best clothes at the time. Another story from the New Salem period was told by the village schoolteacher, Mentor Graham:

The fall after his arrival at New Salem, Lincoln was a neighbor of mine, and performed many kind acts during a time that sickness was prevailing in the neighborhood. At one time my own family, consisting of nine persons, were all sick excepting myself. I was unable for several weeks to do any work, and we were without means and in much distress. I was walking past Lincoln's boarding-house one day when he came out and asked me about the family. I told him my little girl was dead. He appeared much affected. When I came back he handed me ten dollars, probably all the money he had in the world. I had not asked him for any and did not suppose he knew that I needed it.

A final example, a story related by his close friend, Joshua Speed, concerns some small birds that had been blown from their nest onto the road Lincoln and his friends were traveling. In the face of much jeering, Lincoln stayed behind to restore the birds to their nest, explaining when he caught up with his unsympathetic friends, "Gentlemen, you may laugh, but I could not have slept well to-night, if I had not saved those birds. Their cries would have rung in my ears." This remark suggests that Lincoln, who would have been in his twenties at the time, had come to an understanding with himself about his tenderheartedness, that he accepted this condition as a fact of life, realizing that it did no good to pretend that his mind could safely ignore what his feelings could not.

We naturally think of Lincoln's inherent tenderheartedness as an asset, but assets can get you into trouble. When Lincoln discovered that he was more attracted to another woman than the one he was going with, Mary Todd, he was told by his friend Speed that he must tell Mary as much to her face, which he did. But when Mary reacted by blaming herself and breaking into tears, Lincoln instinctively took pity on her, drew her down on his knee, and kissed her. Not until he returned to Speed's store and Speed explained to him what this meant did he realize that his impulsive act, which Speed called "a bad lick," had effectively blocked his own retreat and renewed the affair he had set out to end.

Although he eventually broke with Mary Todd, her claim that he was honor-bound to marry her and the idea that he was the cause of her unhappiness continued to plague him. "That still kills my soul," he wrote Speed. "I cannot but reproach myself, for even wishing to be happy while she is otherwise."[4] His inability to rid himself of these intense guilt feelings about the pain he had caused Mary contributed to his decision to hastily renew their courtship a few months later and marry her on two hours' notice. The result was something of a mismatch, to say the least, and Lincoln's inborn tenderheartedness was more than a little to blame.

This all has to do with the first form of the identity question I referred to: "Who essentially am I?" "Who or what is the real me?" The form of the question that allows for some choice is "Who do I want to be?" Here, I think, we have a great many clues from reports of his early life through which we can see Lincoln in the act of making choices and thus defining himself. This is particularly clear in what he distanced himself from, or rejected. For example, in a homogenous community where most people were passionate about politics and were almost universally boosters of Andrew Jackson, the young Abraham Lincoln, well before voting age, decided he was anti-Jackson. This is evidence not only of a strong individuality, but of courage and self-confidence. In a world where almost everyone smoked or used tobacco, Lincoln chose not to. In a world where everyone drank whiskey, for reasons of health as well as sociability, Lincoln decided to abstain. He tried it, like everyone else, but eventually he gave it up because he didn't like what it did to him (he said it left him "flabby and undone"). Just consider, for a moment, the peer pressure he must have repeatedly endured to relent, to be a good fellow and join the party. After proving himself a formidable fighter, in a place where fighting was commonplace and nearly unavoidable, he opted for the more civilized and rule-bound contests of wrestling, and became a peacemaker, actively breaking up and preventing fights. Most decisive of all, perhaps, was his rejection of his father's and his community's way of life. He was, as he said, brought up to farm work, but he had no wish to remain a farmer and sought some other form of making a living as soon as he was free to do so. These conscious choices, of which we have a fairly clear record, constitute the actions of a decidedly distinctive personality, a person with a wish and a will to be different.

If we can thus find indications of the young Lincoln asking and coming to grips with the basic questions of "Who am I?" and "Who do I want to be?" there was another important question that troubled him probably more than it does most, and one that brings us back to the feelings of apprehension that I mentioned earlier, namely "What is my destiny?" or, more pointedly, "What is fated to happen to me?" While most of us are no doubt visited by such a question from time to time, probably very few are haunted by it, but this seems to have been the case with the young Abraham Lincoln. As far as I have been able to determine, Lincoln was a fatalist all his life. He was born into a family and community whose religion was Calvinistic and predestinarian, and this may well have shaped the contours of his imagination from an early age. While he never seems to have embraced his family's Baptist beliefs, and remained a skeptic all of his life, he readily admitted that he was superstitious and that he believed, as he often said in later years, "What is to be will be, and no prayers of ours can reverse the decree."[5]

This would seem to be a statement about the futility of protesting or resisting the inevitable, but a favorite quotation he took from Shakespeare's *Hamlet* suggests something further: "There's a divinity that shapes our ends, / Rough-hew them as we will."[6] What is acknowledged here is a controlling hand—not just blind destiny, but destiny with a purpose. At a crossroads in his life, he revealed in a letter to his friend Speed that he took precisely this view, quoting scripture to drive home his point: "I always was superstitious; and as part of my superstition, I believe God made me one of the instruments of bringing your Fanny and you together, which union, I have no doubt He had fore-ordained. Whatever he designs, he will do for *me* yet. 'Stand *still* and see the salvation of the Lord' is my text just now."[7]

What is important to grasp about this incident, particularly in view of its invocation of scripture, is that Lincoln was *not* saying, as some have suggested, "God will take care of me." He was saying, "Something has been ordained to happen to me, but I don't know what it is." For while Lincoln always believed in God, he was never a professed Christian, let alone a hopeful one; he did not believe in personal salvation or redemption. For certain of the basic Christian doctrines he had, especially when young, sharp criticisms and even ridicule that he had picked up from such eighteenth-century rationalists as Thomas Paine and Constantin de Volney. As time went on, it became more and more apparent to Lincoln's closest friends that far from being a hopeful man in his basic outlook and temperament, the opposite was true: he was a profoundly gloomy man, troubled by dreams and other portents, and haunted by fears and apprehensions. His law partner famously reported that Lincoln had several times told him privately, "Billy, I fear that I shall meet with some terrible end."[8]

Students of Lincoln have taken this revelation to refer to a fear of death, perhaps even a horrible death. Particularly in the perspective of his assassination, this is certainly what it sounds like, but I would like to put forward a couple of *other* possibilities that I believe, along with death, were frighteningly real for the young Lincoln. The first is quite well documented and concerns the profound emotional depression that overtook him in the winter of 1840–41. Most of the preceding year had been dedicated to the presidential election campaign for the Whig party's candidate, William Henry Harrison, Old Tippecanoe. In the stimulation and excitement of the campaign, Lincoln had initiated a courtship with the visiting Kentucky belle, Mary Todd. Perhaps to his surprise, she responded eagerly, which made for a difficult situation when he discovered, shortly after the election in November, that he was more attracted to another girl, Matilda Edwards, than he was to Mary. This is the point referred to earlier, at which he tried to break up with Mary but, because of his instinctive empathy with people in distress, ended up by renewing the relationship, albeit unintentionally. Because the evidence is so fragmentary and elusive, what happened next is very hard to sort out. Apparently Lincoln continued his attentions to Matilda Edwards, which, together with Mary's continued flirtations with other men, provoked a confrontation between them in which Lincoln renewed his plea to end the relationship. Mary Todd apparently told him he was behaving dishonorably and that he was honor-bound to marry her. There may have been a formal occasion about this time at which Mary expected their engagement to be announced and at which Lincoln failed to appear. Whatever the precipitating cause, Speed said that Lincoln went off the deep end and became suicidal, that he had to be taken in hand by his friends, who took the precaution of removing all knives and razors from his presence. He recovered his composure, but his emotional life began a downward slide that ended a month later with Lincoln in deep depression and, for at least a week, essentially dysfunctional.

Not only the reminiscences of his close friends but Lincoln's own letters during this period testify to his profoundly depressed state of mind. He wrote his partner John T. Stuart, "I am now the most miserable man living. If what I feel were equally distributed to the whole human family, there would not be one cheerful face on the earth. Whether I shall ever be better I can not tell; I awfully forbode I shall not. To remain as I am is impossible; I must die or be better, it appears to me."[9] When he continued for some time in this condition without showing much improvement, his friend Speed said he warned him that he must rally himself or die, to which Lincoln replied that he was "more than willing" to die, except that "he had done nothing to make any human being remember that he had lived."[10] Here we have Speed recalling that Lincoln, in his deepest anguish, revealed to him the reason he wanted, in spite of his unrelieved misery, to go on living. His ultimate purpose in life was to do something that, in Speed's words, "would redound to the interest of his fellow man was what he desired to live for." Moreover, Speed testified that Lincoln, as president, reminded him of this earlier conversation and told him that he believed that, in issuing the Emancipation Proclamation, his "fondest hopes" had finally been realized.[11]

What this suggests is that Lincoln, even as a young man, knew what he wanted in life: he wanted to be remembered for doing something worthwhile. In 1838, a few years earlier, he had talked in his Lyceum Address about the willfulness of men with great egos, like Napoleon, who could not be expected to concern themselves with the welfare of their country or their fellow citizens inasmuch as they sought to be remembered by imposing their will on others. In his despondency in the winter of 1841, Lincoln apparently specified that his own purpose in life was quite different: to be remembered for something "that would redound to the interest of his fellow man." In these circumstances, it seems reasonable to think that the "terrible end" that Lincoln told Herndon he constantly feared might refer, at least in part, to the frustration of what he had called his "fondest hopes," that is, of never achieving recognition for a truly memorable and beneficent act. I think we get a rather clear reflection of this when Lincoln, after the 1858 debates with Douglas, consoled himself on his defeat in a letter to his old friend Anson Henry: "I am glad I made the late race. It gave me a hearing on the great and durable question of the age, which I could have had in no other way; and though I now sink out of view, and shall be forgotten, I believe I have made some marks which will tell for the cause of civil liberty long after I am gone."[12] Here he acknowledged that he had achieved at least part of his goal; the lasting good that he has done is specifically referred to as compensation for not being personally remembered.

The other "terrible end" that I believe the young Lincoln feared, one that is not well-documented and, indeed, is almost unrecognized in Lincoln biography, is madness. I referred earlier to his emotional collapse in the winter of 1841 as a result of his botched courtship with Mary Todd and his futile pursuit of Matilda Edwards. A similar condition had come upon him some five and a half years earlier, when the young woman to whom he was then engaged, Ann Rutledge, unexpectedly died of brain fever. The extended bereavement that this calamitous event brought on was such that his friends in New Salem, where he resided at the time, feared that he had lost the will to live and had become suicidal. Herndon learned the details of this incident from the people Lincoln himself confided in and who helped him through this difficult period. These two well-documented episodes indicate that in spite of his great physical strength, his strong intelligence, his self-assurance, his popularity and ebullient sense of humor, the young Lincoln had acute emotional vulnerabilities. He thus knew what it was to lose his composure and to find himself in the grip of powerful emotions that he could not control, but which, in fact, took control of him.

If we look for them, there are indeed indications that the young Lincoln was deeply concerned about such loss of control. His strong commitment to logic and rationality come immediately to mind. Living at the height of the romantic age, he steadfastly opted for the rationalism of the eighteenth-century Enlightenment and the arguments of writers like Volney and Paine. His two early public addresses, of which we have complete texts, the Lyceum Address of 1838 and his Temperance Address of 1842, both end with conspicuous appeals to Reason. In the Lyceum Address, the subject is the survival of American political institutions, which, he says, were established by the ardent beliefs and efforts of the founding generation but are now threatened by lawlessness and the passions of the mob. "Passion has helped us," Lincoln told his audience, "but can do so no more. It will in future be our enemy. Reason, cold, calculating, unimpassioned reason, must furnish all the materials for our future support and defence."[13] This appeal to Reason as a solution for a troubled political system is all the more conspicuous for being unexpected; one would think that suggesting a revival of the passions of the founders would be much more like it. The peroration of the Temperance Address, which celebrates the prospect of a temperance revolution, is even more unbuttoned and provocative: "Happy day, when, all appetites controled, all passions subdued, all matters subjected, *mind,* all conquering *mind,* shall live and move the monarch of the world. Glorious consummation! Hail fall of Fury! Reign of Reason, all hail!"[14] With no apparent sense of the irony involved, the final subduing of all passions is here passionately extolled, and the reign of Reason is announced by pulling out all the rhetorical stops. I point this out not to take a cheap shot at the young Lincoln but to call attention to the telling disjunction between medium and message. Nonetheless, these two dramatic perorations are revealing evidence that Lincoln had become passionate on the subject of Reason as a safeguard in situations that threaten disorder. As David Herbert Donald has recently pointed out, these two perorations point unmistakably to what Donald called one of Lincoln's "deepest concerns: the overthrow of reason."[15]

In 1846, Lincoln sent a literary friend a series of poems he had written that were inspired by a visit two years earlier to the Indiana neighborhood of his boyhood. "In the fall of 1844," Lincoln explained, "thinking I might aid some to carry the State of Indiana for Mr. Clay, I went into the neighborhood in that State in which I was raised, where my mother and only sister were buried, and from which I had been absent about fifteen years. That part of the country is, within itself, as unpoetical as any spot of the earth; but still, seeing it and its objects and inhabitants aroused feelings in me which were certainly poetry; though whether my expression of those feelings is poetry is quite another question."[16] The first poem Lincoln sent his friend was about the qualities of memory and the strangeness of revisiting a childhood scene where fully half of the people one expected to meet are dead. The second, which was a continuation of the first, was about an "insane man," Matthew Gentry, who had gone unexpectedly mad, maiming himself and trying to kill him own mother. "He is three years older than I," Lincoln wrote, "and when we were boys we went to school together. He was rather a bright lad, and the son of *the* rich man of our very poor neighbourhood. At the age of nineteen he unaccountably became furiously mad, from which condition he gradually settled down into harmless insanity. When, as I told you in my other letter I visited my old home in the fall of 1844, I found him still lingering in this wretched condition. In my poetizing mood I could not forget the impressions his case made upon me."[17]

That the impressions that had been made upon him were quite strong is implicit in Lincoln's remark, but the poem itself is vivid testimony to the magnitude and depth of those impressions. Here are the first several stanzas:

> But here's an object more of dread
>     Than ought the grave contains—
> A human form with reason fled,
>     While wretched life remains.
>
> Poor Matthew! Once of genius bright,
>     A fortune-favored child—
> Now locked for aye, in mental night,
>     A haggard mad-man wild.
>
> Poor Matthew! I have ne'er forgot,
>     When first, with maddened will,
> Yourself you maimed, your father fought,
>     And mother strove to kill;
>
> When terror spread, and neighbours ran,
>     Your dange'rous strength to bind;
> And soon, a howling crazy man
>     Your limbs were fast confined.
>
> How then you strove and shrieked aloud,
>     Your bones and sinews bared;
> And fiendish on the gazing crowd,
>     With burning eye-balls glared—
>
> And begged, and swore, and wept and prayed
>     With maniac laugh[ter] joined—
> How fearful were those signs displayed
>     By pangs that killed thy mind!

And when at length, tho' drear and long,
　　　Time soothed thy fiercer woes,
How plaintively thy mournful song
　　　Upon the still night rose.

I've heard it oft, as if I dreamed,
　　　Far distant, sweet, and lone—
The funeral dirge, it ever seemed
　　　Of reason dead and gone.

To drink its strains, I've stole away,
　　　All stealthily and still,
Ere yet the rising God of day
　　　Had streaked the Eastern hill.[18]

Many of Lincoln's biographers have pointed out these Indiana poems as evidence that their author was not a major poet, but in their haste to demonstrate their acuity as literary critics they have overlooked the more important circumstance that the Matthew Gentry poem is a firsthand autobiographical account of an important event in their subject's early life. It qualifies as an important event because the poem attests that Lincoln himself, as a young man, was personally affected by the case of Matthew Gentry's madness, even to the extent of slipping away from home in the middle of the night in order to listen to the strange music made by the moaning of his schoolmate. This concern is reinforced by Lincoln's seeking out Gentry when he visited his old Indiana neighborhood and what he told his literary friend about not being able to "forget the impressions his case made upon me."

Given the young Lincoln's dread of disorder and the discovery that he had acute emotional vulnerabilities that could get the better of him, it seems to me highly likely that one version of the "terrible end" that the young Lincoln constantly feared was that he might become, like Matthew Gentry, suddenly and unaccountably mad. We have no direct testimony to this effect, but I would like to offer a parallel case that may shed light on Lincoln's situation.

The philosopher William James was, like Lincoln, a brilliant and ambitious man, who, also like Lincoln, suffered temporary mental breakdowns in his early years and struggled with chronic depression the rest of his life. In his book *The Varieties of Religious Experience,* James reported an extraordinary case that he later admitted was actually his own description of an experience he had as a young man. Here is what James wrote:

> Whilst in [a] state of philosophic pessimism and general depression of spirits about my prospects, I went one evening into a dressing-room in the twilight to procure some article that was there; when suddenly there fell upon me without any warning, just as if it came out of the darkness, a horrible fear of my own existence. Simultaneously there arose in my mind the image of an epileptic patient whom I had seen in the asylum, a black-haired youth with greenish skin, entirely idiotic, who use to sit all day on one of the benches, or rather shelves against the wall, with his knees drawn up against his chin, and the coarse gray undershirt, which was his only garment, drawn over them enclosing his entire figure. He sat there like a sort of sculptured Egyptian mummy, moving nothing but his black eyes and looking absolutely non-human. This image and my fear entered into a species of combination with each other. *That shape am I,* I felt, potentially. Nothing that I possess can defend me against that fate, if the hour for it should strike for me as it struck for him.[19]

"After this," James continued, "the universe was changed for me altogether."[20] Whether or not the Matthew Gentry incident was a transforming experience for Abraham Lincoln is difficult to determine, but the parallels are provocative. Just as the image of the idiot suddenly imposed itself on James as an indelible symbol of his own acute vulnerability, Lincoln's poem strongly suggests that the example of Matthew Gentry may have had the same effect on him. If the most fortune-favored boy in the neighborhood of his growing up could suddenly and unaccountably lose his sanity and become a danger to his family and himself, one can readily guess what this suggested to the fatalistic young Lincoln about the precariousness of his own situation.

I began by calling attention to the questions of identity that I believe Lincoln faced as a young man and by suggesting that his anxiety about the future is a dimension of his experience that his biographers have not yet adequately considered. Why, I hope you are asking, is this significant? I think it comes down to this: Abraham Lincoln was the remarkable man he was, and thus the exceptional president and leader he was, in part because he lived from his young manhood onward with a relentless anxiety about his own personal destiny, his fate. He knew he was different from those around him and tried to act accordingly, showing strong independence from the time of his childhood. He knew he was unusually gifted and had great potential, but the example of Matthew Gentry suggested that those whom fortune favors have no special immunity against the unfathomable decrees of fate. And his experiences at the death of Ann Rutledge in 1835 and at the collapse of his courtship with Mary Todd in 1840–41 suggested that there were dark forces within him that he could not control, that could, in fact, take control of *him* and draw him under. As a counterweight to the superstition that he accepted as part of his nature, he deliberately cultivated rationality and logic, just as he cultivated humor and hilarity as a counterweight to the depression that increasingly plagued him. From an early age, he cherished a noble aspiration, a tenacious desire to accomplish something truly worthy for which he would be remembered, but it existed in tension with a terrible fear that he might not prevail.

We frequently hear that true champions are people who never doubt the eventuality of their own success, whose belief in themselves sweeps all before it, and whose philosophy is to take no counsel of their fears. These are, indeed, heroic qualities and well beyond the capabilities of most of us. In this light, it seems important to recognize that Abraham Lincoln, our greatest national hero, was apparently not such a person. He believed in himself, and that to an extraordinary degree, but his belief was balanced by a fearful conviction that even the noblest human aspirations and the worthiest efforts are subject to inscrutable contingencies and limitations. It was part of what he called the "doctrine of necessity," and it made its mark not only on his youth but on the man he would become.

## CHAPTER 3

# Mary and Abraham: A Marriage

## Jean H. Baker

"M arriage is a noose." "When a man takes a wife, he ceases to dread hell." "Marry in haste and repent in leisure." "A woman is necessarily an evil, and he that gets the most tolerable one is lucky"—and so on. There is an edgy, bridegroom-beware quality to the old proverbs that make marriage into a joking matter, with the joke on women. Today, yesterday's derisive sayings may seem as far removed from contemporary reality as some of the herbal remedies of an earlier age. But unlike calomel and the wild datura vine, these reproachful wisdoms from the past still carry authority and reflect our uncertain attitudes about the matrimonial state. We remember them because marriage is a universal, habitual human behavior—the ultimate in institutional survivals, however modified. We also remember them because marriage is so little studied, and this vacuum of historical information returns us to the folklore of the past.

Consequently, evaluations of the Lincoln marriage are largely subjective. Lacking context and for that reason varying tremendously, they float outside of historical analysis and remove a typical middle-class marriage from its moorings. Writes David Donald in the most authoritative biography ever written about Lincoln, "For all their quarrels, [the Lincolns] were devoted to each other. In the long years of their marriage Abraham Lincoln was never suspected of being unfaithful to his wife.

She, in turn, was immensely proud of him and was his most loyal supporter and admirer."[1]

But listen to what Michael Burlingame has written in *The Inner World of Abraham Lincoln* in a 58-page assessment of the Lincoln marriage, 56 pages of which are a condemnation of Mary Lincoln: "In 1864 [the President] pardoned a soldier who had deserted to go home and marry his sweetheart, [saying] 'I want to punish that young man . . . probably in less than year he will wish I had withheld that pardon." According to Burlingame, who argues that Lincoln regretted his marriage as much as he expected the young soldier to rue his, the Lincolns' marriage was a "fountain of misery."[2] Burlingame is certain that Mary Lincoln is responsible for this fountain of misery, without any acknowledgment that proverbs, peers, and popular culture had taught Lincoln to joke about marriage, although never his own.

Mostly the depictions of the Lincoln marriage as a disaster focus on Mary Todd Lincoln's failings. Of course, it has always been women who are held responsible for the quality of a marriage, for many reasons not the least of which is that men write history and have especially controlled the Lincoln story. After her husband was assassinated, Mary Lincoln told the biographer Josiah Holland that during their courtship she had "trespassed" on her husband's "tenderness of character."[3] Such a sense of guilt is hardly an unusual feeling for any recent widow or widower to acknowledge. But listen to how Douglas Wilson interprets the commonplace reaction of a widow. He writes: "Had she been a man, [Lincoln] would have known how to respond [to this trespass on his tenderness]: he could have ridiculed her in public, planted a malicious piece about her in the newspaper, or knocked her and left her a-kicking."[4] (These are things that, on at least one occasion, Lincoln did to various adversaries.) Certainly the pinnacle of this judgmental style of interpretation by opposing quotations emerges in the title of Michael Burlingame's short book—*Honest Abe, Dishonest Mary.*

My response is that we have too many historians deciding that they don't like Mary Lincoln and with extraordinary vehemence extrapolating their personal judgments onto the marriage. Douglas Wilson and Michael Burlingame don't like Mary Lincoln; that does not mean that Abraham Lincoln did not, nor, more relevantly, does it mean that the compact that Mary Todd and Abraham Lincoln fashioned in the nearly

23 years of their marriage was not a satisfying one from which both partners gained emotional support, physical satisfaction, and intellectual intimacy.

To be sure, an unsuccessful Lincoln marriage is historically serviceable. For the president's daily association with a woman he supposedly loathed makes him ever more the martyr of American mythology. The president who dealt so generously with the afflicted in public affairs learned, in this understanding, to do so through his private life with a shrew: "Lincoln daily practiced tolerance of a cantankerous female who was neither his first nor his greatest love."[5] And those who assess the Lincoln marriage as unhappy have provided their hero with some alternatives.

First there is Ann Rutledge, a woman who is often portrayed as Lincoln's first and *only* love. I must protest. Granted that Lincoln may have loved Ann Rutledge and may even have been engaged to her (she apparently was less loyal and was betrothed in her brief life of 22 years to two other men before becoming engaged to Lincoln), still Ann Rutledge died in 1835.[6] Lincoln married seven years later. According to the most rabid enthusiasts of the Ann Rutledge legend, Lincoln adored her throughout his life. Perhaps the reason has something to do with the hauntingly beautiful poem by Edgar Lee Masters from his *Spoon River Anthology* that expresses the romantic longing of men caught in the reality of humdrum relationships with wives transformed in their imaginations, according to one proverb, "from good girls to bad wives": "I am Ann Rutledge who sleep beneath these weeds/Beloved in life of Abraham Lincoln/Wedded to him not through union/but through separation."

But poetry is not historical evidence, and we do not have any creditable evidence of this enduring love from its principal, save an offhand comment in 1860 that he thought of her often. Hearsay evidence is not admissible, at least in most courts, and Lincoln's is no comment of an enduring passion. Instead it is more the testimony of his lifelong obsession with death. Now mine is not the evidence of scholars, but a half-century later I remember my first love with nostalgic affection. He happened to have been killed in an automobile accident while I was in college. Still I find it absurd for me and for anyone to hold that he was an only love and that I never got over him, even though I still think of him. There are, to paraphrase F. Scott Fitzgerald, second acts in American love lives.

Recently a new contender for Lincoln's affection has emerged in Douglas Wilson's *Honor's Voice: The Transformation of Abraham Lincoln.* Her name is Mathilda Edwards, and she was 17 years old and living at Elizabeth and Ninian Edwards's home when she supposedly became Lincoln's great love just before he, age 33, married Mary Todd. To establish this point, both Burlingame and Wilson make much of two sources from the Herndon collection. Lincoln's friends James Matheny and Joshua Speed, the latter said to be himself in love with Mathilda Edwards, reported that Lincoln fell in love with Miss Edwards.

But there is conflicting evidence that they do not consider. Elizabeth Edwards, who lived in this Springfield household on Second Street, twice told Herndon that there was nothing to the relationship between Mathilda and Abraham Lincoln. Interviewed in 1865 and again in 1887, Elizabeth Edwards, who is the most credible witness on the matter, denied that Lincoln loved Mathilda. Quoting from an interview with Elizabeth Edwards, "I asked Miss Edwards . . . if Mr. Lincoln ever mentioned the subject of love to her. Miss Edwards said O my word, he never mentioned such a subject to me. He never even stooped to pay me a compliment." And then Elizabeth goes on to say, "Mr. Lincoln loved Mary." Asked again in 1887, Elizabeth Edwards reiterated, "It is said that Miss Edwards had something to do in breaking Mary's engagement with Lincoln—it is not true. Miss Edwards told me that Lincoln never condescended to pay her even a poor compliment: it was the flirtation with Douglas that did the business."[7]

What the promotion of other women to Lincoln's true loves accomplishes is to undermine Mary Lincoln and to place an anecdotal vise on the Lincoln marriage, which makes Lincoln's wife into someone he did not want to marry and who, in retaliation, made his life, according to William Herndon, into a hell. Remember neither Abraham nor Mary ever left even a shred of documentary evidence that either of them loved anyone else. In fact, after Lincoln's assassination, Mary Lincoln wrote a friend that Lincoln had always assured her that she was his *only* love.[8]

Conveniently for the anyone-but-Mary school, there is another teenager waiting in the wings who may represent the millennium's candidate for Lincoln's true love. Sarah Rickard was the sister-in-law of

Lincoln's friend William Butler. After the president's death, Rickard reported to Herndon that Lincoln had proposed marriage to her, and she had refused him because he seemed almost like an older brother.[9] In any case, with the addition of Sarah to his list of girlfriends, Lincoln, a man universally viewed as uncomfortable with women, is transformed into a veritable Don Juan.

The reason for this controversy over the Lincoln marriage is our flawed understanding of the history of that institution. While we easily locate Lincoln the Republican partisan and officeholder within his political times, we do not put his marriage within the context of nineteenth-century courtship and marriage. There is an additional reason. Given the culture of their time, the Lincolns did not leave much documentary evidence about their relationship, and this silence, especially since many of their letters to each other burned in a fire, has encouraged an ensuing battle of quotations from outsiders over the state of their marriage. Unlike today, when young adults feel comfortable asking the president of the United States about his underwear, most middle-class Americans 150 years ago were reticent about their relationships with spouses. They closed their bedroom doors to the prying eyes of outsiders. Besides being off-limits, marriage is not a topic that most historians are interested in, especially those who write about Lincoln. Instead it is consigned to the woman's world.

In recent years, sociologists and historians have begun to study marriage as a legal arrangement, a social custom, a gender practice, and a sexual statement that changes over time. Critical in this regard for the Lincolns was the fact that the patriarchal marriage of the eighteenth century that placed men as the rulers of the household was giving way in mid-nineteenth century America to a more companionate ideal in which wives and husbands sought mutual love and affection as individuals creating a satisfying partnership. Some, though not all, Americans of this period held a romantic vision of marriage as the joining together of individuals with unique personalities who adored each other because that newfound entity of the nineteenth century—their essential self—had discovered a complementary soul.[10] In what follows I would like to place the Lincoln marriage in the context of the scholarship that we have on courtship, wedding, marriage, and parenting, using mostly the words and behaviors of the marriage's two principals and avoiding the memories of their contemporaries. Perhaps that way we can end the divergence of opinion—"the battle of the quotations"—that has led historians to create a contentious subfield of Lincoln studies.

## Courtship: "A Man Chases a Woman Until She Catches Him"

For most young women in midcentury America, the period of courting was a time of gaiety and fun. During this time females exerted an authority they lost when they married and by common law became one with their husbands—and he legally the one. Certainly this was the case with the Kentucky belle Mary Todd who, as her brother-in-law Ninian Edwards said, "could make a bishop forget his prayers."[11] She was having a good time at the parties in Springfield, Illinois, after she settled in her sister Elizabeth's home in the late 1830s.

By this time, the earlier considerations of cows and land and marriages controlled by parents had given way to considerable power exerted by young women themselves over whom they would marry. Marriage was no longer a property arrangement, nor an agreement between families. By way of comparison, in the 1730s Benjamin Franklin sought a dowry from a possible bride in order to pay for his printing press, and when the mother of his intended refused, he promptly ended the courtship.[12] But in the new republic of the United States, arranged marriages disappeared.

Indeed, European travelers pointed to the freedom of mate choice as one of the signal differences between Europe and the United States. But within an institution in which men enhanced their standing and satisfied their wants, American wives often lost their ambitions. Alexis de Tocqueville, the perceptive French observer of the United States, noticed as much in *Democracy in America:* "In America a woman loses her independence forever in the bonds of matrimony . . . a wife submits to stricter obligations . . . her husband's home is almost a cloister."[13] Mary Lincoln had observed as much about an institution she once called "the crime of matrimony." "Why is it," wrote Mary Todd to one of her friends, "that married folks always become so serious?"[14]

Even if they could choose their mate without parental interference, still young middle-class women had to marry because they were denied any respectable means of earning a living save as teachers and governesses, at the same time that any means of self-protection within marriage was denied them. But their courting power was solely that of a veto. As one young American woman Eliza Southgate noted, "We have the liberty of refusing those we don't like, but not of selecting those we do."[15] Mary Todd had done to that several suitors. Once married, women were without rights as citizens; but in a catch-22, if they stayed single, they were ridiculed as spinsters. Thus for young American women, marriage was a necessity; it was the way they earned their living. But they surely had reasons to hesitate.

In an era when divorce was not a recognized statutory procedure and required in most instances special legislative action or a petition to a special court, marriage to a bad husband—to an alcoholic (and this was a period of the highest per capita alcohol consumption in our history) or to a wife-beater was a life-threatening mistake. The annals of nineteenth-century misery were full of women who fled their husbands to avoid abuse and were ordered home by the courts.

Meanwhile, men had reasons to hesitate before marrying, for as breadwinners they were responsible for providing for their wives and children. For a man like the upwardly mobile and very conscientious Abraham Lincoln, such circumstances gave cause for concern. As Abraham Lincoln wrote in 1837, "Whatever woman may cast her lot with mine, should any ever do so, it is my intention to do all in my power to make her happy and contented."[16] And that required a sufficient income to establish a household with a young woman who was accustomed to a standard of living far above that of Lincoln's childhood. "Men," writes a student of courtship, "hesitated to commit themselves to marry—until they felt emotionally ready and could be sure of acquiring the necessary financial resources. Emotional preparedness for marriage was simply defined: If a young man fell in love with a woman, he wanted—some day—to marry her."[17]

And as every study of marriage in the nineteenth century makes clear, many engagements were disrupted as the principals stepped back from their courtship to contemplate the permanency of their future condition. As we know, this was the case with Mary Todd and Abraham Lincoln. Sometime in 1840 they had reached an agreement that they might marry; and then, on what Lincoln called "the Fatal First" of January 1841, they broke off their engagement. A year and a half later they were courting again; and as all the world knows, they married in November of 1842.

Many historians have taken the disruption of their courtship as a sign that Lincoln did not love Mary Todd, and they assume without any preponderance of evidence that he was the one who ended their engagement. Then, according to this interpretation, he renewed his troth because he valued honor over breaking his word or because he worried, having been attached for debt in New Salem, that he might be charged with breach of promise. I find these explanations implausible. Isn't it more dishonorable, especially in an age when true love is becoming the conventional practice, to marry a woman you don't love? And as for a breach of promise suit, this judicial procedure was infrequently used in the 1840s when a new tradition of courtship based on mutual love had replaced a previous generation's interest in property arrangements. In a resounding statement of her own commitment to the new way of courtship and marriage, Mary Todd wrote a friend in 1840 " . . . my hand will never be given where my heart is not."[18]

Besides, where is Mary Lincoln in this masculinized equation during a period in her life when she had considerable power? Well, in this misogynist rendering she is humiliated, marries Abraham Lincoln for vengeance, and spends the rest of her life succeeding in making her husband miserable, according to William Herndon in an interpretation that has influenced contemporary positions. Here we have left the common-sense world that should accompany historians and have entered the dramas of Italian opera as well as the gender wars. There is no compelling documentary evidence on why their engagement was broken or who broke it, so the field is rife for speculation.

The clash of contradictory opinions ranges from Ninian Edwards's assertion that Mary Todd released Lincoln from his pledge, through Elizabeth Edwards's position that her sister's flirting with Stephen Douglas disrupted the relationship, to Abner Ellis, the Springfield postmaster's, opinion that Mary backed out of the engagement. "Hur refusal to comply actually made Mr. L sick."[19] And among modern historians, interpretations move from Ruth Randall's arguments that the Edwards family opposed the marriage and so Lincoln gave it up, to my view that she was furious when he was late to a party.

Douglas Wilson, an historian of Lincoln's early private life, contends that the Lincoln courtship was superficial. He argues that when Lincoln got to know Mary better he found out that he did not like her, but as a man of honor felt compelled to marry her. But Wilson overlooks two things—one specific to Mary Todd and the other to courting in the early nineteenth century. He forgets that Mary Todd had first come to Springfield in 1837 (although he notes it in an exculpatory footnote) at almost exactly the same time that Lincoln had arrived from New Salem. She had then gone home, to return a year later. Hence their acquaintanceship was probably longer than he maintains. Furthermore, a courtship in which the lovers write those delightful "Lost Townships" letters published in the *Sangamon Journal* is hardly a superficial one in which the couple does not know each other.

These famous letters have been used in a variety of different ways to infer a number of things about Lincoln and the duel he almost fought with James Shields. Initially Lincoln had made fun of Shields, the Illinois state auditor, in a devastating satire published in the *Sangamon Journal*. Learning that Lincoln had written them, Shields challenged the chagrined author to a duel that was only forestalled by last-minute negotiations. But Mary Todd had also written one of these letters, and for her and her future husband they stand as an amusing public means for the reconciliation of a private relationship. "I know he's a fighting man . . . ," wrote Mary Lincoln, "but isn't marrying better than fighting, although it tends to run into it." In Mary's final effort, written within weeks of her marriage, "Happy groom! Is sadness far distant from thee? The fair girls dream only of past times and glee."[20]

The second point is that we are imposing our twentieth-century standards of courtship if we think that Mary Todd did not know Abraham Lincoln very well. In the nineteenth century, the public courtships of earlier periods were no longer observed by the community. Instead courting, which usually began with friendship, had moved inside, where outsiders were closed out. The mid-nineteenth century was a transitional period in this process, as what had been a public affair became more private and sheltered, often in the twentieth century in the back seat of an automobile. The Lincoln courtship occurred at an historical moment when some courting was out of the house and very public, taking place during picnics, sleigh rides, and Springfield's dancing parties—

all of which are mentioned by Mary Todd. But as often, a romance developed in walks down country lanes, on parlor sofas such as the horse-hair one in the Edwards's home, and in the bower of trees surrounding the house.[21] That is why there were few sightings of Abraham and Mary in busybody Springfield before their marriage in the fall of 1842.

And many mid-nineteenth-century courtships were briefer than those of the twentieth century. "Before marriage," writes John Gillis, "young people made and unmade relationships with bewildering rapidity, keeping open their options for a much longer period than young people do today."[22] This was a generation that did not know the meaning of going steady. Surely the number and variety of both Mathilda Edwards's and Mary Todd's beaux suggest different, less uniform courting arrangements than exist in our times.

On the other hand Lincoln, according to Charles Strozier and David Donald, had trouble moving from the familiarity of all-male gatherings to intimacy with a woman. According to Strozier, both Speed and Lincoln "found solace in discussing their forebodings about sexuality—their intimate maleness substituted for the tantalizing and frightening closeness of women." In Donald's words, "(Lincoln) was worried about how to go about transforming the adored object of chaste passion into a bed partner."[23] One measure of Lincoln's uncertainty was his age when he married. He was 33 years old, which is seven years older than the typical groom of this period. Most men in Springfield married at 24, and even those who had come to the city as bachelors were routinely married by 31.[24]

Other historians cite Lincoln's letters to his friend Joshua Speed as evidence of his uncertainty about marrying. In this interpretation, only after Speed answered that he was more contented married than single did Lincoln become involved with Mary Todd again. Yet if we place the Lincoln courtship within its contemporary context, such inquiries emerge as routine occurrences. [25] What Abraham Lincoln and Mary Todd did in delaying their marriage was such a commonplace episode that we don't have to use it as a predictive factor for their future happiness together.

In fact, the timing of the transition to marriage was the most controversial aspect of marrying, and especially young men often wrote their friends to inquire as to their evaluation of marriage. Abraham Lincoln was no different than Daniel Webster and Henry Channing and thousands of other American men when he sought counsel from a male friend about his experience. The real point here is that both Joshua Speed and Abraham Lincoln were nervous about marriage. For self-made men, the creation of their own family circle might inhibit the independence and autonomy they had so carefully crafted for themselves in a male environment in new urban settings. It was the great dilemma of the nineteenth century facing middle-class males: was a manly life compatible with the domesticity imposed by this new cultural ideal of companionate marriage? And on the other hand, could they be true men of the republic who grounded their civic spirit in the creation of a family unless they married?[26]

### The Wedding: "A Wedding Is Destiny and Hanging Likewise"

Much has been made of the suddenness of the Lincoln wedding. In the event's classic symbol, the cakes were still warm; the bridesmaids recruited the day of the wedding; and there were only 30 guests. The groom is reported to have said that he was going to hell—a sentiment that other grooms of the time frequently seconded as they anxiously contemplated an uncertain future state. Note here those pessimistic proverbs about marriage that have infiltrated our cultural heritage. "He that marries late marries ill." "Marry in haste and repent at leisure." They represent just the kind of dark popular wisdom that Lincoln would latch onto to comment about marriage as a public event, but they do not indicate his private feelings about his own marriage. In fact he would acknowledge his marriage as a matter of "profound wonder." Rather than being interpreted as the awe that a 33-year-old man felt at the matrimonial state, even this comment has been interpreted to display his ambivalence about his marriage to Mary Todd.[27]

For the detractors of Mary Lincoln, the swiftness of the marriage sustains the proverb that a quick marriage is a bad one. In fact, after the very public disruption of their courtship, Mary Todd had told her sister that "it was best to keep the courtship from all eyes and ears."[28] Again our lack of historical understanding about weddings has contaminated the Lincoln story. Weddings of the nineteenth century were shorter and simpler affairs than they are today. Indeed, getting married on what would seem to us the spur of the moment was quite common.

For example, among the Adlai Stevenson family of nearby Bloomington during this period, several brides and grooms undertook similarly hasty (in our eyes, but not theirs) marriages.[29] In 1855, Lucy Stone and Henry Blackwell were married before breakfast, and on their way to New York by eight o'clock in the morning. The point is that there was no standardized wedding ritual, and while there were plenty of so-called prescription manuals that prescribed etiquette on a variety of other issues, few dealt with weddings. Nor were marriages obligatory family events as they are in contemporary America. Brides did not wear fancy satin gowns of lacy white; the concept of an organized catered reception was two generations away; any need for months of planning amid wedding consultants was unnecessary.

If we can move the Lincolns away from their uniqueness and use them to sustain generalizations about the history of weddings, their wedding took place at a transitional point in the history of middle-class American marriages. In the wonderful anecdote of the occasion, Judge William Brown, who was accustomed to more rustic civil ceremonies, cried out after the groom had promised to endow the bride with all his goods and chattels, lands, and tenements: "The statute fixes that, Lord Jesus Christ, God Almighty, Lincoln." Still Lincoln had contemplated his wedding long enough and loved his bride sufficiently to place an engraved gold ring on her finger with the inscription "LOVE IS ETERNAL."[30]

## The Marriage: "A True Wife Is Her Husband's Better Half"

Like their courtship and wedding, the Lincoln marriage is encrusted with conflicting quotations about its level of satisfaction. Certainly it is worth remembering that one observer's bad marriage may be another's heaven. Both Professors Burlingame and Wilson ask the question, how could Lincoln have married such a dreadful woman? But we could ask as well, what did Mary Todd see in Abraham Lincoln, the hardly handsome or gentrified product of the prairies of Kentucky, Indiana, and Illinois who still wore pants that were too short and who once burst into a party saying the "girls smelt good." In any case the marriage, a crucial one for these two who had cut themselves off from their surviving parents and birthplaces, endured amid compromises on both sides. Mary

Lincoln acknowledged the completeness of the relationship and its companionship, once writing a friend that her husband had been "always lover-husband-father-all to me."[31]

And as for the close-mouthed Lincoln, it was his behavior, not his words, that testified to the strength of the relationship, whether it was his often-expressed desire to have Mary Lincoln home ("I really wish to see you," he telegraphed in 1863), his nursing of his wife after the death of their son Eddie in 1850 and the birth of Tad in 1853, and his appearance at the Springfield railroad station three nights in a row during a snowstorm in January 1861 to meet his wife who was returning from New York. Certainly the president shared some of the turmoil of his presidential life with her, meticulously advising her when she should come home if she took Tad out of Washington during the bad weather season. "Don't come on the night train; it is too cold," he warned in December 1864 with the solicitude that marked his relations with her. "I would be glad to see you and Tad," he telegraphed, as he acknowledged her deep interest in army matters and often sent news from the Virginia front. He encouraged her to join him in the last days of the war when he went several times to Virginia, and he was holding hands with her during the performance of *Our American Cousin* when he was assassinated. Even his failure to be at home—a chronic condition for nineteenth-century professional men—must be viewed in the context of nineteenth-century marriages where complaints by wives about their husband's absences were common.[32]

Leaving the impressionistic judgments aside, I would like to take three arenas of the Lincolns' life that brought the couple close together and then discuss several that drew them apart.

## Sources of Congeniality: "Be One with Me in All Things"

Most observers of the Lincoln marriage have been impressed with their sexuality. Sex was one of the bonds that made this marriage between two very different human beings a success. Again some male historians have argued without any evidence that the Lincolns' sex life ended after Tad's difficult birth in 1853 because Mary Lincoln did not have any more children. Alternatively it is supposed to have ended in 1856 when the Lincolns enlarged their house at Jackson and Eighth and no longer

shared a bedroom, a conclusion that removes the couple from the growing affluence of midcentury middle-class Americans who sought bigger
houses with more bedrooms. By the 1850s, many middle-class couples
slept in separate bedrooms. For example, Letitia and Adlai Stevenson of
nearby Bloomington did so, and managed to add to their family. Despite malevolent speculation, there are almost no gynecological conditions resulting from childbirth that prevent sexual intercourse save a
prolapsed uterus, which, given Mary Lincoln's lifestyle, she clearly did
not suffer from. Again, the removal of the Lincoln marriage from its life
and times has distorted our view on these matters.

Listen to the letters that Abraham and Mary Lincoln wrote to each
other in 1847–1848 when Mary Lincoln had gone to Lexington to visit
her family and Abraham Lincoln, an Illinois congressman, was living in
a boarding house in Washington during winter. Lincoln had encouraged
her departure; she was cooped up in two small rooms with two children
under five, but as he acknowledges, "In this troublesome world we are
never quite satisfied. When you were here, I thought you hindered me
some in attending to business." Now he wants her back. "Come along
as soon as possible," he writes in June 1848, signing himself "affectionately" and "most affectionately." "I shall be impatient till I see you. . . .
Come as soon as you can."[33] It is not the lament of a man who hates his
wife. Nor are his telegrams to Mary Lincoln in the White House when
she has left for the summer and he hopes that she will come back soon.

Earlier Mary had written a long letter to him that had a strain of
sexuality in it: "How much, I wish instead of writing, we were together
this evening. I feel very sad away from you. . . . With love I must bid
you good night." Then she scratched through with love, knowing that
this night at least she would not physically love her husband.[34] Several
times Mary Lincoln is quoted by neighbors as wishing that Mr. Lincoln
were home more often so that she could love him more. And while
women are ever accused of dressing for other women, Mary Lincoln's
low-cut dresses and flirtatious style certainly drew attention to her, but
they also pleased her husband.

On more than one occasion, her husband praised her stylishness in
the presence of bystanders. He noticed when she adopted low necklines.
"Whew," the president was quoted as saying, "our cat has a long tail
tonight." Always moved by her looks in the way of long-married couples

who pass imperfections lightly by (and Mary Lincoln did not age well), he praised his wife's appearance. Once Lincoln remarked at a White House reception, "my wife is as handsome as when she was a girl, and I a poor nobody then, fell in love with her and what is more, have never fallen out."[35]

Indeed, Mary had become pregnant almost immediately after their wedding, and while this was not unusual for American brides in an era without many effective means of artificial contraception, what is interesting about the Lincoln marriage is that the couple controlled their fertility. Robert Todd was born in August 1843, followed by Eddie in early 1846. There were no more children until after Eddie's death in 1850, and then immediately so. Willie was born in December 1850, followed, because he needed a playmate, by the fourth and last Lincoln son, Thomas "Tad" in April 1853. Compare this to Mary Lincoln's family of origin. Her father Robert Smith Todd had seven children by his first wife and after she died after childbirth, another eight by his second wife.

But by the 1850s, especially in towns and cities, couples like the Lincolns were responding to the fact that children were not potential units of labor available for work on the family farm as Lincoln had been for his father, but rather were projects that required considerable venture capital. That is one reason why the American fertility rate dropped from seven in 1800 to a fraction over six in 1820 and to a little over four in 1850. The reason was birth control, by which I mean any kind of action taken to prevent having children whether it be coitus interruptus, long-term breast feeding, or the devices such as condoms and "womb veils" that arrived in the Springfield post office in mysterious brown paper wrappers.[36]

Planning a family requires an intimacy about sexual relations that for aspiring couples meant shared companionate power over reproduction, as sex, according to a recent student, "became a powerful pervasive subject in the 19th century with birth control a part of it."[37] In an age when sexuality was being separated from reproduction and partners discussed the timing of their children, there was mutuality and openness about a critical aspect of the intersecting lives of wives and husbands.

At home there was also little tension in the Lincolns' life as parents, and parenting, sex, and money matters are the habitual arenas in which couples of both the nineteenth and twentieth centuries disagree. As we know from them and from their neighbors, both Mary and Abraham were permissive parents. Once on a train to Lexington, a fellow traveler was appalled at the behavior of what Lincoln affectionately called "the Little codgers."[38] Eddie and Robert were racing through the train, disturbing the other passengers. Lincoln's law partner William Herndon has left disgruntled accounts of the boys' visits to the law office he shared with Lincoln, where they dropped orange peels and pulled out legal files—with never a reprimand from their ever-approving father. In the White House, the children's antics, which included once waving a Confederate flag and aiming a toy cannon at the cabinet, continued unchecked by any parental intervention. According to Mary Lincoln, her husband took pleasure that his children were "free-happy and unrestrained by parental tyranny. . . . 'Love is the chain whereby to lock a child to its parents.'" Or as the First Lady said, "We never controlled our children much."[39]

Fully engaged with the children—in a way that more traditional parents were not—Mary and Abraham gave birthday parties in their honor at a time when such celebrations were unusual. Mary dressed up and played a part in Robert's reenactment of Ivanhoe, giving advice to the brave knights to be more merciful than brawny. Neighbors remembered parties at the Lincolns' where the boys were trotted downstairs to recite poetry, usually Shakespeare and Burns. And when her half-sister Emilie Helm was soon to be a mother, she offered her own self-portrait as a "happy, loving, laughing Mama."[40]

Besides sex and their children, Mary Todd and Abraham Lincoln shared the politics of what Mary Lincoln liked to call the affairs of "our Lincoln party." Indeed the relationship between Mary and Abraham Lincoln is laced together with examples of their mutual interest in partisan politics. The daughter of a father who participated in Kentucky politics as a Whig state senator, Mary Lincoln was one of those nineteenth-century women who were interested in "the great game of politics." There were others, and we are in the process of finding out about the tangential, but nevertheless important, ways in which American women participated in parades, went to rallies, and even gave speeches in the 1840s and 1850s.[41] Mary Lincoln was such a woman; and even in the White House, the couple discussed the composition of his cabinet, as well as matters relating to the war and politics.

This was a couple who transformed a mutual interest in public events into a love affair. They had always shared an admiration for Henry Clay, Mary's neighbor in Lexington, and Whig politics. During the days of their courting, they had discussed election returns, and Mary Todd had commented in a letter to a friend about Lincoln's presence in the offices of the Whig newspaper during the 1840 election when, according to James Conkling, "some fifteen or twenty ladies were collected to listen to the Tippecanoe Singing Club." During their courtship, Lincoln gave Mary a list of the state legislative returns, and she tied it with a pink ribbon.[42]

After their marriage, Mary Lincoln maintained her interest in the male sphere of politics. It was partly her interest in public issues that brought her to Mrs. Spriggs's tiny Washington boarding house when Lincoln was a congressman in 1847. Few wives from the Midwest, much less mothers with small children, uprooted their households to be with their husbands in Washington, and Mary Lincoln was one of the few. And when Lincoln wanted to become the commissioner of the Land Office, it was his wife who undertook a letter-writing campaign. This shared interest in politics was one of the significant ways in which she related to her husband.

Lincoln's political career stalled in the 1850s, and it was Mary Lincoln who constantly encouraged him in his two unsuccessful senatorial campaigns. An ascension from Vandalia, the first capital of Illinois, to the White House would have left little room for a wife's advice. Instead, Lincoln's jagged course across the partisan landscape of nineteenth-century American party politics left plenty of opportunity for shared discussions of political strategies. At home, Lincoln received not only the applause that a typical wife might bestow; he received heartening reinforcement as well as intelligent discussion of ambitions that were mutual. "Mary insists that I am going to be Senator and President of the United States too," Lincoln told a reporter and then shook with laughter at the absurdity of it. Henry Whitney, a lawyer who traveled the circuit with Lincoln, recounted a similar incident.[43]

But this interest in politics made Mary Lincoln unpopular with some of Lincoln's friends, certainly with his secretaries in the White House, and ultimately with many historians. Women's lives in this period were to be led in private, not public. Women were not to hold discussions about politics and know the difference among Whigs, Know-Nothings, and Democrats. Women were not supposed to meddle in patronage matters. And certainly Mary Lincoln excelled in the latter. She sought positions for her relatives, and when she failed to get her way, she intercepted cabinet officers and pressed officials at her receptions. Often she pleaded in the name of the presidential "we."

To the extent that politics involves matters of power and authority, as first lady Mary Lincoln was consistently political. When she began her crusade to fix up the White House, which she, and others, thought resembled a shabby old hotel, she did so because she believed that it would be a physical statement of the power of the Union during the Civil War. She knew that the impressions of foreign ambassadors, especially those from Great Britain and France, were critical to the future of the republic. But the White House was her home, and in the separated spheres of the nineteenth century she was enacting what historians of women have classified as "domestic feminism." She was decorating a home for her family, and doing so at a time in which women were beginning to enter the public domain as consumers.

## Avenues of Separation:
## "Alas for Those Who Love and Cannot Blend"

Of course, like others', this was not a marriage without conflict, although the stories of marital anguish—always for Lincoln rather than his wife—are overblown. The episodes of Mary Lincoln's pot-throwing and knife-wielding promoted, incredibly, into possible maricide are exaggerated and exceptional. But their avenues of separation involved differences in temperament and taste. He was frugal; she was sometimes a spendthrift. He was plebeian; she was to the manor born. On her bad days she was volatile and lost her temper; on his he was depressed and distracted. Often he was remote, and he was frequently absent from home. Certainly the president was embarrassed by his wife's spending during the Civil War, both on her clothes and on the White House—the flub-a-dubs that he complained about.

In one spectacular public instance, he was mortified by her behavior on the parade grounds near Malvern Hill in March 1865. She had arrived late to the parade grounds, and when she saw him riding alongside the handsome Mrs. General Ord, Mary Lincoln berated him before the high command of the Union Army. But like summer storms, these fits of temper and jealously subsided and the couple reconciled in a few days.[44]

Clearly there were outsiders who saw their marriage as a difficult relationship; clearly Mary Lincoln had a temper that she displayed to the world, instead of, one might conjecture, internalizing her complaints against her husband in silent anger or indifference. Clearly her husband was frequently inattentive to her, "deficient," as one woman once said of him, "in those little links which make up the great chain of woman's happiness. . . ."[45]

## Conclusion: "A Union of Opposites"

In these differences Abraham Lincoln and Mary Todd Lincoln complemented each other—not in the ancient way of marriage as a little commonwealth with the husband and father as ruler and the wife and mother as subject. Rather, their relationship was part of the companionate ideal of a new closeness of husband and wife—the "tender passion" of a nineteenth-century marital style based on difference—the union of opposites of a generation that sought congeniality of interests even as it established the paradox of separate spheres. Or as Mary Lincoln perceptively commented about her marriage, "for I well know how deeply grieved the P feels over any coolness of mine . . . fortunately for both my Husband and myself . . . our lives [together] have been eminently peaceful."[46]

Partly this mutuality grew because both spouses crossed over the boundaries that divided husbands and wives into separate spheres and that often established marriages grounded in parallel lives of different work, habitats, traits, and emotions. Given Mary Lincoln's interest in politics, her life overlapped with Abraham Lincoln's in an unusual shared endeavor, while he, with his egalitarian approach to their mutual authority in the home and with the children, entered the traditional woman's world. "Mr. Lincoln," according to his nephew, was always "a home man."[47] Today we expect marriages to be based on symmetrical roles with both partners sharing work, play, leisure activities, housekeeping, and child-raising. The Lincoln marriage puts us on the road to that kind of relationship and, from this perspective, is very modern.

The best way to remember the Lincoln marriage is to consider individual marriages arranged along a spectrum from total alienation to
warm, empathetic relationships of intimacy. Somewhere along this line
the Lincoln marriage falls. Placed in the context of other middle-class
marriages of this period that separated husbands and wives into different spheres, the Lincoln marriage seems a close one. That is not to say
that there were not squabbles and the frequent rain showers of Mary
Lincoln's temper, which were matched by the lack of spousal congeniality occasioned by Lincoln's melancholy and episodes of neurasthenia. It
is to say that its bad moments have been vastly exaggerated.

Remember this marriage was bound together by three strong
bonds—sex, parenting, and politics—and keep in mind that story, cor-
roborated by several observers, that when Lincoln learned he had won
the Republican nomination and later the presidency, he hurried home,
saying as he turned the corner, "Mary, Mary *we* are elected." It is as
good a testament to the profound respect and affinity the Lincolns had
for each other as any I can think of.[48]

## CHAPTER 4

# Military Fantasies

### Gerald J. Prokopowicz

In July 1863, at the Pennsylvania crossroads town of Gettysburg, the Union Army of the Potomac under George Gordon Meade won a momentous victory over Robert E. Lee's Army of Northern Virginia. In three days of intense fighting, Meade's army inflicted 28,000 Confederate losses, while suffering 23,000 killed or wounded of its own, including three of its seven corps commanders. On the fourth day of the confrontation between the two forces, the battlefield was comparatively quiet. Lee sent a seventeen-mile-long wagon train of wounded men back toward Virginia, but defiantly kept the rest of his troops in place on Seminary Ridge, daring Meade to attack him. Meade, however, showed no sign of wanting to continue the fight, and Lee at last ordered the rest of his army off the battlefield. After waiting another day to be certain that Lee was retreating, Meade pursued cautiously.

In Washington, D.C., where reports from Meade's headquarters arrived via a chain of semaphore and telegraph stations, sometimes within the hour, President Abraham Lincoln's elation at the reading of the Union victory was mixed with concern that Meade might lose the advantage he had gained. From the moment in June when the Confederates had marched north into Maryland, Lincoln had wanted the Army of the Potomac not simply to chase Lee back to Virginia, but to follow him, attack him, cut him off from his base, and destroy him. Now, with Lee's weakened forces trapped between Meade's troops and the rain-swollen Potomac, all this seemed possible. The end of the war was in sight, Lincoln thought, if only Meade would attack. But the president found the tone of his general's dispatches disconcerting, especially when Meade spoke of "efforts to drive from our soil every vestige of the presence of the invader." "Will our Generals never get that idea out of their heads?" Lincoln fumed. "The whole country is *our* soil."[1]

What happened next left Lincoln nearly beside himself with frustration. Meade did not attack, Lee crossed the Potomac safely at Williamsport on July 14, and the war seemed no closer to its end than ever. Major General Henry Wager Halleck, Lincoln's military chief of staff, immediately informed Meade of Lincoln's unhappiness with the result of the campaign, prompting Meade to offer his resignation. To soothe Meade's injured pride, Lincoln sat down that same afternoon to write the general a letter of thanks and apology. "I am very—*very*—grateful to you for the magnificent success you gave the cause of the country at Gettysburg; and I am sorry now to be the author of the slightest pain to you," he began. But even as the words flowed from Lincoln's pen, his emotions overcame him again:

> I do not believe you appreciate the magnitude of the misfortune involved in Lee's escape. He was within your easy grasp, and to have closed upon him would, in connection with our other late successes, have ended the war. As it is the war will be prolonged indefinitely. . . . Your golden opportunity is gone, and I am immeasurably distressed because of it.

So distressed was Lincoln that he had begun to wonder aloud about going to the headquarters of the Army of the Potomac and, under his constitutional power as commander in chief, taking personal control of the army in order to complete the pursuit and destruction of Lee's forces. "Nothing I could say or do," he lamented to his secretary John Hay, "could make the Army move." And he added to his son Robert: "If I had gone up there, I could have whipped them myself."[2]

Traditionally, historians have dismissed this extraordinary suggestion as nothing more than an expression of Lincoln's frustration, like an
angry baseball fan yelling "Hey, I coulda caught that one myself" at a
$2-million-a-year utility infielder who has dropped an easy pop fly. But
there is reason to believe that Lincoln meant what he said. This was not
the first time that Lincoln had spoken of taking personal command of
the Army of the Potomac. On January 12, 1862, Lincoln had discussed
military strategy with an old friend, Illinois Senator Orville H. Browning. Since General in Chief George B. McClellan had typhoid fever and
the three main federal armies were showing no signs of preparing to
take aggressive action, Lincoln told Browning that he was "thinking of
taking the field himself." After McClellan recovered from his illness, he
brilliantly outflanked the rebels by moving the Army of the Potomac by
sea to the Virginia Peninsula, but there he lost his nerve and advanced
so slowly that Lincoln reportedly said, "If McClellan is not using the
Army, I should like to borrow it for a while." When Lincoln speculated
on July 15, 1863, that he might have led the army to victory after Gettysburg, John Hay confirmed in his diary that the president "had that
idea" before.[3]

Not only did Lincoln regularly speak of playing a more direct role
in the conduct of the war, on occasion he acted out his fantasy of participating in the fighting. During a visit to McClellan's headquarters on
the Peninsula in May 1862, Lincoln, accompanied by Secretary of War
Edwin Stanton and Treasury Secretary Salmon Chase, sailed in a revenue cutter across Hampton Roads toward the Confederate-held city of
Norfolk. In a moment of surreal adventure, Lincoln and Stanton
boarded a smaller boat, sailed to the southern shore, disembarked, and
strolled on the Confederate beach for a few dangerous moments. Based
on the president's report that the coastline was more navigable than had
been supposed, Union infantry went ashore at the same spot the next
day and captured Norfolk.

As president, Lincoln traveled little, but when he did leave the
White House it was often to get a closer look at the war. He did not
have to go far in July 1864, when Jubal Early's rebel raiders approached
within shooting distance of Washington. Lincoln took the opportunity
to ride out to Fort Stevens on the outskirts of the city to observe the
fighting. There he stood on the parapet amid the whistling of enemy

bullets while sensible veteran officers took shelter behind the walls; according to legend, one of those officers was future Supreme Court Justice Oliver Wendell Holmes, Jr., who did not recognize the president and yelled at him to "Get down you damn fool." Lincoln got down, but his appetite for danger was apparently not sated. The following year, during his trip to Grant's headquarters at City Point in April 1865, he dared to enter the city of Richmond on foot before the embers had cooled from the fires that marked the rebels' withdrawal, and toured the former capital of the Confederacy escorted only by his young son Tad and a few sailors.

These stories raise two questions. First, for what purpose did Abraham Lincoln, a lifelong politician with almost no military experience, so consistently seek to participate more directly in the war? Second, what would have happened if Lincoln had gone beyond speculation and observation, and assumed the leadership of the Army of the Potomac? The questions are interrelated. Lincoln felt both a personal and public imperative to demonstrate his willingness to share the risks of war, as a matter of honor as well as political leadership. He also saw, as the war went on, that few of the men he was appointing to command were any more qualified or capable than he was. But the particular leadership abilities that made him a great president would not necessarily have made him a great general, or even a good one, and it was fortunate for the Republic that he kept his fantasies in check long enough to allow leaders like Grant and Sherman to emerge and relieve him of the need to imagine himself guiding the Union to victory on the battlefield.

The primary motive for Lincoln to go to war in person was the opportunity to make a public display of his personal bravery. Physical courage, Lincoln knew, was an important aspect of political as well as military leadership in a society that lionized war heroes like George Washington and Andrew Jackson. As a young man, Lincoln had learned firsthand the political value of courage, when he moved to the rough and tumble frontier village of New Salem in 1831 and quickly won the respect of the local ruffians by outwrestling their leader, Jack Armstrong. A year later, when the men of New Salem answered the state's call for militia to drive Chief Black Hawk and his people away from their ancestral lands, Lincoln was among the volunteers. So impressive had been his demonstration of courage against Armstrong that

Lincoln was elected captain of the New Salem company, a victory that gave him more satisfaction, he wrote in 1860, than any other success in his life.

Lincoln saw no action in the Black Hawk War, but as a congressman in 1848 he used his brief wartime experience to mock Democratic presidential candidate Lewis Cass's pretensions of military heroism. Lincoln took the trouble to attack Cass's military record because he knew that for many voters, a candidate's bravery in battle seemed to matter more than his views on the issues of the day. This lesson was driven home for Lincoln when his Whig party won the presidential elections of 1840 and 1848 by nominating former generals William Henry Harrison and Zachary Taylor, whose political qualifications were questionable but whose physical courage was beyond doubt.

If courage was a desirable quality in a leader, honor was indispensable. As Douglas Wilson has persuasively argued, it was Lincoln's interest, even obsession, with his personal honor that led him to do things in his personal life that otherwise made no sense at all. His 1837 proposal of marriage to Mary Owens, despite her "weather-beaten" appearance and "want of teeth," was a particularly grotesque example. Lincoln felt obligated by his honor to follow through on what he thought she thought was a promise to marry her if she returned to Springfield from Kentucky, which she did. It was fortunate for all concerned that Owens's common sense exceeded Lincoln's, prompting her to reject his reluctant, honor-driven offer. In his next matrimonial venture, Lincoln found himself engaged to marry Mary Todd, but had second thoughts that contributed to the breaking of the engagement. Soon, however, he found the pain of violating his honor (as he perceived it) worse than the prospect of a life with Mary, and so asked for her hand a second time, resulting in marriage in 1842.[4]

A third affair of honor in which Lincoln found himself embroiled, also in 1842, involved Illinois State Auditor James Shields, an adversary whom Lincoln apparently found a good deal less intimidating than either Owens or Todd. When Shields challenged Lincoln to a duel over an insulting newspaper article, Lincoln accepted. Dueling was illegal in the state, but Lincoln, the lawyer who had preached "reverence for the laws" as the "political religion" of the nation in his 1838 Lyceum Address, placed his personal honor above the spirit if not the letter of the law. He proposed to meet Shields at a location in Missouri, just across the Mississippi River, where they would fight using "Cavalry broad swords of the largest size" while standing in a ten-foot square. Lincoln may have proposed the absurd terms of the contest in the hopes of turning the whole thing into a joke, but he was not laughing when he showed up on the appointed day, prepared to eviscerate the much smaller Shields. At the last moment, friends of the two men found a way to resolve their quarrel; Lincoln was later embarrassed by the incident and made it a point never to discuss it, but the fact remained that he had been willing to risk his political career and his very life rather than compromise his reputation for personal courage.[5]

One might imagine that as president of the United States, Abraham Lincoln in 1861 could consider his honor validated and his leadership confirmed, without the need to make further displays of his bravery. But the outbreak of the Civil War changed the definition of leadership, by elevating the importance of courage. The volunteer armies of both sides were led largely by amateur officers who found that most of the skills that had brought them success in civil life were of little use on the battlefield. These officers may have known how to make grand speeches, negotiate deals, win friends, fix machines, or raise prize crops. But most of them could no more maneuver a company across a pasture than Lincoln could in his Black Hawk War days, when he once found himself leading his men toward a fence with a gate in the middle. Unable to remember the proper words of command to send his line of men endwise through the gate, he ordered them to halt, fall out, and reform in five minutes, on the other side of the fence. The typical Civil War volunteer officer, innocent of military training or experience, could not base his claim to leadership on technical competence; only by demonstrating superior bravery could he hope to win the respect of his troops.

President Lincoln was a volunteer captain writ large; his lack of military experience meant that he, too, had to find a way to demonstrate his fitness as a war leader. His awareness of the importance of courage as an element in wartime leadership was sharpened in February 1861, when he completed his inaugural journey from Springfield to Washington by traveling incognito through Baltimore to avoid a rumored assassination plot. Political cartoonists had a field day with the spectacle of Lincoln sneaking into the capital like a spy rather than a head of state, exaggerating the cloth cap that he wore in place of his characteristic stovepipe hat into a full set of Scottish regalia complete with kilt, or (more humiliating still by the prevailing standards of male honor) portraying him as dressed in women's clothing.

Two other events early in Lincoln's presidency focused his attention on his personal obligations as a war leader. The first was the death of young Colonel Elmer Ellsworth at Alexandria, Virginia, on May 24, 1861. Ellsworth, a young Lincoln protégé who had accompanied the inaugural party by train from Illinois, made a profligate display of his bravery by marching his regiment across the Potomac to Alexandria and climbing out onto the roof of a hotel to tear down a Confederate flag that was visible from the White House. For his trouble, Ellsworth was shot by the hotel keeper and became the first Union officer to die in the war.

Lincoln had long used metaphors of combat in his speeches describing the struggle against the expansion of slavery; in Peoria in 1854, he characterized the response of antislavery men to the Kansas-Nebraska Act as a hand-to-hand battle fought with brutal weapons: "[W]e rose each fighting, grasping whatever he could first reach—a scythe—a pitchfork—a chopping axe, or a butcher's cleaver." When he sat to write a moving letter of condolence to the parents of Elmer Ellsworth, killed by a real shotgun rather than a metaphorical farm implement, he must have reflected on his personal responsibility for the consequences of Ellsworth's bravery. Lincoln had never shown any lack of the political courage that he called for in his followers; now that he was asking for much greater sacrifices, what price should he be prepared to pay?[6]

Five months later, at the battle of Ball's Bluff, Virginia, Lincoln's old political crony Edward Baker was killed in action while leading his troops to defeat. Unlike Ellsworth, Baker was of the same generation as Lincoln. In the 1840s, Lincoln, Baker, and John J. Hardin had agreed to support one another in turn, seeking to be Whig party candidates for Congress; and in 1846, Lincoln named his second son Edward Baker Lincoln in his friend's honor. That same year, John J. Hardin volunteered to serve in the Mexican War, where he was killed at the Battle of Buena Vista, four months after Lincoln was elected to Congress on a platform opposing the war. When Baker fell at Ball's Bluff, Lincoln could not have helped noting that he was the lone survivor of the old

Whig leadership of Sangamon County; the others had courageously sac-rificed their lives for their country. Moreover, Baker's death was a re-minder to Lincoln that his age was no excuse for not serving; his con-temporaries were showing themselves quite capable of going to war, and dying, just as nobly as young Colonel Ellsworth.

As president, Lincoln could not very well go to the front at the head of a brigade, as Baker did. But he did do all he could to demonstrate, publicly and privately, that he was as willing as any man to put every-thing he had, including his life, at risk in the Union cause. After the scotch cap fiasco, Lincoln swore off any further measures designed to protect him from assassination, and made it his practice to ride alone at night to the Soldiers' Home, or walk to the War Department without escort, almost daring his enemies to make attempts on his life. He took irrational risks in the face of the enemy, at Norfolk, Fort Stevens, and Richmond. He accepted the death of his favorite son, Willie, as a price he had to pay, since he was asking equally painful sacrifices of so many other families, and he overrode his wife's desperate wishes in allowing his oldest boy, Robert, to join the army, for the same reason. Under the draft law that was enacted midway through the war, conscripted men were permitted to hire substitutes rather than serve in person, and while Lincoln was exempt from the draft (by age as well as occupation), he nonetheless took the trouble to hire a substitute, John Staples of Penn-sylvania, to go to war in his place. In sum, he did everything required by the letter of the law and the code of honor that he could do to par-ticipate in the war, short of going to the front and taking personal com-mand of the Army of the Potomac.

While that was more than enough for the public and for posterity, it was apparently not enough to satisfy Lincoln's own sense of honor. When he looked at those who were doing the fighting, he must have seen few reasons why he should not be among them. That he was a head of state did not necessarily excuse him from going to war, for though no English king had led his troops into action since George II at Dettingen in 1743, other European monarchs continued to combine military and political leadership throughout Lincoln's lifetime. On June 24, 1859, for example, while attorney Abraham Lincoln was engaged in filing legal papers on behalf of his clients, three of the crowned heads of Europe (Napoleon III of France, Franz Josef I of Austria, and Victor

Emanuel II of Piedmont) were personally directing their armies in battle at Solferino. While Lincoln might have laughed at the idea that he should model his behavior after that of the kings and emperors of the Old World, he could not so easily dismiss the example set two years later by his Southern counterpart Jefferson Davis, who reacted to news of the battle at Bull Run by riding to the battlefield, eager to inspire his generals and rally his troops with his martial presence.

In 1861, the idea of president-as-general was by no means as outlandish as it would later seem. George Washington had ridden into Pennsylvania in 1794 at the head of the militia that he had called from neighboring states to suppress the Whiskey Rebellion; and during the Nullification Crisis of 1832, Andrew Jackson had warned South Carolina that he would not hesitate to lead troops into the state and hang John C. Calhoun, if necessary, to vindicate the authority of the federal government. These examples must have carried weight with Lincoln, for whatever he may have thought of Jackson's politics (or Washington's), he regarded the two men as models of male behavior. He invoked them both in his angry reply to a delegation from Baltimore that urged him to yield to Southern demands in April 1861: "[Y]ou would have me break my oath and surrender the Government without a blow. There is no Washington in that—no Jackson in that—no manhood nor honor in that."[7]

While the demands of manhood and honor pushed Lincoln into making public displays of his courage, the ineffectiveness of his generals pulled him toward the idea of going to war in person. Physically, he would have been up to the task. He was fifty-two when the war began, younger than Robert E. Lee and much younger than his own general in chief, Winfield Scott. He was strong, still able to lift an ax by its handle and hold it with his arm outstretched, as he demonstrated one day in the White House to an amused party of onlookers, none of whom could do the same. He had great stamina, relatively good health, and could ride a horse competently, if not with elegance. As a youth on the Indiana frontier, he had learned how to endure hardships; and as a lawyer riding the Eighth Judicial Circuit in Illinois, he had regularly traveled great distances in all kinds of weather, lodged in spartan quarters, eaten poor food, and experienced with his fellow lawyers the camaraderie of an all-male world. Indeed, the relish with which he later recalled his circuit-riding years suggests that he might even have found military campaigning an enjoyable alternative to domestic life in the White House.

Intellectually, Lincoln was no less qualified than many of the generals whom he appointed. He would have been little hampered by his lack of a formal military education, any more than he had allowed his lack of a formal legal education to stop him from becoming the foremost courtroom lawyer in his state. If volunteer officers like John Logan or Nathan Bedford Forrest could command armies successfully without a West Point diploma, there is no reason to suppose that Abraham Lincoln could not have done the same. Lincoln himself sometimes doubted the value of formal educational qualifications for officers. "I personally wish Jacob R. Freese, of New-Jersey, to be appointed a Colonel for a colored regiment," Lincoln wrote to Stanton of an officer candidate who had failed a qualifying examination in 1863, "and this regardless of whether he can tell the exact shade of Julius Caesar's hair." The curriculum at West Point before the Civil War was, after all, aimed at turning out junior officers with engineering skills, not at producing leaders of great armies, for which antebellum America had little need. It is widely noted that Lincoln took time during the war's first winter to borrow from the Library of Congress a military textbook written by General Halleck, apparently to teach himself the fundamentals of military science much as he had taught himself law or the geometry of Euclid years earlier. More significant is that Lincoln did not bother to follow up his initial reading with further study, once he realized that army-level strategy is a matter more of common sense and politics than of technical military skill.[8]

That Lincoln had the strategic insight to be a successful general is clear. As the war progressed, he demonstrated an increasingly sure grasp of the basic principles of war. In September 1861, he drafted a "Memorandum for a plan of campaign" that was the closest thing to an overall strategic plan produced by anyone in the federal administration, with the exception perhaps of Scott's much-derided Anaconda Plan. In his advice to his generals, Lincoln displayed an intuitive understanding of such concepts as the advantage of interior lines and the importance of focusing on the objective. At the outset of the Gettysburg campaign, Lincoln calmly replied to Major General Joseph Hooker's proposal to go south and take Richmond while Lee was invading the North: "I think *Lee's Army,* and not *Richmond,* is your true objective point." When Grant explained his plan for the Union armies in the East and West to act at the same time, either advancing or pinning down the enemy in their front, Lincoln was delighted to find a general who shared his idea that, as he put it, "Those not skinning can hold a leg."[9]

In imagining how Lincoln would have fared as a general, not too much should be made of his skill as a strategist. Unsuccessful generals like McClellan and Hooker were able to conceive of strategic plans no less brilliant than those of Grant or Sherman. It was the character of the plans' authors that determined success or failure, more than the nuances of their strategies. Here again, Lincoln compares favorably with many of his generals. Unlike McClellan, who sullenly blamed the sorry outcome of his cleverly designed Peninsula campaign on the administration, Lincoln was not afraid to take responsibility for failure as well as success. Unlike the luckless Ambrose Burnside, who in December 1862 relentlessly sent brigade after brigade up Marye's Heights at Fredericksburg long after any chance of victory was gone, Lincoln could admit when he had made a mistake; consider his humble letter to Grant after Vicksburg, in which he confessed that he had doubted Grant's strategy in approaching the city from the south, and then wrote, "I now wish to make the personal acknowledgment that you were right, and I was wrong." Unlike George Meade, who regularly called councils of war to gain the advice of his generals, Lincoln did not rely overmuch on his advisors, and made some of his most important decisions without, or even against, the advice of his cabinet. Unlike Don Carlos Buell (or William Rosecrans, or especially McClellan), Lincoln was neither a procrastinator nor a perfectionist, yet neither was he rash, for he had learned during his long political career how to accept temporary delay and even defeat while pursuing a larger overall goal.[10]

Lincoln's performance in the role of commander in chief provides further evidence of how well he might have done in the field. Early in the war, he occasionally usurped the authority of his subordinates and concerned himself with details better left to those on the scene. During the Confederate invasion of Kentucky in 1861, for example, he sent numerous telegrams directing the movements of individual regiments and gunboats. By the summer of 1862, Lincoln had learned to delegate such minutia and to focus on larger issues, so that when Confederate cavalry raiders again entered Kentucky in August 1862, sowing panic among local authorities, Lincoln responded with a single message to Major General Halleck: "They are having a stampede in Kentucky. Please look to it."[11]

Yet for all of Lincoln's qualifications, it remains almost impossible to picture Honest Abe as a man on horseback. Although he equaled or excelled most of his generals in physical health, mental acuity, strength of character, and ability to learn, he remained a profoundly unmilitary figure. When General William Rosecrans complained about some imagined snub he received in the parceling out of promotions, Lincoln answered, "Truth to speak, I do not appreciate this matter of rank on paper as you officers do." Lincoln did not see the world as his professional officers did, in regard to rank or anything else. His was the world of politics, characterized by compromise, negotiation, persuasion, and deal-making, a world in which even those who attained the highest levels of success were still ultimately responsible to and at the mercy of their constituents. The military world, based on hierarchy, obedience, and command, was alien to him. He regarded his brief immersion in it during the Black Hawk War as a subject for self-mockery. In an 1852 speech lampooning Democratic presidential candidate Franklin Pierce's claims of military glory, Lincoln described the last muster of the Springfield militia:

> Among the rules and regulations, no man is to wear more than five pounds of codfish for epaulets, or more than thirty yards of bologna sausages for a sash; and no two men are to dress alike, and if any two should dress alike the one that dresses most alike is to be fined. . . . Flags they had too, with devices and mottoes, one of which latter is, "We'll fight till we run, and we'll run till we die."

Lincoln honored those who served the nation in the army and navy, but it is safe to say that the values, ideals, and practices of the military world left Abraham Lincoln distinctly unimpressed.[12]

Conversely, many of Lincoln's traits that served him well in the courtroom and on the campaign trail would have been out of place on the battlefield, beginning with his sense of humor. It's difficult to name a funny general, perhaps because the horror and misery of war are not laughing matters. In 1862, Lincoln experienced a public relations debacle after his visit to McClellan's headquarters at Antietam, when a report circulated that he had asked his companion Ward Hill Lamon to sing a comic ditty called "Picayune Butler" while he toured the scene of the recent battle. Anti-Lincoln cartoons pictured the president calling for a funny song, oblivious to the dead and dying soldiers at his feet. Even his own cabinet at times criticized his habit of reading funny stories in moments of national drama, a habit that Lincoln justified as a way of releasing tension and preserving his mental health. Effective though it was as a tool for persuasion or comic relief, Lincoln's humor would have found no safe political outlet while he was leading men to their deaths.

Similarly, Lincoln's fundamental gentleness and mercy, which contributed to his greatness as a president, would have sabotaged him as a military commander. For Lincoln, one of the few reliefs from the cares of office was the opportunity to pardon soldiers who had been convicted of desertion, sleeping on guard duty, and other violations of the Articles of War, if he could find any extenuating circumstances. "[I]t makes me rested, after a day's hard work," he told Schuyler Colfax, "if I can find some good excuse for saving a man's life. . . ." But if these pardons rested Lincoln, they made more work for his generals, some of whom claimed that Lincoln's well-known tenderness made it harder for them to enforce discipline. For Lincoln to succeed as a general, he would have had to deny himself the comfort of caring about individuals, and followed instead the example of William T. Sherman, who observed in the summer of 1864: "I begin to regard the death and mangling of a couple thousand men as a small affair, a kind of morning dash. And it may be well that we become so hardened."[13]

Generals like Sherman, Grant, Thomas, Lee, Jackson, and the other great commanders of the war were not ignorant of the terrible sacrifices they asked of their men (Sherman claimed "I value their lives as much as my own"); but they were hardened to war's costs, to the point that they did not hesitate to act with malice toward the enemy, and charity for none. Further, these generals shared a supreme egotism that allowed them to send thousands of young men to their deaths with equanimity, confident that they were making the right military decisions. Men who lacked such self-assuredness were bound to fail. When McClellan, for all his bluster, wrote to his wife after the battle of Antietam, "Those in whose judgment I rely tell me that I fought the battle splendidly & that it was a masterpiece of art," he revealed as pathetic a lack of self-confidence as one can imagine coming from the pen of a person in his position. The great generals believed in themselves, and did not rely on the judgment of others to validate their actions.[14]

Lincoln had no lack of confidence in his ability to make political and moral decisions; but in military matters, he frankly sought to rely on the judgment of others. In the war's first year, he met frequently with his general in chief, first Winfield Scott and then McClellan; and when he lost faith in McClellan, he traveled to West Point to consult again with the retired Scott. In July 1862, when he called Henry "Old Brains" Halleck to Washington to become general in chief, he expected Halleck to serve as his personal military adviser. In December 1862, when a number of high-ranking officers in the Army of the Potomac disagreed with the strategy proposed by the army's commander, Ambrose Burnside, Lincoln shrank from mediating the conflict and referred it to Halleck. "If in such a difficulty as this you do not help," he wrote to his general in chief, "you fail me precisely in the point for which I sought your assistance." That others sensed Lincoln's lack of confidence in his military judgment is suggested by the difficulties he experienced in trying to motivate his generals to act more aggressively. From McDowell at Bull Run, to McClellan on the Peninsula, to Buell in East Tennessee, to Meade after Gettysburg, to Thomas in Nashville, Lincoln sent a stream of orders, suggestions, pleas, and threats to try to spur his generals into action. In every case, as he admitted to John Hay in reference to Meade, "[N]othing I could say or do could make the army move."[15]

As president, Lincoln was able to employ his political skills, especially his gift of persuasion. He was able to strike an exquisite balance between mercy and determination, and to identify and define the complexities and ambiguities of a war in which "both [sides] read the same Bible, and pray to the same God; and each invokes His aid against the other." The demands of battlefield command would have changed this. To Lincoln's personal and political detriment, he would have had to forego persuasion for command. He would have been denied the opportunity to express the basic kindness of his nature, suppressing his conciliatory side for long stretches of time, perhaps until it atrophied.

His sympathy for the Southern people would have been tested by daily confrontations with them, as enemy soldiers, as sullen prisoners, as implacable guerillas, as bitter refugees.[16]

Worse, he would have found himself in situations where success only comes to those who, by training and temperament, are certain of their actions. Lincoln's humble awareness that "events have controlled me" as much as he controlled events may have made him a better man, but it would not have made him a better general. Lincoln's recognition of the humanity of the enemy, and his sympathy for even the miscreants among his own soldiers, would have been no advantage on the battlefield. In short, Lincoln could not have commanded well without betraying the qualities for which he is best remembered.[17]

But what if Lincoln had indulged his fantasy of military command not for months at a time but just once, in July 1863? What if he had taken over at the moment when, as he wrote in the letter addressed to Meade, "Our army held the war in the hollow of their hand & they would not close it." Could he have closed it? Could Abraham Lincoln have sealed the fate of the Army of Northern Virginia and ended the war in an afternoon? There is no good reason to think so. Historians have debated this hypothetical situation at excruciating length, but the fact remains that no Civil War field army was ever attacked and destroyed on the battlefield. In only one battle, at Nashville in December 1864, was a field army defeated so badly that it could not fight again, and that occurred only after John Bell Hood had used up his depleted, demoralized, ill-fed Army of Tennessee in a series of suicidal attacks against George Thomas's defensive works at Franklin. But Robert E. Lee was not John Bell Hood; one Pickett's Charge had been enough for him, and he would fight all his remaining battles with his men behind breastworks or in trenches, or sheltered by woods from the terrible federal artillery. He would not throw his men away again. Had Meade, or Lincoln, attacked Lee's army after Gettysburg, the results would have differed little from those of the Wilderness, Spottsylvania, or Cold Harbor: thousands more dead and wounded, but both armies still capable of fighting.[18]

Once Lee's men began to rely on prepared defensive positions instead of fighting in the open, they posed a tactical conundrum for the attacking forces that would continue to puzzle military thinkers until the end of the First World War. Abraham Lincoln, for all his virtues, did not have the answer to that problem. Fortunately, for his reputation and for the fate of the nation, Lincoln's virtues did include a high degree of self-knowledge. After gaining the therapeutic value of writing his letter criticizing Meade for failing to destroy Lee's army, Lincoln filed it away, unsent. After venting his emotions by telling young John Hay that "If I had gone up there I could have whipped them myself," Lincoln returned to the business of being president, and let the idea remain forever a fantasy.

## CHAPTER 5

# Abraham Lincoln and Jefferson Davis as Commanders in Chief

## David Herbert Donald

T he Constitution of the United States of America and the Constitution of the Confederate States of America use identical language to define the war powers of the chief executive: "The President shall be commander in chief of the army and navy."[1] Thus endowed with equal authority, one Civil War president directed a supremely successful victory, while the other led his country as it stumbled to disaster.

In tracing the reasons for Union triumph—or Confederate defeat—historians, while not neglecting economic, diplomatic, political, and military factors, have often attempted to explain the outcome of the war in terms of the relative skill with which Abraham Lincoln and Jefferson Davis exercised these war powers granted by their respective constitutions. Indeed, in what may have been the first of the important Gettysburg College conferences on the Civil War, the great historian David M. Potter argued that the South lost the Civil War because of Jefferson Davis's inadequacies as commander in chief, and went on to suggest that, had the Confederacy and Union swapped chief executives, the outcome of the conflict might have been entirely different.[2]

## I

Before accepting that conclusion, though, students might do well to consider just how the two rival presidents understood the role of commander in chief. The similarities in their conceptions and in their actions are striking.

Both presidents believed their constitutional responsibility as commander in chief included that of general in chief. At the outbreak of hostilities they had little choice.[3] The Confederacy, as a new nation, had no army, and President Davis had to devise a basic strategy for the war. Lincoln's resources were equally limited. The United States army consisted of about 16,000 men, mostly stationed on the Indian frontier. The president had no general staff, no army war college, to advise him. He could turn only to the aged General Winfield Scott, whose judgment both about the secession crisis and the way to prosecute a war proved lamentably defective, and to a few bureau chiefs in Washington, who were unused to thinking beyond their narrow departmental responsibilities. So it fell to the president to determine strategy.

The basic plans Lincoln and Davis hit upon were, in effect, mirror images: the Union needed to prosecute an offensive war that would prevent the Confederates from winning their independence; it must cut off the South from foreign assistance, push back the Southern armies, and disestablish the Confederate government. Conversely, the Confederacy had to fight a defensive war, holding back the Union armies until Northerners grew weary of attempting to compel their allegiance. Davis called this his "offensive-defensive" strategy,[4] which would essentially hold all Confederate territory while lashing out from time to time with raids and attacks on the enemy forces. Though both Lincoln and Davis were severely criticized for lack of strategic vision, it is hard to see that either had other viable options. What is more important here is that both presidents conceived the determination of basic strategy as a duty imposed by their constitutional obligation as commanders in chief.

Both presidents understood that, as commanders in chief, they had also the ultimate responsibility for organizing their nations' forces. Davis made an early decision to rely on a departmental command structure, in which each departmental commander was responsible for defending his district. Thus, at the end of 1861 there were, in addition to the main army of Joseph E. Johnston, the Army of Northwest Virginia commanded by Robert E. Lee, the Department of West Florida, commanded by Braxton Bragg, the Department of Fredericksburg commanded by T. H. Holmes, and so on and on.[5] This command structure has been much criticized, and certainly it often resulted in a lack of cooperation and coordination even between the armies that lay adjacent to each other. On the other hand, in view of the vast extent of the Confederacy, the absence of an effective communications network, and the strong parochialism of Southern states and communities, it is hard to see what other plan of organization the Confederate president could have adopted. As the war went on, many of these departments were consolidated, and a drastic reorganization in 1863 grouped all Confederate armies in the Western theater under the command of Joseph E. Johnston.[6] Johnston's inability to assume functional control over armies that stretched from East Tennessee to Vicksburg suggests that Davis's first decision in favor of small geographical commands had not been entirely a mistake.

Lincoln, for his part, began with a very similar command structure. Thus John C. Frémont commanded the Missouri department, William T. Sherman commanded the Department of the Cumberland, Robert Patterson commanded the military departments of Pennsylvania, Delaware, Maryland, and the District of Columbia, and so forth. Believing that these local commanders had a better knowledge of the field and a closer acquaintance with the local populace, Lincoln delegated operational control to them. As in the Confederacy, these regional commands were consolidated as the war dragged on. Thus, toward the end of 1863 Lincoln combined most of the Union forces in the West—the former departments of the Ohio, the Cumberland, and the Tennessee—into a new Division of the Mississippi, which Ulysses S. Grant commanded.

In addition to selecting a general strategy, both commanders in chief thought it their duty actively to participate in drawing up detailed plans for military operations. Repeatedly they called conferences of their top generals and civilian advisors to discuss tactics. For instance, in April 1862, when Joseph E. Johnston opposed plans to stop McClellan's advance on the Peninsula and favored a retreat to the defenses of Richmond, Davis summoned Johnston, Lee, James Longstreet, and other advisers to assess the situation; after protracted discussion, in which he heard both sides of the question, the president, as commander in chief, made the decision that McClellan must be checked before he reached the Confederate capitol.[7]

Similarly, in September 1863, when news reached Washington that William S. Rosecrans was under siege in Chattanooga and would likely have to surrender his entire army, President Lincoln attended a conference with Secretary of War Edwin M. Stanton, Secretary of State William H. Seward, Secretary of Treasury Salmon P. Chase, and General Henry W. Halleck, which considered the daring expedient of taking 15,000 troops from the Army of the Potomac and rapidly shipping them by railroad to the Western theater to relieve Rosecrans. Stanton predicted that the force would reach Chattanooga in five days, but the president, aware how slowly the army bureaucracy moved, said he was willing to "bet that if the order is given tonight, it could not be got to Washington in five days." But further discussion made it clear that there was no other way to save Rosecrans's army. The president overcame his doubts and, as commander in chief, directed the reinforcements.[8]

Both Lincoln and Davis kept control over the selection of generals to lead their armies. Neither paid close attention to rank or precedent in making their choices. Davis made mortal enemies when he dated Albert Sidney Johnston's commission before those of Joseph E. Johnston and P. G. T. Beauregard.[9] Similarly, Lincoln gravely offended Rosecrans by giving Ulysses S. Grant a commission bearing an earlier date. Davis attempted to extricate himself from his difficulties by giving involved explanations that rationalized his choices; Lincoln was more honest in writing Rosecrans: "Truth to speak, I do not appreciate this matter of rank on paper, as you officers do. The world will not forget that you fought the battle of 'Stone River' and it will never care a fig whether you rank Gen. Grant on paper, or he so, ranks you."[10]

From time to time each president was tempted to interpret his responsibility as commander-in-chief to mean leading his armed forces on the field of combat. Davis, who was a graduate of West Point, had served in the Mexican War, and had presided over the War Department under President Franklin Pierce, thought that his proper career should have been a military, not a political one, and he longed for an opportunity to lead Confederate troops into battle. Some of his generals, like Joseph E. Johnston, urged him to delegate his civilian responsibilities so that he could take to the field,[11] and Davis seriously considered their proposals. He felt frustrated when the need to make opening remarks to the Confederate Congress kept him from the fighting at First Manassas, and he rushed to the front as soon as he could leave Richmond. Arriving just as the battle ended, he toured the field, conferred with his commanders, and sent back dispatches that made it seem that he had been responsible for the Confederate victory.

But he learned a lesson from the vigorous remonstrances of General Johnston and Beauregard that the president was claiming fame that was rightly theirs, and thereafter he did not personally attempt to lead the Confederate forces. To be sure, as McClellan's army pushed up the Peninsula to the outskirts of Richmond, President Davis often visited the front and conferred with his generals, but he did not take personal charge of the campaign or direct the fighting. In 1863 he made a much publicized visit to the Confederate armies in the West, but his purpose was to inspirit the troops and their quarreling commanders, not to lead the men into battle.

Abraham Lincoln, who had no military experience except for a few months service in the Black Hawk War, was not initially tempted to give personal direction to the Union armies. He began his term with enormous respect for military expertise, especially that of the aged and much honored General Winfield Scott. But when the experts failed to provide victories, he often thought of taking control of the Union armies himself. Not a modest man, he was confident that he could teach himself the art of war as he had once taught himself Euclid's elements of geometry, and he did not see that he could do a much worse job than his bumbling generals. His first attempt to exercise direct control over the operations of the armies was his famous "President's War Order No. 1" of January 1862, in which he directed the commanders of all the armies to begin a simultaneous advance on George Washington's birthday. Intended primarily to spur General McClellan into action, Lincoln's general order became the subject of ridicule, and the president did not again attempt to exert personal control over the Union armies.

But, like Jefferson Davis, he retained an intense interest in military operations. Frequently supporters urged him to take personal command of the Union forces, and from time to time he was inclined to agree with them. When General George Gordon Meade failed to follow up on his victory at Gettysburg, Lincoln for once lost his temper. In a rare confidence, he said to John Hay that he should have taken to the field in person. "If I had gone up there, I could have whipped them myself," he fumed. "Our army held the war in the hollow of their hand and they would not close it."[12] But he soon calmed down and praised General Meade for his "magnificent success" at Gettysburg.

Most of the fighting was too distant from Washington for Lincoln to observe the major battles firsthand, though, like Davis, he visited the Eastern armies frequently. On a trip to the Peninsula in May 1862, while waiting for McClellan to join him, he grew restive because the Confederates still held the south side of the James estuary and Norfolk Naval Yard, where the formidable *Merrimack* was sheltered. Against the advice of the professionals who claimed that it was impossible to land troops anywhere near Norfolk, Lincoln led a scouting expedition, found a landing site, got out on what Virginians called their "sacred soil," and strolled up and down the beach in the bright moonlight. Tied up by other business, he did not participate in the invasion the next day, but his scouting led to the surrender of Norfolk and the sinking of the *Merrimack*. "So," Secretary of the Treasury Chase wrote, "has ended a brilliant week's campaign of the President, for I think it quite certain that if he had not come down, [Norfolk] would still have been in possession of the enemy and the *Merrimack* as grim and defiant and as much a terror as ever."[13]

But Lincoln's Norfolk adventure was an aberration, and, for the most part, he, like Davis, did not attempt personally to direct military operations. Late in the war, in July 1864, when Jubal A. Early's raid threatened Washington, the president—along with Mrs. Lincoln and many other civilians—repeatedly went out to Fort Stevens to see the fighting. His immense height—to which was added that of his stovepipe hat—made him such a conspicuous target for sharpshooters that he had to be ordered down from the parapet.[14] His role was clearly that of an observer, not a commander.

## II

The criticisms leveled against President Lincoln and President Davis further suggest the similarities of their actions as commanders in chief. Both men were subjected to the most scathing denunciations, often from members of their own party or faction. It is easy to compile an anthology of abuse of both presidents, and in the following list of six representative complaints only the specialist can tell which was directed at Lincoln and which at Davis:*

1. "He lacks system, is very slow, does not discriminate between important and unimportant matters, has no practical knowledge of the workings of our military system in the field."[15]

2. "I do not say the cause will fail, but the chances are all against us. . . . Cold, haughty, peevish, narrow-minded, pig-headed, *malignant* he is the cause. . . . While he lives, there is no hope for us."[16]

3. "No man can be found who is equal to this crisis in any branch of the government. . . . If the President had his wife's *will* and would use it rightly, our affairs would look much better."[17]

4. "I do not believe in [the president] at all. . . . He is thick-headed; he is ignorant; he is tricky, somewhat astute in a small way, and obstinate as a mule."[18]

5. The difficulty with [the president] is that he has no conception of his situation. And having no system in his composition he has undertaken to manage the whole thing [the war] as if he knew all about it."[19]

6. "[The president] is a slow, very slow worker. . . . Hence a total absence of vigor; all the revolutionary vigor is with the enemy, in legislation and execution. With us timidity, hair-splitting, and an absence of all *policy.*"[20]

Both men were regularly assailed for being poor administrators. In Davis's case the charge is an unexpected one, because he was a notably

---

*Quotations 1, 2, and 6 are from Davis's critics; quotations 3, 4, and 5 are from Lincoln's.

efficient Secretary of War under President Pierce. But perhaps it was just that experience that contributed to his weakness as Confederate president. He had presided over a War Department that approached a state of rigor mortis; with a minimal staff of aged and incompetent bureaucrats and retired officers, he had transacted most of the department's business himself. He brought to the Confederate war effort the same sense of personal involvement, to the extent that for a time he attempted to read every application for appointment or promotion in the army. A courtly man, with excellent Southern manners, he favored seemingly endless discussion of policy with his advisers; though he firmly retained the right to make all final decisions, he simply wore out his aides in conferences that went on for hours. Consequently he gave the impression of being slow and indecisive.

Almost identical animadversions were made about Lincoln as an administrator. In his case the comments are rather less surprising, because prior to his election to the presidency he had never actually run anything except his two-man law office in Springfield. Critics claimed that, as president, he simply did not know enough about the workings of the federal government, and at the outset he admitted his almost total ignorance about military affairs. He was less given than Davis to prolonged conferences with his advisers, but he spent hours every day listening to the complaints, petitions, and projects of the private citizens who thronged the White House. He confessed that his mental processes were slow, and he did not readily make decisions, preferring, as he said, to allow events to control his actions.

Both Lincoln and Davis were accused, with some justice, of playing favorites in making military appointments. Lincoln supported McClellan long after that general had proved he could never win an offensive campaign, and he stood by Halleck despite storms of criticism, saying wryly that he had to be Halleck's friend since nobody else was. Similarly, Davis had an unaccountable admiration for Albert Sidney Johnston. He held on to the irascible and ineffectual Braxton Bragg until there was practically a mutiny in the army and an uprising in the Congress. When obliged to remove Bragg from command, Davis took revenge on critics by naming Bragg his chief military adviser.

So convinced were Davis's critics of his incompetence that the Confederate Congress, at the instigation of Senator Louis T. Wigfall of

Texas, passed a bill creating the position of general in chief of all the Southern armies, and Davis had to use his veto to fend off this challenge to his powers as commander in chief.[21] Lincoln's opponents, fuming over repeated Union defeats, in December 1862 secured the almost unanimous backing of the Republican caucus in the Senate for a resolution demanding that the president reconstruct his cabinet so as to give more effective leadership to the war effort. Only Lincoln's adroit management of the crisis averted what amounted to a virtual coup d'etat.[22]

In sum, both presidents were under constant attack for their ineptness and inefficiency as commanders in chief. It is hard to know whether it was better to be called, as Lincoln was, thick-headed, ignorant, tricky, and obstinate as a mule or to be characterized, as was Davis, as cold, haughty, peevish, narrow-minded, pig-headed, and malignant.

## III

But for all these similarities, there were major differences in the ways Lincoln and Davis played their roles as commander in chief. Some of these reflected the very different personalities of the two men. Davis, always prickly and unwell nearly all the time he was in the Confederate White House, was quick to take offense when he believed his prerogatives as commander in chief were threatened. After the first battle of Manassas, when Joseph E. Johnston claimed that he ranked next to the president himself in command of the Confederate army in Virginia, Davis tersely endorsed his letter: "insubordinate." And when Johnston continued to make the case that his accomplishments and previous military record entitled him to outrank the other generals, the president replied with stunning finality: the language of Johnston's letter was "unusual; its arguments and statements utterly one-sided; and its insinuations as unfounded as they are unbecoming."[23] The two men, formerly close friends, thenceforth addressed each other in terms of cold formality.

By way of contrast Lincoln handled such issues with a minimum of friction. When considering Joseph E. Hooker to replace Ambrose P. Burnside after the fiasco at Fredericksburg, he learned that his blustering new commander was reported to have said—no doubt after spending too much time in the Washington bars—that a new regime would prevail if Joe Hooker were in command and that both the army and the country needed a dictator. In a beautiful letter the president told Hooker that he was "not quite satisfied" with the general because of these and other political utterances but was going to entrust him with the command anyway. "What I now ask of you is military success, and I will risk the dictatorship," he said, and he went on to urge: "Beware of rashness, but with energy, sleepless vigilance, go forward, and give us victories."[24]

But it is probably a mistake to give too much emphasis to these personal differences between the two commanders in chief. It is not clear that any amount of tact, or even the loftiest Lincolnian rhetoric, could have assuaged the raging egos of Johnston, Beauregard, and Davis's other military critics. Nor is it obvious that Lincoln's letters, skillful as they were, did much to transform McClellan into a fighting general or to make Halleck anything more than what Lincoln called him, "a first-rate clerk."[25]

It is more profitable to look into the different ways in which the two presidents understood the war powers given to them by their constitutions. Though the Supreme Court in the decades before the war had largely followed a narrow, literal interpretation of the Constitution, restricting the powers of the national government to those expressly listed in that document, there had been since the days of Chief Justice John Marshall, Justice Joseph Story, and Daniel Webster a powerful counter-tradition of interpreting the Constitution broadly. In what we would now call an "instrumental" interpretation of the Constitution, these jurists insisted that document was never meant to be an iron hoop girding the trunk of the tree of nationalism. Instead, as William Whiting put it, the Constitution should be viewed as "the tree itself,—native to the soil that bore it,—waxing strong in sunshine and in storm, putting forth branches, leaves, and roots, according to the laws of its own growth, and flourishing with eternal verdure."[26]

This nationalist tradition has always held that the powers of the federal government, extensive as they were, were greatly expanded in times of war or insurrection.[27] In the congressional debates over slavery, former President John Quincy Adams enjoyed taunting the strict-constructionist Southerners with the warning that, in case of secession and war, the war powers implicit in the Constitution gave the government the right to emancipate their slaves. Similarly, Senator Charles

Sumner of Massachusetts, a disciple of Adams, went to the president as soon as he heard of the firing on Fort Sumter to alert him that now "under the war power the right had come to him to emancipate the slaves."[28]

Lincoln was thoroughly familiar with this body of legal doctrine that favored the use of government as an instrument of social policy, and when the war broke out he used it as the basis of his actions. In so doing he was reinforced by the opinions of his attorney general, Edward Bates, and he carefully read the contemporary pamphlets written by legal scholars explaining and defending presidential war powers. For instance, he read Charles J. Stille's *How a Free People Conduct a Long War* (1862),[29] and he attached great weight to Charles P. Kirkland's *A Letter to Hon. Benjamin P Curtis,* which defended the president against charges of "usurpation" and use of "arbitrary power."[30] Perhaps most influential was *The War Powers of the President,* by his solicitor general, William Whiting, which vigorously argued that emancipation of the slaves fell within his war power.[31] These legal authorities helped confirm Lincoln's view that his oath to defend the Constitution imposed on him what he termed "the duty of preserving, by every indispensable means, that government—that nation—of which that constitution was the organic law."

In Lincoln's view the war powers devolved primarily upon the president. Though many Republicans contended that it was the legislative, not the executive, branch of government that was entitled to exercise the war powers, Lincoln insisted that "as commander-in-chief of the army and navy, in time of war, I suppose I have a right to take any measure which may best subdue the enemy."[32]

With the firing on Fort Sumter he showed how broadly he intended to construe the war powers of the commander in chief. Invoking "the power in me vested by the Constitution, and the laws," he called up 75,000 members of the state militias to put down the rebellion.[33] That action was clearly constitutional and authorized by existing laws. But he then went on, without any express constitutional authorization or any legislation of Congress, to expand the regular United States army by ten regiments and by enlisting 18,000 men in the navy. To protect ships from California bearing gold so necessary for Union finances, he dispatched an armed revenue cutter, and he ordered the commandants

at the navy yards of Boston, New York, and Philadelphia each to purchase and arm five steamships in order to preserve water communication with Washington. In case that communication was temporarily cut,
he directed Governor E. D. Morgan of New York and an associate to
act for the United States government in forwarding troops and supplies.
He also authorized the Treasury Department to advance, without security, $2,000,000 to a New York committee headed by John A. Dix to
pay "such requisition as should be directly consequent upon the military and naval measures necessary for the defence and support of the
government." "Whether strictly legal or not," he said later in reporting
these measures to the Congress, they "were ventured upon, under what
appeared to be a popular demand and a public necessity, trusting . . .
that Congress would readily ratify them."[34]

Nor was Lincoln's use of the war powers confined to the first
months of the war, when the Congress was not in session and the president had of necessity to act alone. Employing his rarely-used title as
commander in chief, he ordered the suspension of the privilege of the
writ of habeas corpus, at first in limited areas but eventually through
the North, so that not only supporters of the Confederacy but critics of
the Union government could be imprisoned, without formal charges. In
normal circumstances these prisoners, or their attorneys, would secure
a writ of habeas corpus from the appropriate federal court, and the arresting official would have to produce them in court and bring specific
charges against them, which would be tried before a jury. But with the
suspension of the great writ, army officers were commanded to ignore
all such judicial proceedings. The number of such persons thus arbitrarily arrested may never be fully known; after years of the most laborious
research, Mark E. Neely places it well in excess of 16,000.[35]

In other areas as well, Lincoln exercised his war powers. There was
no general censorship of the press, but from time to time individual
newspapers were suppressed—usually for brief periods of time—and it
was not hard for other editors to learn the lesson. Similarly, there was no
systematic limitation of the right of free speech—but no one could escape the message conveyed by the arrest of former Congressman
Clement L. Vallandigham, who was accused of discouraging enlistments
by saying that the Lincoln administration had needlessly prolonged the
war in order to liberate the blacks and enslave the whites in America.

And, of course, the greatest extension of the war powers was the Emancipation Proclamation, for which Lincoln explicitly invoked his authority as commander in chief.

These measures found no parallels in the Davis administration. Proudly the Confederate president boasted in his February 1862 inaugural address: "Through all the necessities of an unequal struggle there has been no act on our part to impair personal liberty or the freedom of speech, or though, or of the press."[36] In face of invading Union armies, President Davis did think it necessary to suspend the writ of habeas corpus in certain localities; but unlike Lincoln, who acted entirely on his own, Davis first secured authorization from the Confederate Congress, and then only for brief periods. And, of course, Davis made no move that rivaled the Emancipation Proclamation.

It is easy to explain Davis's failure to make a bold assertion of his war powers as commander-in-chief in terms of his personality. Certainly when compared to Lincoln, Davis seemed stiff and unimaginative, but on closer study he proves remarkably flexible and creative in facing the never-ending demands of the war. It is also true that Davis's attitude toward the war powers stemmed to some degree from ideology; long a strict-constructionist, he for years had argued that the federal government had only the powers expressly granted in the Constitution. But Davis realized in assuming the presidency that old ideas had to give way to new necessities, and in the years that followed he often exhibited remarkable adaptability to changing reality.

It is best to understand that Davis's refusal to use his war powers as commander-in-chief stemmed from the situation in which he found himself. From the very beginning he and his fellow Confederates cast themselves not as revolutionists but as the true defenders of the traditional American faith, from which their Northern opponents had so sadly strayed. It was for this reason that, in drafting a Constitution for the new Confederate States of America, the framers deliberately made only the most minor changes in the Constitution of the United States, preserving both the language and the structure of the original. As Davis said when he took his oath as provisional president in February 1861: "We have changed the constituent parts, but not the system of government. The Constitution framed by our fathers is that of these Confederate States."[37]

Starting from this premise, Davis found his subsequent actions as president negatively defined by the steps that Lincoln took. For instance, when Lincoln first suspended the writ of habeas corpus in 1861, Davis immediately responded: "We may well rejoice that we have forever severed our connection with a government that thus tramples on all the principles of constitutional liberty."[38]

That early exchange pretty clearly defined Davis's subsequent reactions to the initiatives of the Lincoln administration. By 1862 he was lamenting "the disregard [that Lincoln and his administration] have recently exhibited for all the time-honored bulwarks of civil and religious liberty." He went on to portray life in the North under the rule of the despot: "Bastiles filled with prisoners, arrested without civil process or indictment duly found; the writ of *habeas corpus* suspended by Executive mandate; a State Legislature [in Maryland] controlled by the imprisonment of members . . . ; elections held under threats of military power; civil officers, peaceful citizens, and gentlewomen incarcerated for opinion's sake."[39]

Having so fiercely and publicly attacked Lincoln's broad use of the war powers, Davis was, of course, estopped from using them himself. Because of that self-imposed constraint, dissent, desertion, and disloyalty grew rampant in the Confederacy. The armies disintegrated as uninhibited state judges liberated conscripts and deserters with writs of habeas corpus. Untrammeled, newspapers voiced criticisms of the administration that were almost treasonous. Local and state officials brazenly defied the orders of the Confederate government. With his hands tied, Davis could do nothing to check the disintegration of his nation.

Herein lies one of the greatest ironies of the Civil War era: Lincoln invoked his war powers to curb disloyalty in the North, where it is not clear that these draconian measures were either necessary or effective. But their chief effect was to inhibit Davis from employing similar measures in the South, where they might have curbed more vigorously the dissent and disloyalty that signally contributed to the collapse of the Confederacy.

## CHAPTER 6

# Apple of Gold in a Picture of Silver: The Constitution and Liberty

## Allen C. Guelzo

I

In the threatening winter of 1861, as the United States was being inched ever closer to the outbreak of civil war by the secession of the Southern states over the issue of black slavery, the newly elected president, Abraham Lincoln, opened up a confidential correspondence with a former Southern political colleague, Alexander Stephens of Georgia. Stephens had made headlines in November 1860, in a speech to the Georgia legislature, urging Georgia not to follow the South into secession. Lincoln sent him a friendly note, asking for a printed copy of the speech—and perhaps warming Stephens to an invitation to come into Lincoln's cabinet as a gesture of mollification toward the South. Stephens wrote back, apologizing that the speech was not yet in print (apart from the newspaper reports of it that Lincoln had read), but taking the opportunity to urge Lincoln to make some kind of conciliatory promise to the South about staying within the bounds of the Constitution, as president, and not threatening to take federal action against slavery in the South, where slavery had enjoyed a kind of constitutional immunity since the beginnings of the Republic. This, Stephens believed, would deflate the secession fire-eaters better than any cabinet offer, adding (with a phrase borrowed from the Book of Proverbs), "A word fitly spoken by you now would be like 'apple of gold in a picture of silver.'"

Lincoln was disappointed that Stephens seemed to think that he intended some unconstitutional aggression against the South. The president-elect could not believe that conciliatory words from him about the Constitution were really necessary: "Do the people of the South really entertain fears that a Republican administration would, *directly,* or *indirectly,* interfere with their slaves, or with them, about their slaves?" The correspondence died on that point of mutual misunderstanding, and Stephens, rather than entering Lincoln's cabinet, eventually became vice-president of the new Southern Confederacy in February 1861. (And nine years later, Stephens would compare Lincoln to Caesar, the destroyer of the Roman republic, and claim that "I do not think he understood" the niceties of constitutional government "or the tendencies of his acts upon them").[1]

But Stephens's anxiety about Lincoln's potential for breaking over the limits of the Constitution stayed in the forefront of Lincoln's thinking, like an irritation he could not rub out. So did the biblical image about apples of gold and pictures of silver, for in January Lincoln wrote out a brief statement on the place of the Constitution in his thinking, perhaps as part of a reply to Stephens, in which Lincoln borrowed precisely Stephens's own image about apples of gold. "Without the *Constitution* and the *Union,* we could not have attained . . . our great prosperity," Lincoln acknowledged, and therefore he had no intention of treating the Constitution lightly. But "there is something back of these, entwining more closely about the human heart," Lincoln insisted, "That something is the principle of 'Liberty to all' that is enshrined in the Declaration of Independence, that 'all men are created equal.'" This was a principle that, for Lincoln, slashed straight across the practice of slavery, and if Stephens expected him to pay attention only to the Constitution and ignore the principles that lay "back of these," he would have nothing to expect but disappointment in Lincoln. The Constitution did not exist merely for its own sake, as though it were only a set of procedural rules with no better goal than letting people do what they pleased *with* what they pleased; it was intended to serve the interests of "the principle of 'Liberty to all,'" which meant that the Declaration was "*the* word, *'fitly spoken'* which has proved an 'apple of gold' to us." The Constitution, and the federal Union the Constitution created in 1787,

> are the *picture* of silver, subsequently framed around it. The picture was made, not to *conceal,* or *destroy* the apple; but to *adorn,* and *preserve* it. The *picture* was made *for* the apple—*not* the apple for the picture.[2]

There is no doubt but that the Declaration of Independence was the central statement of Lincoln's political idealism. "I believe that the declaration that 'all men are created equal' is the great fundamental principle upon which our free institutions rest," he wrote in 1858; and two months after his correspondence with Stephens, at Philadelphia's Independence Hall, Lincoln declared that "I have never had a feeling politically that did not spring from the sentiments embodied in the Declaration of Independence." What he hated about the enslavement of blacks was not only its crass disregard of the natural equality of all human beings, but the way it forced "so many really good men amongst us into an open war with the . . . Declaration of Independence, and insisting that there is no right principle of action but self-interest." And it was the Declaration's promise of equality that Lincoln made the chapter and verse of his great call for a "new birth of freedom" in his most memorable public speech, the Gettysburg Address.[3]

But this was precisely what, at bottom, divided Lincoln and Alexander Stephens. For Stephens, the Declaration was a great mistake; and the Constitution was indeed a set of procedural rules, intended to teach no particular system of political morality, or any other morality for that matter. "The prevailing ideas . . . at the time of the formation of the old Constitution were, that the enslavement of the African was in violation of the laws of nature," Stephens said on March 21, 1861. "Those ideas; however, were fundamentally wrong. They rested upon the assumption of the equality of races. This was an error." And resting the Constitution on the Declaration was the equivalent of building the national house on "a sandy foundation."[4]

And there have been, long after Stephens and even among Lincoln's admirers, those who have wondered whether Stephens was right, or at least right in apprehending that Lincoln had taken entirely too cavalier an attitude toward the Constitution. According to the conservative political scientist Willmoore Kendall, Lincoln did not merely set the Declaration and the Constitution into what he imagined was a proper relationship of apples of gold and pictures of silver; he used the Declaration to demolish the Constitution in the name of his own egalitarian ideology. "What Lincoln did . . . was to falsify the facts of history, and to do so in a way that precisely *confuses* our self-understanding as a people," Kendall argued. Gottfried Dietze, a political conservative like Kendall, saw Lincoln's appeal to the Declaration as the "apple of gold" as a democratic pretense that allowed him to demote the Constitution to a mere piece of framery, so that Lincoln would be free to pursue dictatorial glory as president. Lincoln, said Dietze, was "a democratic Machiavellian whose latent desire to achieve immortality broke forth at the first opportunity offered by . . . the Civil War." Or if not glory, Lincoln used the pursuit of equality as an excuse for granting himself "unprecedented and virtually dictatorial powers as president," and so tear down the restraints of the Constitution so that he could satisfy a kind of political Oedipus complex. According to Dwight G. Anderson, Lincoln would use the appeal to equality in the Declaration in order to "put himself in Washington's place as the father of his country." For Anderson, Lincoln as president only posed as a defender and maintainer of the Union and the Constitution, while in reality "he actually was transforming it."[5]

And even among Lincoln's admirers, there is a running current of discomfort at Lincoln's apparent willingness to set the Constitution below the Declaration. The great Lincoln biographer, James G. Randall, the equally great historian James Ford Rhodes, and the path-breaking political historian William Dunning all agreed that Lincoln rode roughshod over the Constitution in pursuit of dictatorial powers, although they were quick to add that Lincoln's "wholesome regard for individual liberty" and "the legal-mindedness of the American people" kept him from turning into an outright tyrant. More recently, voices on the political left like Garry Wills, Charles L. Black, and Mark Tushnet have actually applauded Lincoln for dumping the Constitution in favor of the Declaration. According to Wills, the Gettysburg Address, by invoking the Declaration of Independence at the beginning rather than the Constitution, changed "the recalcitrant stuff of that legal compromise, bringing it to its own indictment." At Gettysburg, Lincoln performed "one of the most daring acts of open-air slight-of-hand ever witnessed by the unsuspecting" and "changed the way people thought about the Constitution." (Willmore Kendall, in Wills's reading, was actually quite right: Wills merely chose to cheer what Kendall chose to deplore). Howard Jones echoes Wills's judgment by describing the war as "an instrument" Lincoln used "for reshaping the Union of the Constitution into the more perfect Union envisioned by signers of the Declaration of Independence." Even Phillip Paludan, who offers the most realistic and persuasive middle path between Kendall and Wills, can only insist that Lincoln was indeed a Declaration-of-Independence egalitarian, but a *process* egalitarian who believed "that equality would be realized only through the proper operation of existing institutions."[6]

What runs as a common thread through all of these comments, favorable and unfavorable alike, is the peculiar sense that, in varying degrees and for good or ill, Lincoln really does represent a sacrifice of the Constitution to the Declaration. Lincoln's own image of the "apples of gold in the picture of silver" has offered easily quotable support for that, since it suggests all too broadly that the Constitution's importance is largely that of an instrument for implementing the Declaration's ideals. As Lincoln said to a political rally in June 1858: "be ever true to Liberty, the Union, and the Constitution—true to Liberty, not selfishly, but upon principle—not for special classes of men, but for all men, true to the union and the Constitution, as the best means to advance that liberty."[7] Did Lincoln sit at the other extreme from Alexander Stephens, and did he regard the Constitution as a wax nose, to be reshaped according to his own egalitarian idealism? If either Wills or Kendall are even close to being right, the answer would have to be *yes*, to both questions.

The difficulty with resting in this opinion is that we still live under this Constitution, and the Civil War was fought to keep it in place; and very nearly all the advances in civil equality made in this century have been based on appeals to the Constitution. Certainly, no civil rights litigation has achieved success by ignoring the Constitution and directing judges' attention to the Declaration. Casting Lincoln as both Wills and Kendall do—as a subverter of the Constitution—makes Lincoln into a sort of political monster rather than a hero. So what did Lincoln intend when he spoke of the Constitution as a "picture of silver"? And before we confidently conclude that Lincoln had to tear down the Constitution in order to pave the way for equality, what did Lincoln mean by *equality?* For it may turn out that Lincoln was more of a constitutionalist than meets the eye, and a very different sort of egalitarian than we think.

II

It is surprising that Abraham Lincoln, a lawyer's lawyer, would find himself defining the relationship of the Declaration and the Constitution in terms of illustrations and pictures rather than a precise legal equation. But Lincoln was not the only one with that problem. This was because there was no simple consensus in the American Republic as a whole about how the Constitution was supposed to function, and nowhere was that more dramatically demonstrated than in the ferocious political contests between the Democratic party of Andrew Jackson and Stephen A. Douglas, and the Whig party of Henry Clay and Abraham Lincoln.

Born in the great political triumph of Thomas Jefferson and his followers in the presidential election of 1800, the Democratic party saw itself as the party of a virtuous countryside, a party of independent landowners who would keep liberty pure by preventing the fledgling American merchant class from concentrating too much lethal political power in its own hands. For the Democrats, the Constitution was a procedural rulebook, and for the most part, only a procedural rulebook. It prescribed only the minimum of guidelines for public life and left the balance to the self-government of American individuals. It bothered the Democrats not at all if those self-governing individuals galloped off in a hundred different cultural and moral directions. Any attempt to prescribe a common cultural standard not only stepped beyond the Constitution, but amounted to a conspiratorial concentration of power. "So long as the individual trespasses upon none of the rights of others, or throws no obstacle in the way of their free and full exercise," wrote Orestes Brownson, "government, law, public opinion even, must leave him free to take his own course."[8]

This heady brand of do-your-own-thing populism (made all the headier by the leadership, first, of Jefferson, and then of Andrew Jackson) had two basic flaws: nations of landowners tend not to do well if they are ever sucked into war with nations of merchants; and, landowners (far from being always virtuous) can just as often be suspicious, provincial, and lecherous. The first of those flaws showed up in the War of 1812, when radical Jeffersonians led by Henry Clay brought the United States into a war in which the American Republic came within an ace of having its ill-equipped and underweight armies of farmers wiped out by the British. Clay, the sadder but wiser politician, backed away from Jefferson and began insisting that, if the United States wanted its liberty to survive, it had better investigate the acquisition of a little power—and so Clay created the Whig party to promote a national banking system to encourage commercial development (and a national tariff to protect it) and a general combination of business and government in joint effort.

This enraged Democrats. "Our plan may be stated in a phrase of the utmost brevity," erupted Democratic journalist William Leggett, "for it consists merely in the absolute separation of government from the banking and credit system." Clay's so-called American System for the promotion of commerce and industry would only lay open the path to frightening accumulations of power, both inside and outside the government. Once accumulated, that economic power could then be used in political ways—to buy votes for public works projects that benefited the powerful, to finance campaigns for the imposition of evangelical Protestant morality on the working class (like the New York City religious revivals underwritten by the wealthy Whig merchants, Arthur and Lewis Tappan), and, even more threatening, to back movements for the abolition of black slavery (which the Tappans were also financing). To Democrats like Leggett, such concentrations of power, and the capacity for social mischief they created, were wildly unconstitutional. The Constitution nowhere gave any sanction to proposal for national banks, national roads, or national meddling with slavery—at least not explicitly.[9]

But *explicitly* was just Clay's point—what the Constitution did not expressly forbid was not *un*constitutional, and so hey-ho for the National Bank. Add to this the guidance given to American jurisprudence by Joseph Story and James Kent in favor of absolutizing contract law and inhibiting state restraints on commerce, and the breakup of state restrictions on banking and interstate business supervised by Chief Justice John Marshall and the Marshall court, and the way was open to "constitutionalizing" the entire field of domestic economic policy. Instead of the Constitution enjoying a sacred consensus above mere policy disputes, the Constitution in the early republic became the site of every one of those disputes.[10]

The second flaw in the Democratic reasoning—the unreliability of rural virtue—was something with which Abraham Lincoln was all too well acquainted. "I presume I am not expected to employ the time assigned me, in the mere flattery of the farmers, as a class," Lincoln warned the Wisconsin State Agricultural Fair when he was invited to speak there in 1859. "I believe there really are more attempts at flattering them than any other; the reason of which I cannot perceive, unless it be that they can cast more votes than any other." Born in rural Kentucky poverty to the very model of independent Democratic farmers, Lincoln disliked agricultural work and everything attached to it almost from the beginning; and as soon as he came of age in Illinois, he left the farm for the town and the city and never looked back, to become a storekeeper and then a lawyer, two professions that were the point guards for American commercial development. It was this that made Lincoln a Whig from the start and drove him into politics (even before law), and which made "the name of Henry Clay . . . an inspiration to me." It also determined Lincoln's view of the Constitution, and, as we shall see, gave his understanding of the Declaration an unexpectedly economic twist.[11]

It is only if we suppose that Lincoln thought of nothing but the Declaration—only if we ignore his immersion as a highly partisan Whig in the 1830s and 1840s, along with the general propensity of all political partisans then to "constitutionalize" policy debates—that we will be surprised to find Lincoln closely preoccupied with the integrity of the Constitution far earlier than with the Declaration of Independence. For despite the suggestions of some of his critics, Lincoln in the 1840s devoted more attention to the interpretation of the Constitution, and to a far more restrained notion of the Constitutional interpretation at that, than Wills, Kendall, or Randall claimed. His earliest extended political statement, the Springfield Young Men's Lyceum Address on "The Perpetuation of Our Political Institutions" (from January 1838), closes with a ringing denunciation of the role of "passion" in politics (and *passion* was understood to be the Democratic style, as opposed to Whig "reason") and a call for "*general intelligence, [sound] morality* and, in particular, *a reverence for the constitution and laws.*" In 1848, as a Congressman advocating Clay's programs of tax-supported "internal Improvements," Lincoln attacked proposals to amend the Constitution as a mistake leading to ruin:

> No slight occasion should tempt us to touch it. Better not take the first step, which may lead to a habit of altering it. Better, rather, habituate ourselves to think of it, as unalterable. It can scarcely be made better than it is. New provisions, would introduce new difficulties, and thus create, and increase appetite for still further change. No sir, let it stand as it is. New hands have never touched it. The men who made it, have done their work, and have passed away. Who shall improve, on what *they* did?[12]

Of course, as a Whig, he was more inclined to grant exceptions to this stiffness in handling the Constitution when it came to the pet projects of the Whig party. Participating in his first national political campaign in 1840 as a Whig speechmaker, Lincoln attacked the Democrats' successful dismemberment of the national banking system under Andrew Jackson and Martin Van Buren, a dissolution grounded in Jackson's claim that the Constitution gave no express sanction to a national bank. "As a sweeping objection to a National Bank . . . it often has been urged, and doubtless will be again, that such a bank is unconstitutional," Lincoln told a Springfield audience in December 1839. "Our opponents say, there is no *express* authority in the Constitution to establish a bank," Lincoln observed, but as a good Whig, he replied, "The Constitution enumerates expressly several powers which Congress may exercise, superadded to which is a general authority to make 'all laws necessary and proper,' for carrying into effect all the powers vested by the Constitution of the Government of the United States." A national banking system was as good a means of satisfying that need as any of the simple substitutes the Democrats were proposing; therefore, on Lincoln's expansive logic, "is it not clearly within the constitutional power of Congress to do so?"[13]

But this only meant that he read the Constitution as a Whig might read it, not that he had no regard for it whatsoever. Far from it: his first brief sliver of national notoriety was his attempt to force President Polk to reveal his own constitutional high-handedness in triggering the Mexican War, riding roughshod over "the provision of the Constitution giving the war-making power to Congress." In 1852, he had actually criticized the campaigners for an immediate abolition of slavery as the enemies of constitutional government. "Those who would shiver into fragments the union of these States; tear to tatters its now venerated constitution; and even burn the last copy of the Bible, rather than slavery should continue a single hour," Lincoln said in a eulogy for the recently deceased Henry Clay, "together with all their more halting sympathizers, have received and are receiving their just execration."[14]

But *as* a Whig, he was also inclined to read the Constitution as more than merely a procedural document, which secured liberty but refused to do more than express neutrality on what was done with that liberty. The same spirit in the Whigs that looked to create a powerful economic republic also looked to sponsor a powerful spirit of nationalism, which would triumph in the creation of a single American national identity rather than a diversity of local, regional, or state identities. "I wish to be no less than National in all the positions I may take," he wrote in 1854. What Lincoln found great in Henry Clay, as he said in 1852, was that "Whatever he did, he did for the whole country. . . . Feeling, as he did, and as the truth surely is, that the world's best hope depended on the continued Union of these States, he was ever jealous of, and watchful for, whatever might have the slightest tendency to separate them." And taken one step further, the Whigs also encouraged the creation of unified concepts of public morality, and attracted large-scale support from Protestant evangelicals who feared that the Democrats, in the name of personal liberty, had simply become the party of moral indifference to right and wrong.[15]

Lincoln never professed very much in the way of religion; but almost as a way of compensating for his lack of religious profile, he cultivated an unbending moral uprightness that won him the reputation, which has come down even to our times, as what his Springfield law partner William Herndon called "a safe counselor, a good lawyer, and an honest man in all the walks of life." And it was his moralism that led him into conflict, after 1854, with slavery. Lincoln's opposition to slavery always had strong moral overtones. "I have always hated slavery," he declared in his great debates with Douglas in 1858; and in 1854, he explained, "I object to it because it assumes that there CAN be MORAL RIGHT in the enslaving of one man by another."[16]

Lincoln did not articulate just what constituted the basis of that moral outrage. (As Southern defenders of slavery delighted to point out, the Bible was singularly silent on condemning slavery, so it would be difficult for him to find a source for antislavery moralism there). Certainly, one part of this moral loathing for slavery was Lincoln's tendency to associate slaveholding with low-life, nouveau riche forms of loose moral living. He once told a political ally that slavery "was the most glittering ostentatious and displaying property in the world" and was "highly seductive to the thoughtless and giddy headed young men who looked upon work as vulgar and ungentlemanly." And in his 1842 Temperance Society Address in Springfield, Lincoln spoke of the "victory" of Reason arriving only "when there shall be neither a slave nor a drunkard on the earth"—implying that slavery and drunkenness were twins.[17]

Another, larger claim for moral indignation was that slavery violated natural law. "The ant who has toiled and dragged a crumb to his nest, will furiously defend the fruit of his labor, against whatever robber assails him," Lincoln wrote in 1854. Slavery, which robbed the slave of the fruit of *his* labor, was just as much an outrage on the part of the human laborer. This was "so plain, that the most dumb and stupid slave that ever toiled for a master, does constantly know he is wronged." And even if the Bible had nothing explicit to say against slavery, Lincoln believed that natural theology did. "I think that if anything can be proved by natural theology, it is that slavery is morally wrong."[18]

But above all, slavery violated the spirit of the Declaration of Independence, and it was in this context—as a contradiction of the secular morality of the Declaration of Independence—that the Declaration first begins to assume, in the 1850s, a significant place in Lincoln's rhetoric. "To us it appears natural to think that slaves are human beings; men, not property," Lincoln said in New Haven in 1860, "that some of the things, at least, stated about men in the declaration of independence apply to them as well as to us." In that case, the enslavement of blacks was a step away from the moral road of the Declaration, and a step away from liberty and toward the enslavement of everyone. "Then we may truly despair of the universality of freedom, or the efficacy of those sacred principles enunciated by our fathers—and give in our adhesion to the perpetuation and unlimited extension of slavery." Slavery was a moral spot on the garment of freedom as laid down in the Declaration. "Our republican robe is soiled, and trailed in the dust," he said in 1854 in the tones of a parson demanding repentance from his flock: "Let us repurify it. Let us turn and wash it white, in the spirit, if not the blood of the Revolution. . . . Let us readopt the Declaration of Independence, and with it, the practices, and policy, which harmonize with it." Only that will save the Republic from the embarrassment of slavery; and in that case, "we shall have so saved it, that the succeeding millions of free happy people, the world over, shall rise up, and call us blessed, to the latest generation."[19]

The standard Democratic response was to point out that, morality and the Declaration notwithstanding, the Constitution sanctioned slavery, left it untouched in the States where it was legal, and maybe even untouchable everywhere else, too. As legal historian Paul Finkelman has remarked, "The word 'slavery' was never mentioned in the Constitution, yet its presence was felt everywhere." The slaveholding states were granted extra representation in Congress based on a census count of three-fifths of their slave populations; recovery of slave runaways—euphemistically described as persons "held to Service or Labour"—was made a matter of interstate comity throughout the Union; the Atlantic slave trade was guaranteed existence for 20 years; and the Constitution's prohibition on export duties gave granted unearned favors to slave-based agricultural products.[20]

Some of the most extreme Southern Democrats argued that the Declaration not only had nothing to do with the Constitution, but it had actually been a philosophical mistake for the United States to adopt such ideas in its founding documents. Northern Democrats, like Lincoln's great Illinois rival, Stephen A. Douglas, would not go so far as to reject the Declaration out of hand, but they would argue that the Declaration's ideas about freedom and equality applied only to white people. "In my opinion the Signers of the Declaration of Independence had no reference whatever to the negro, when they declared all men to have been created equal," Douglas remarked in the great debates of 1858. And this left him free to deal with the Constitution purely as a procedural document that made no claims to any moral judgments whatsoever. It was not that Douglas actually favored slavery; it was that he believed that the rights of black people were "a question which each State in this union must decide for itself." This was because "our government was formed on the principle of diversity in the local institutions and laws, not that of uniformity."[21]

The response of many antislavery Whigs in the 1840s and Republicans in the 1850s was to concede this point and flee from the Constitution to the Declaration as some sort of alternative standard of government.[22] And for Lincoln, too, the Declaration surfaces in the 1850s as a vital authority to appeal to when Democrats reached out to white racial prejudice as a way of silencing Northern unease with slavery. But Lincoln showed no sign that he believed the Constitution now had to be reshelved to a lower point, or that he had ever believed other than that the Constitution was a moral document, with moral implications about liberty and equality that coincided perfectly with the Declaration.

As the image of the apple of gold and the picture of silver indicates, Lincoln believed that the Declaration and the Constitution needed each other. The Declaration was a statement of foundational natural rights, and natural rights that were shared everywhere by every human being. But it was not, and could not be, a statement about civil or political rights, which were a different thing altogether. "I have said that I do not understand the Declaration to mean that all men were created equal in all respects"—the details of specific civil and political rights were up to each community to grant. And the granting of such rights was very much a power left to the states in the early nineteenth century, within the very general framework of the federal Constitution. Even up through the last weeks of his life, Lincoln was reluctant to commit the federal government to a national statement about black civil rights, because the Constitution gave the federal government no power to delimit those rights. (Not that Lincoln had no concern for black civil rights: this is why he delicately pestered reconstruction governors like Michael Hahn to enfranchise the freedmen, because civil rights like the franchise were understood, before the Reconstruction Amendments, to be the proper constitutional bailiwick of the states.) But in the basic natural rights that belonged to everyone, Lincoln believed that blacks and white alike shared a common, equal ground that forever forbade one race from enslaving the other. "Though it does not declare that all men are equal in their attainments or social position, yet no sane man will attempt to deny that the African upon his own soil has all the natural rights that instrument vouchsafes to all mankind." And in no case was that natural equality more evident than in the case of economic rights. Every man, "in the right to put into his mouth the bread that his own hands have earned . . . is the equal of every other man, white or black."[23]

This did not mean, however, that the Declaration and the Constitution were two entirely different sorts of document, the one strictly about ideas and the other strictly about technical process. A close reading of the historical context of the Constitution would demonstrate that the Constitution was animated by the same moral commitment to liberty as the Declaration. True, the Constitution gave some measure of legal sanction to slavery, but this was only because the choice in 1787 was between making those concessions and getting a national Constitution, or a descent into national anarchy and misrule; and only because the authors who made those concessions made them in the expectation that slavery would gradually die out anyway on its own. "You may examine the debates under the Constitution and in the first session of Congress and you will not find a single man saying that Slavery is a good thing," Lincoln wrote in 1859, "They all believed it was an evil."[24]

Whatever immunities the Constitution originally conferred upon slavery, "I believe that the right of property in a slave is not distinctively and expressly affirmed in the constitution." For instance: "There was nothing said in the Constitution relative to the spread of slavery in the Territories, but the same generation of men said something about it in [the] ordinance of [17]87," the Northwest Ordinance that restricted the spread of slavery into the old Northwest Territory. What was more, "they placed a provision in the Constitution which they supposed would gradually remove the disease by cutting off its source. This was the abolition of the slave trade," once the initial 20-year sanction for it had expired:

a European, be he ever so intelligent, if not familiar with our institutions, might read the Constitution over and over again and never learn that Slavery existed in the United States. The reason is this. The Framers of the Organic Law believed that he Constitution would *outlast* Slavery and they did not want a word there to tell future generations that Slavery had ever been legalized in America.[25]

Lincoln did not feel any necessity for setting the Constitution and the Declaration in tension with each other because he supposed that the common intentions of their common authors on the point of equality and liberty spoke sufficiently well for themselves. And this, he explained, was why he had not stepped forward as an antislavery partisan before 1854 and the adopting of the Kansas-Nebraska bill, permitting the extension of slavery into the western territories. "I have always hated it, but I have always been quiet about it until this new era of the introduction of the Nebraska bill began. I always believed that everybody was against it, and that it was in the course of ultimate extinction. . . . The adoption of the Constitution and its attendant history led the people to believe so." The "theory of our government is Universal Freedom," Lincoln said in 1854, "'All men are created free and equal,' says the Declaration of Independence. The word 'Slavery' is not found in the Constitution."[26]

And so he continued to believe. Unlike many fellow Republicans, Lincoln would not demand an end to the obnoxious provisions of the Fugitive Slave Law of 1850, because however much he disliked the operation of it, it was guaranteed to the South under the Constitution. As Lincoln wrote Joshua Speed in 1855, "I confess I hate to see the poor creatures hunted down, and caught, and carried back to their stripes, and unrewarded toils." But "I also acknowledge *your* rights and *my* obligations, under the constitution, in regard to your slaves," and he wanted Speed to appreciate "how much the great body of the Northern people to crucify their feelings, in order to maintain their loyalty to the constitution and the Union." Lincoln declared at the end of the Lincoln-Douglas debates, "I have neither assailed, nor wrestled with any part of the constitution. The legal right of the Southern people to reclaim their fugitives I have constantly admitted. The legal right of Congress to interfere with the institution in these states, I have constantly denied." In 1859, he actually advised Salmon Chase to restrain the Ohio state Republican committee from asking for a repeal of the Fugitive Slave Law to be included in the 1860 Republican national campaign platform. "The U.S. Constitution declares that a fugitive slave *'shall be delivered up.'*"27

But to argue from that premise that the Constitution somehow gave slavery the broad right to plant itself in new areas, and sprout new dominions for itself under the shelter of Douglas's argument that the Constitution made no moral judgments about what people did in those new dominions, was actually a denial of the whole intention of the Constitution. Even when the infamous *Dred Scott* decision in 1857 seemed to suggest that the Constitution actually did protect the extension of slavery into the territories, Lincoln refused to see it as any reason to surrender confidence in the ultimate justice of the Constitution. In his mind, *Dred Scott* was not an interpretation of the Constitution, but a perversion of it.

> If this important decision had been made by the unanimous concurrence of the judges, and without any apparent partisan bias . . . it then might be, perhaps would be, factious, even revolutionary, to not acquiesce in it as a precedent. But when, as it is true, we find it wanting in all these claims to the public confidence, it is not resistance, it is not factious, it is not even disrespectful, to treat it as not having yet quite established a settled doctrine for the country.

And yet, even at that moment, Lincoln would not call for defiance of the Court, but rather for patience in awaiting a new decision. "We do not propose that when Dred Scott is decided to be a slave, that we will raise a mob to make him free," Lincoln warned during the Lincoln-Douglas debates, "If . . . there be any man in the republican party who is impatient of . . . the constitutional obligations bound around it, he is misplaced, and ought to find a place somewhere else." This is not what we expect to hear from a man who sits lightly by the Constitution. But it is what we expect to hear from one who believes that the Constitution was written to pursue, more than just procedural goals, a set of moral goals.28

## III

For Lincoln, the place of the Declaration of Independence as an apple of gold was not intended to diminish the importance of the Constitution as a picture of silver; nor was a description of the Constitution as a means to realizing the goals set out in the Declaration a way of writing off the Constitution. Much as he appealed to Douglas's followers in 1856 to "Throw off these things, and come to the rescue of this great principle of equality," he also added, "Don't interfere with anything in the Constitution. That must be maintained, for it is the only safeguard of our liberties." Nor was he exaggerating for political effect when, en route to his inauguration in 1861, he remarked, "When I shall speak authoritatively, I hope to say nothing inconsistent with the Constitution, the union, the rights of all the States, of each State, and of each section of the country." Moreover, as an "old Henry Clay Whig," he persisted in taking a minimalist view of his own powers as president under the Constitution. "My political education strongly inclines me against a very free use of any of these means, by the Executive, to control the legislation of the country. As a rule, I think it better that congress should originate, as well as perfect its measures, without external bias."[29]

The tragedy of what happened with the secession of the Southern states and the beginning of the Civil War was that, with such views of the Constitution, Lincoln as president was actually a better safeguard for the continued existence of slavery in the South than secession. If it were a case, Lincoln explained in his First Inaugural, where a majority was forcibly depriving a minority of their constitutional rights, secession—or rather, revolution—might well be justified. "But such is not our case. All the vital rights of minorities, and of individuals, are so plainly assured to them . . . in the Constitution, that controversies never arise concerning them." Nor should they be worried that his private intentions might somehow subvert these rights. "By the frame of the government under which we live, this same people have wisely given their public servants but little power for mischief; and have, with equal wisdom, provided for the return of that little to their own hands at very short intervals." Just as only Nixon could have gone to China, only Lincoln, with the moral weight of the Republican party, could have enforced national respect for the Constitutional safeguards that prevented interference with Southern slavery.[30]

But this did not happen, and secession plunged the nation into a situation for which the Constitution granted little guidance. Just as the

Constitution granted no right to secede, it granted the president no direction about how to proceed with the seceders. His guiding star in that case, however, was not the Declaration, but again the Constitution, and his insistence that the Constitution was permanent and unbreakable. "My opinion is that no state can, in any way lawfully, get out of the Union, without the consent of the others," he told Thurlow Weed in 1860, "and that it is the duty of the President, and other government functionaries to run the machine as it is." Just as slavery was a violation of the spirit of the Declaration, secession was a violation of the whole idea of constitutional government. "A majority, held in restraint by constitutional checks, and limitations, and always changing, with deliberate changes of popular opinions and sentiments, is the only true sovereign of a free people." But secession was an insult to the notion of majority rule and constitutional government, a flight "to anarchy or despotism."[31]

The constitutional uncertainties of dealing with secession led Lincoln into a series of actions in the spring of 1861 that were, by his own public admission, of debatable constitutionality in peacetime: suspending the writ of habeas corpus, authorizing the raising of a national army, spending public money to buy supplies, imposing a blockade. What Lincoln reminded his critics was that this was not peacetime, but war, and war of such a nature that no one who wrote the Constitution had ever anticipated, and war that had broken out while Congress was not only in between sessions, but which was in fact still in the midst of completing Congressional elections. (Lincoln's decision in April not to call a special session of Congress before July 4, 1861, was dictated in large measure by the fact that, under the old staggered system of congressional elections, a number of key border-state Congressional districts had not yet finished balloting for new representatives.) When the western counties of Virginia organized their own Provisional Government of Virginia, and then plunged ahead to petition for separate statehood, Lincoln was equally reluctant to sanction what amounted to a disregarding of the Constitution's prohibition on setting up new states out of old ones without the old state's approval (Article 4, section 3) and to discourage a loyalist movement which had been formed at great hazard to support Constitutional government. He was forced finally to come down on the side of the West Virginians—not, significantly, because they represented the triumph of egalitarianism (the West Virginia state constitution actually provided for a gradual emancipation, rather than the full emancipation Lincoln had already announced as his policy for states still in rebellion), but because their movement represented the spirit of the Constitution, if not its precise specification. There is a difference, Lincoln observed, "between secession against the constitution, and secession in favor of the constitution," and there was nothing unconstitutional in taking notice of the difference. "It is said," Lincoln concluded, "the devil takes care of his own. Much more should a good spirit—the spirit of the Constitution—take care of its own. I think it can not do less, and live."[32] Similarly, the exigencies of the war meant that the executive branch of the government swelled to gargantuan size under Lincoln's administration, leading Lincoln's critics to claim that Lincoln was the original author of "big government." But these charges generally miss how dramatically the federal government shrank back to its prewar proportions after 1865, and stayed that way for another half-century. Congress, fully as much as the executive branch, filled the role of "big government" during the war: each wartime Congress, the 37th and 38th, each doubled the number of bills passed by the record 27th Congress of 1841–1843.[33]

It also needs remembering how comparatively limited Lincoln's early extra-Constitutional wartime gestures were. The original unilateral suspensions of the writ of habeas corpus were only operative in areas of military confrontation; the recruiting and supplying of the armies were submitted to Congress for post facto approval, and, despite the clamor of offended Democrats during the war, wartime arrests and limitations of civil liberties were extraordinarily few, especially by comparison with the Red Scares and wholesale confinement of Japanese-Americans in this century's American wars. And one good measure of Lincoln's cautious constitutionalism is the care with which he strove to justify even these measures. He was meticulous in seeking out legal opinions to support actions as commander in chief as minor as the appointment of a temperance representative as an officer or the remission of a fine imposed on a restaurant owner for selling brandy to a wounded soldier; he rigidly segregated decisions that he believed as commander in chief he needed to take to "best subdue the enemy" from meddling in "the permanent legislative functions of the government."[34]

Like his Whig predecessors, Lincoln was troubled by any expansion of government built on nothing more than raw executive power. The adoption of measures on the sole ground that "I think the measure politically expedient, and morally right" bothered Lincoln. "Would I not thus give up all footing upon constitution or law? Would I not thus be in the boundless field of absolutism? Would it not lose us . . . the very cause we seek to advance?" And he submitted himself to the most obvious of all tests of constitutionality, the reelection campaign of 1864, which he could easily have suspended by bayonet, but which never seems even to have crossed his mind as a possibility. In fact, his only recorded discussion about a response to an unfavorable electoral verdict was the extraction of a promise from all his cabinet that they would abide by the legal results. As Don Fehrenbacher remarked, "he placed the principle of self-government above even his passion for the Union" and "affirmed his adherence to the most critical and most fragile principle in the democratic process—namely, the requirement of minority submission to majority will."[35]

It was, in fact, a matter of frustration to the most radical members of Lincoln's own party that he seemed so unwilling to step out from behind the Constitution and deal with the Confederate states as they thought he ought. Despite the clamor of Charles Sumner, Ben Wade, and Zachariah Chandler in Congress, Lincoln never seriously entertained any notion of destroying the identity of the rebel states, and aimed at a speedy reconstruction with those state identities intact. He issued the Emancipation Proclamation only after he had satisfied his own mind that it could be applied strictly as a military measure, under his own authority as commander-in-chief in time of war, and only with strict application to those parts of the Confederacy still in actual rebellion.

Even then, his preface to the Proclamation identified its "object" as "practically restoring the constitutional relation between the United States, and each of the states . . . in which states that relation is, or may be suspended, or disturbed." (He refused, for instance, Salmon Chase's urging to extend the Proclamation to federally occupied parts of Virginia and Louisiana on the grounds that these areas were no longer under his purview as military zones, and that the Proclamation "has no constitutional or legal justification, except as a military measure.") He admitted to Alexander Stephens at the Hampton Roads Conference in February 1865, that as the proclamation was a war measure and would have effect only from its being an exercise of the war power, as soon as the war ceased, it would be inoperative for the future. It would be held to apply only to such slaves as had come under its operation while it was in active exercise. . . . So far as he was concerned, he should leave it to the courts to decide.

He appeared, as Mark Neely has remarked, "to some antislavery advocates at the time and to many historians since to have been strangely stricken with a paralyzing constitutional scrupulousness." Conscious of his constitutional limitations as president, rather than simply attempt to enforce it by bayonet, Lincoln turned in 1864 to having emancipation, in more sweeping form, written into the Constitution as the Thirteenth Amendment. It is hardly likely that a "dictator," or an egalitarian ideologue who believed that the Declaration of Independence trumped all questions, would even have bothered.[36]

There is no easy formula for describing the living connection between Lincoln's well-known awe for the Declaration and his restrained constitutionalism. It is doubtful whether he himself had one, at least explicitly, and his best effort at describing it was only a biblical metaphor. He had no constitutional theory as such, if only because he believed that the original intent of the founders was actually quite easy to discover in the text of the Constitution and in the writings of the founders—which, preeminently, included the Declaration of Independence. But he was convinced that such a connection existed, that as the Declaration set out a political ideal for all Americans, the Constitution remained the single greatest vehicle for realizing, implementing, and occasionally restraining that ideal.

This does not make Lincoln, by any stretch of the imagination, into either Kendall's or Wills's closet revolutionary, undermining a Constitution that he resented as an obstacle to either ambition or liberty. Gideon Welles, Lincoln's secretary of the navy and a former Democrat who was keen to scent Republican improprieties, remarked that:

Mr. Lincoln . . . though nominally a Whig in the past, had respect for the Constitution, loved the federal Union, and had a sacred regard for the rights of the States. . . . War two years after secession brought emancipation, but emancipation did not dissolve the Union, consolidate the Government, or clothe it with absolute power; nor did it impair the authority and rights which the States had reserved. Emancipation was a necessary, not a revolutionary measure, forced upon the Administration by the secessionists themselves, who insisted that slavery which was local and sectional should be made national.

It is one of the great oddities of modern American life that (as Michael Sandel has written) our political discourse has tended to follow not the path of Lincoln, but the path of Stephen A. Douglas, toward insisting that the Constitution provides only a procedural framework in which morally unencumbered individuals scream in protest at any attempt to "legislate morality." To the extent that Sandel is right, perhaps Abraham Lincoln is a revolutionary after all, for our times, if not for his own.[37]

## CHAPTER 7

# Toward Appomattox,
# Toward Unconditional Surrender?

### William C. Harris

On November 7, 1864, Abraham Lincoln, after a bitter campaign, won reelection to the presidency. Both contemporaries and modern historians have viewed the election as a mandate for the "unconditional surrender" of the Confederacy and, as one scholar has expressed it, an affirmation of Lincoln's "strategy of total war to overthrow the [South's] social and political system."[1] Historians have written that by this time Lincoln and the Northern people had adopted a policy of requiring the unconditional surrender of the rebel forces to be followed by the subjugation of the South to the Northern will. Phillip S. Paludan, in the standard account of the North during the war, has contended that General in Chief U.S. Grant's war-making demanded unconditional surrender terms. "The happy conjunction of [Grant's] initials [U.S.] with the phrase 'unconditional surrender,'" Paludan wrote, "guaranteed that no one would easily forget the character of the war."[2] Scholars have also seen Lincoln's presumed decision after the election to either compromise with the Radical Republicans or adopt their position on the postwar reconstruction of the South as evidence of the president's turn toward an unconditional surrender policy and a revolutionary settlement for the South. Recent historians have concluded that Lincoln, free of Northern conservative and border-state political considerations, was willing to accept the disfranchisement of Southern whites, the punishment of Confederate leaders, the confiscation of rebel property, and the imposition of political and civil rights for the freed blacks.

Confederates, though with far greater vehemence, held a similar view of the radical meaning of Lincoln's reelection. The Southern press and leaders declared that the success of "the Northern tyrant," Lincoln, meant that the war would go on until the South had won its independence; the alternative, they announced, was the suppression of the freedom of its people by a heartless antislavery regime. The *Savannah Republican* asserted that the election had "accomplished one valuable purpose: it will set to rest forever all issues but one—subjugation or independence." Such a perceptive Confederate as Josiah Gorgas, Jefferson Davis's Pennsylvania-born ordinance chief, reflected this ominous view of Lincoln's reelection when he wrote in his diary: "There is no use in disguising the fact that our subjugation is popular at [*sic*] the North, and that the War must go until this hope is crushed out" or our society destroyed. Confederate War Clerk John B. Jones rendered a similar judgment. "The large majorities for Lincoln in the United States," he gravely confided to his diary, "clearly indicate a purpose to make renewed efforts to accomplish our destruction."[3]

Before and after the election, Confederates had been influenced by the Northern Copperhead or peace press, and even moderate Democratic journals like the *New York World,* to believe that a victory for Lincoln and the Republicans would result in the subjugation of the South. Seizing upon the harsh rhetoric of Radical Republicans like Charles Sumner and members of the Committee on the Conduct of the War, the *World* declared that Southerners, faced with the extinction of their liberties under Lincoln, will logically draw the inference they must fight to the bitter end to avoid such a calamity. Former President Millard Fillmore, from his home in upstate New York and on the eve of the election, reinforced this foreboding view when he publicly charged that the Republicans "propose to exterminate the South or hold it by a military subjugation." Fillmore asserted that "to maintain this Union by force of arms, merely, would require a standing army that would exhaust all the resources of the nation, and necessarily *convert our government into a military despotism.*"[4]

Lincoln had no such radical purposes in mind. Safely reelected on a platform to preserve the Union and end slavery, he actually expected to achieve these objectives by continuing his lenient reconstruction plan put forth in December 1863 and by the avoidance of unconditional surrender terms that could derail his conciliatory policy, create anarchy in the South, and prevent the restoration of "a Union of hearts and hands as well as of States."[5] The story of Lincoln's policy for the organization of loyal governments in the South and the restoration of the rebel states to their "proper practical relation with the Union" is instructive.[6] Initiated in four states during the war, Lincoln expected his reconstruction policy to serve as the basis for postwar governments in the South. After his reelection, Lincoln placed his highest priority on ending the war and in securing a constitutional amendment abolishing slavery everywhere in the United States. He also sought congressional seating of Union representatives from the reorganized Southern governments, specifically Louisiana and Arkansas. The president's attempts to achieve peace, though having some relevance to his reconstruction policy, can be separated from his efforts to secure the political restoration of the South.

Soon after his reelection in a meeting with his cabinet, Lincoln asked whom he should treat with in the South and how peace negotiations should be opened. According to Secretary of Navy Gideon Welles, the president, who was in the process of drafting his annual message to Congress, was anxious to end the war now that his policy had been sustained at the polls and rebel hopes for success had been shattered. Both Welles and Secretary of War Edwin M. Stanton reminded Lincoln of his nonrecognition policy regarding the Confederate government and strongly advised him to continue the practice of working through state "entities" and individuals who wanted "to return to their duty" in the Union.[7]

On December 6, Lincoln sent his annual message to Congress. The president devoted a long passage in the message to demonstrate the Union preponderance in the war. With the Southern people obviously in mind, the president reaffirmed the government's determination to carry out the purposes of the war. Significantly, Lincoln announced that "the abandonment of armed resistance to the national authority on the part of the insurgents [was] the only indispensable [sic] condition to ending the war on the part of the government." In the same sentence, he insisted that he would retract nothing regarding the Emancipation Proclamation. The president admitted that "no attempt at negotiation with the insurgent leader could result in any good," since Davis would not accept reunion. "What is true, however, of him who heads the insurgent cause, is not necessarily true of those who follow. . . . Some of them, we know, already desire peace and reunion," and their numbers should soon increase. The rebels "can, at any moment, have peace simply by laying down their arms and submitting to the national authority under the Constitution." Lincoln declared that "if questions should remain" after the war, "we would adjust them by the peaceful means of legislation, conference, courts, and votes, operating only in constitutional and lawful channels."[8]

Clearly, Lincoln's peace terms, except for the addition of the important emancipation requirement, had not fundamentally changed since 1861, when in his July 4 message to Congress he promised that the government would violate no constitutional rights of Southerners once they had ceased their rebellion. These terms, along with emancipation, would be repeatedly expressed after his 1864 reelection, beginning with his December 6 message to Congress. They hardly constituted "unconditional surrender" terms, as some historians have claimed. According to *Webster's Third International Dictionary,* "unconditional" is defined as "not limited in any way: not bound or restricted by conditions or qualifications." Lincoln's surrender terms fell far short of this definition as applied to the Southern forces. Indeed, Lincoln did not use the word "surrender" to describe the military conditions for ending the war. He simply indicated that the Confederate forces must cease their fighting and go home. As affirmed in his annual message, Lincoln reserved the right to issue pardons to rebel leaders, which he promised would be forthcoming unless they prolonged the war.[9] When asked whether Jefferson Davis, the archvillain in the minds of most Northerners, should be permitted to flee, the president remarked that, unbeknownst to him, he hoped the insurgent leader would escape the country, thereby avoiding the difficult problem of what to do with him after the war.[10] The word "subjugation" also was foreign to Lincoln's thinking regarding the postwar South. Subjugation, by definition in the case of war, is the act of conquering by force and compelling the defeated foe to submit "as a subject to the government of another." The president's policy was to restore Southerners to equal status in the nation once they had laid down their arms and affirmed their loyalty to the Union, not force them to be subjects of the victorious North. Lincoln insisted that the Southern states had never left the Union. They had simply fallen into the hands of scheming and unscrupulous political leaders who were maintaining their power by means of a military despotism. According to Lincoln, white Southerners would have to accept emancipation, though as a temporary arrangement he would acquiesce in an apprenticeship system for former slaves. Thus, only to a limited extent under Lincoln would the South be subjected to the domination of the North.

Northern opinion in late 1864 and early 1865 generally supported Lincoln's peace terms. Conservative, or moderate, newspapers and journals of the president's wing of the Republican party especially applauded the part of his annual message promising to restore the constitutional rights of white Southerners as soon as they ceased their rebellion. These publications reminded their readers that Lincoln advanced no new peace terms and declared that the Southern people, as distinct from their tyrannical leaders who could never agree to reunion, should find the president's terms acceptable. *Harper's Weekly* told its readers that "the prospects of peace as set forth by the President are exactly what every faithful citizen supposed them to be. When the men who began this war upon the Government lay down arms, and yield to the Constitution and the laws and acts in accordance with it, the war will end" and rights would be restored. John W. Forney, the proprietor-editor of the *Washington Chronicle* and the *Philadelphia Press,* wrote: "It is not, and never has been, the policy of the Administration to degrade the seceded States." Lincoln's sole purpose, Forney insisted, was to bring Southerners "back to the embraces of the Government of their fathers." Meanwhile, until Southerners had ended the tyranny of their leaders and submitted to Union authority, the war would continue.[11]

Already, many Northerners, as well as Lincoln, could see encouraging signs in the South, particularly in North Carolina and Georgia. Forney's influential *Washington Chronicle,* preferring to ignore the defiant voices resonating from the rebel states, reported on January 4, 1865, that "disaffection at the South [was] becoming more and more manifest." The Southern masses were rapidly "recovering from the folly and infatuation into which they were plunged by wily leaders," the *Chroni-*

*cle* claimed. "They are beginning to learn that there is no such feeling of hatred and invincible antagonism to them [in the North] as they once believed. They are finding out that . . . we neither seek to oppress nor to pull [them] down; that all we ask is obedience to the law." The *Chronicle,* reputedly Lincoln's newspaper organ in the national capital, insisted that the North "would spare them every humiliation the moment they avow themselves ready to assume their constitutional obligations" in the Union. The Northern press reported that even some prominent members of the Confederate Congress, like Senator William A. Graham of North Carolina and Representative Henry S. Foote of Tennessee, had declared the Southern war for independence a failure and were seeking an end to the carnage and the destruction of their society.[12]

Lincoln, however, did not lack for Northern critics of the peace that he had outlined in his annual message. Democrats and ultraconservatives claimed that the president did not go far enough in extending the hand of peace to Southerners. The *New York World,* the leading Democratic newspaper, proposed that, since Lincoln had attained his party's original goal of prohibiting the expansion of slavery in order to insure its extinction, the president should leave slavery under state control where, the *World* argued, it was collapsing as a result of the war and "the irresistible compulsion of economic laws." Such a state's rights concession would satisfy the secessionists and lead to a quick restoration of the Union as it existed before the war. With something of this sort in mind, Garret Davis, an ultraconservative Unionist of Kentucky, introduced in the Senate a series of resolutions proposing a national convention that would draft constitutional amendments to placate Southerners regarding slavery and state's rights if they returned to the Union. Davis also called for an amendment prohibiting blacks from becoming citizens of the United States. The Kentucky senator's flight of fancy reached its height when he proposed the consolidation of New England into two states for the obvious purpose of reducing Republican political power in the restored Union. Samuel S. Cox, the Democratic leader in the House of Representatives, advanced a more rational ultraconservative approach to peace: he offered a resolution requiring Lincoln to send or to receive commissioners from the South for the purpose of ending the war on the basis of reunion alone.[13] Republicans in Congress easily brushed aside both of these peace proposals.

A potentially more serious challenge to Lincoln's peace terms than that of the Democrats and ultraconservatives came from Radicals in Lincoln's party. Still seething from his pocket veto of the Wade-Davis Bill in July and troubled by the president's lenient reconstruction plan, Radicals expressed concern that Lincoln in his haste for peace would compromise true freedom for blacks. Despite his insistence that he would stand by his Emancipation Proclamation and would seek a constitutional amendment abolishing slavery, Radicals had long viewed Lincoln as soft and indecisive on slavery and willing to temporize in order to shorten the war. They also objected to Lincoln's generous amnesty and pardoning policy, which, if carried out, would end all hope for the confiscation of rebel property and would lead inevitably to an early return of Southern leaders to power. Some Radicals like Senator Charles Sumner of Massachusetts were beginning to advocate the enfranchisement of blacks as a means for protecting the fruits of Union victory in the postwar South.

The president's policy, Radicals contended, meant the premature reconstruction of "half-abolitionized" states like Louisiana and Arkansas and the demand that their representatives be seated in Congress. A black correspondent to the *New Orleans Tribune,* while applauding the president's emancipation policy, questioned the wisdom of his peace plan requiring rebels simply to lay down their arms and pledge future loyalty. Both this writer and the *Boston Commonwealth,* the leading Radical newspaper in New England, expressed alarm regarding Lincoln's statement that "if questions should remain" after the war, "we would adjust them by . . . legislation, conference, courts, and votes, operating only in constitutional and lawful channels." Such a policy, the *New Orleans Tribune* correspondent declared, was "fraught with evils of great magnitude" for black freedom and the Union after the war.[14]

Encouraging reports of defeatism and disaffection from the South in December and early January, along with Lincoln's willingness to open negotiations on the basis of Union and emancipation only, inspired "amateur peace negotiators," as the *New York Herald* referred to them, to offer their services to bring the two sides together. The most important effort was initiated by Horace Greeley, the Republican editor of the *New York Tribune.* As if to obtain vindication for his role in the ill-fated Niagara Falls conference with Confederates during the summer,

Greeley again sought to play the role of peacemaker. Admitting that he was not "a favorite with our great ones" in Washington after the summer debacle, Greeley wrote Francis Preston Blair, Sr., an old Jacksonian wirepuller, who, along with his son Montgomery, had the ear of Lincoln and also friends in the South, that he should go to Raleigh and pull North Carolina out of the rebellion. Northern newspapers had reported that peace talk was rampant in the North Carolina General Assembly, and the state, according to Greeley, with encouragement from Blair, would quickly agree to negotiate a separate peace with the Union under Lincoln's lenient terms. Greeley told Blair that other Southern states would immediately follow North Carolina's example.[15]

Blair agreed with Greeley's assessment of the opportunity for peace and also that he should play a role in initiating negotiations. But instead of launching the peace effort in Raleigh, Blair sought a pass from President Lincoln to go to Richmond in an unofficial capacity and sound out Jefferson Davis himself on a peace plan. Burned by the Niagara Falls affair, Lincoln reluctantly granted Blair a pass through the lines. The president, wanting to avoid the embarrassment of another failed private peace initiative, told Blair that he did not want to know what he had in mind when he visited the rebel capital. What the old Jacksonian had in mind was a fanciful peace scheme involving an armistice between North and South followed by a joint military intervention against the French in Mexico. Such an operation, Blair believed, would prepare the way for reunion. Blair upon his arrival in Richmond on January 12 outlined his plan to Davis. The Confederate leader endorsed the part of Blair's scheme regarding an armistice, which, he thought, would surely produce Confederate independence, but he informed Blair that he could only negotiate on the basis of "two countries."[16]

When Blair reported his talks to Lincoln, the president found the two-country condition entirely unacceptable and informed Davis, through Blair, that he could agree only to negotiations on the principle of "one common country." Still, Lincoln was encouraged by Blair's report, probably more by his account of the defeatism he found among prominent members of the Confederate government than by Blair's talks with the insurgent leader himself. Though careful not to divulge specific information regarding Blair's mission, Lincoln left the impression with White House visitors that the old Jacksonian's trip to

Richmond "was far more successful than he anticipated . . . and that peace is much nearer at hand than the most confident have at any time hoped for."[17]

Ignoring Lincoln's requirement for talks, Davis appointed a three-member peace commission to meet with Union authorities. The commission was headed by Alexander H. Stephens, who, though vice president of the Confederacy, was a harsh critic of Davis and viewed by many as amenable to a negotiated peace even if it meant reunion. Lincoln, hoping that Davis would accept the one-country principle, on January 30 directed Major Thomas T. Eckert, head of the U.S. Telegraph Office in the War Department, to go to the front near Petersburg, meet with the Confederate commissioners, and ascertain if they were prepared to negotiate on his condition. If they agreed to the one-country principle, the president directed that General Edward O. C. Ord, commanding in the area, permit the commissioners to pass through the federal lines.[18]

The next day, January 31, Lincoln, in anticipation of the success of Eckert's mission, sent Secretary of State William H. Seward to Fort Monroe, Virginia, to talk to the commissioners. In his instructions to Seward, the president mentioned his precondition for negotiations and then outlined "three things [that] are indispensable" to peace. These were: 1) "the restoration of national authority throughout all the States"; 2) "no receding, by the Executive of the United States on the Slavery question" as indicated in his last annual message to Congress "and in preceding documents"; 3) "no cessation of hostilities short of an end of the war, and the disbanding of all forces hostile to the government." Lincoln indicated that "all propositions . . . not inconsistent with [those three] will be considered and passed upon in a spirit of sincere liberality." Finally, he directed Seward not "to definitely consummate anything" but to report to him what the Confederate commissioners "may choose to say."[19]

Major Eckert arrived at General U.S. Grant's headquarters on February 1, immediately talked to the Confederate commissioners, and determined that they were not prepared to accept Lincoln's one-country stipulation for peace negotiations. When Lincoln received Eckert's telegraphic dispatch reporting the meeting, he prepared to recall both the major and Secretary of State Seward from Virginia. However, early on the morning of February 2, the president received an important dispatch from General Grant that quickly changed his mind. Grant indicated: "I am convinced, upon conversation with [the rebel commissioners] that their intentions are good and their desire sincere to restore peace and union. . . . I fear now that their going back without any expression from anyone in authority will have a bad influence." The commanding general declared that he hoped Lincoln would have an interview with the commissioners. "Their letter to me was all that the Presidents [sic] instructions contemplated" as a precondition for peace negotiations.[20]

Lincoln immediately telegraphed Grant that he would meet "the gentlemen" personally at Fort Monroe "as soon as I can get there." Within two hours, the president had departed Washington for Fort Monroe, where Seward was already waiting. According to the *New York Herald* correspondent, Lincoln, upon leaving Washington, expressed confidence that peace could soon be achieved.[21] Joining Seward on board the *River Queen* in Hampton Roads near Fort Monroe, the president and his secretary of state met with the Confederate commissioners for four hours on February 3.

At Hampton Roads, Lincoln repeated his liberal peace terms while rejecting the Confederate proposal for a cease-fire followed by a joint military expedition against the French in Mexico. In response to Alexander H. Stephens's question, "is there no way to put an end to the present trouble?" Lincoln bluntly informed him that it could be done only if those resisting the Union ended their resistance. At the same time, Lincoln and Seward attempted to reassure the Confederate commissioners that the Washington government would not pursue a policy of subjugation or suppression of constitutional liberties after Southerners had laid down their arms. Lincoln declared that once "the National Authority was recognized, the States would be immediately restored to their practical relations to the Union." The president indicated that he supported federal compensation for slaveholders, provided their states abolished the slave institution. He cited a figure of $400,000,000 as "a fair indemnity for the loss to owners." Lincoln, however, as Stephens later wrote and some historians have assumed, did not suggest that the Thirteenth Amendment, which had been initiated by Congress three days earlier and sent to the states for action, could be ratified prospectively by the Southern states to take effect in five years.[22]

When no agreement could be reached on peace, Senator Hunter, for the Confederate side, offered his conclusions regarding the conference. He declared that the talks left nothing for the South but "unconditional submission" to the North. Seward immediately challenged the use of the words "unconditional submission" to describe the Union government's position. The South, by returning to the Union and "yielding to the execution of the laws under the constitution of the United States, with all its guarantees and securities for personal and political rights, . . . could [not] be properly considered as unconditional submission to conquerors, or as having anything humiliating in it." When Hunter expressed doubt, Lincoln told him that he had the sole power to pardon and restore property, and, as he had said before, he would exercise that authority "with the upmost liberality." The president insisted that he had no desire to withhold any rights from Southerners once the fighting had ceased.[23] The peace terms that Lincoln offered at Hampton Roads could not conceivably be construed as requiring the unconditional surrender of the South and its subjugation by the North, as Senator Hunter concluded. Along with Hunter, President Davis and other die-hard Confederates also claimed that Lincoln's terms meant "unconditional surrender" and defiantly called on Southerners to continue the fight in order to avoid the suppression of their liberties. Many Southerners, however, knew better, but they were in no position in early 1865 to accept Lincoln's offer of peace.

Despite the failure of the Hampton Roads Conference, Lincoln, who had always exaggerated the strength of Unionism in the South, still hoped that the Southern states would recognize the inevitability of defeat and, in order to avoid further bloodshed and ruin, would accept his peace terms and recall their troops from the war. Upon his return to Washington, the president, in a bold effort to spur Southern action for peace and reunion, drafted a proposal, in the form of a joint resolution for congressional approval, to compensate the slave states, including the border states, for the loss of their slave property. As he had suggested at Hampton Roads, the amount would be $400,000,000 in U.S. bonds to be distributed to the states in proportion to their 1860 slave population. One half of the bonds were to be distributed if by April 1 "all resistance to national authority" had ceased. The remaining one half would be given if by July 1 the Thirteenth Amendment had become a part of the Constitution. Lincoln promised that when these conditions had been met he would declare the rebellion ended, all political offenses pardoned, and confiscated property, except for slaves, returned to owners.[24]

When presented to the cabinet, Lincoln's compensation proposal received a cold reception. The cabinet unanimously rejected any plan to compensate slaveholders for their slaves. With victory in sight and the Thirteenth Amendment in the process of ratification, it was too late to revive the compensation issue. Though dismayed and evidently surprised at the cabinet's strong opposition to his proposal and probably realizing that Congress would never approve compensation, Lincoln dropped the scheme. Later, Secretary of Navy Welles recorded in his diary: "The earnest desire of the President to conciliate and effect peace was manifest" in the meeting, "but there may be such a thing as so overdoing as to cause a distrust or adverse feeling."[25]

In retrospect, Lincoln's willingness to extend liberal terms to the South and compensate slaveholders revealed his intense desire to end the fighting, since the collapse of the Confederate armies and Union victory now seemed imminent and, he believed, the continued bloodshed and suffering unnecessary. As Professor Gabor Boritt has written, Lincoln, though never a pacifist, had long deplored the necessity for war. As a congressman opposing the Mexican War during the late 1840s, he characterized "military glory as that attractive rainbow, that rises in showers of blood—that serpent's eye, that charms to destroy." For President Lincoln, the Civil War proved necessary to preserve the Constitution and the republic of the founding fathers and, by 1863, the destruction of the fundamental cause of the conflict—slavery. In a moment of great anguish during the war, Lincoln revealed his inner conflict to Democratic congressman Daniel W. Voorhees. "Doesn't it seem strange that I should be here" directing this terrible war, he declared. "I [am] a man who couldn't cut a chicken's head off—without blood running all around me" and my lamenting the sight of it.[26]

In his policy toward the South, the president was also influenced by a fear that unless a conciliatory hand was extended, die-hard rebels would resort to guerrilla tactics after the surrender of the Confederate armies, as was then occurring in Missouri and Kentucky, where no organized rebel force existed. Lincoln had long feared that the war, unless contained within its conservative objectives, would degenerate into "a remorseless and violent revolutionary struggle," culminating in anarchy. Gideon Welles later reported that in the early months of 1865 Lincoln "frequently expressed his opinion that the condition of affairs in the rebel States was deplorable, and [he] did not conceal his apprehension that, unless immediately attended to, . . . civil, social, and industrial relations [would] be worse after the rebellion was suppressed." Similarly, journalist Alexander K. McClure recalled that during the last months of the war Lincoln indicated increasing concern about postwar Southern poverty. According to McClure, the president "feared almost universal anarchy in the South when the shattered armies of the Confederacy should be broken up." "It was this grave apprehension," McClure wrote, "that made Lincoln desire to close the war upon such terms as would make the Southern people and Southern soldiers think somewhat kindly of the Union to which they were brought back by force of arms."[27]

Even after the failure of the Hampton Roads Conference and despite their earlier opposition to his peace initiative, Northern critics, including some Radicals like Thaddeus Stevens and Democrats like Samuel S. Cox, now praised the president's peace effort. Lincoln's handling of the Hampton Roads affair clearly enhanced his influence and his authority to set the terms for peace. The New York Tribune approvingly announced that the president "has made it plain to the impartial world, as it will be made plain to the Southern masses, that [they] can have peace on the simple condition of fidelity to their country and obedience to her laws." The people of the loyal states, the Tribune confidently reported, will now "rally with enthusiastic energy to the support of their Government" in its policy for ending the war. "We shall very soon have achieved a substantial, honorable and enduring Peace," the Tribune predicted.[28]

Four weeks after the Hampton Roads Conference, Lincoln, while at the capitol signing bills on the last day of the congressional session, received a startling dispatch from General Grant. The commanding general reported that as a result of a recent conversation between Union General Edward O. C. Ord and Confederate General James Longstreet, General Lee had proposed a "military convention" between the opposing army commanders in Virginia for the purpose of concluding the

war. Grant, through Secretary of War Stanton, asked Lincoln for instructions in the matter. At first the president was inclined to authorize
the meeting, perhaps not realizing that Lee also had a political settlement in mind. But Lincoln quickly changed his mind, reportedly after
Stanton angrily reminded him that peace terms should be decided by
the president and not the generals in the field. Lincoln then dictated the
following message for Stanton to send Grant: the president "wishes you
to have no conference with General Lee unless it be for the capitulation
of Gen. Lee's army, or on some minor, and purely, military matter"; the
president holds all political questions in his own hands; "and will submit them to no military conferences or conventions."[29]

The next day, Lincoln took the oath of office for his second term
and delivered a brief inaugural address that reached rhetorical heights
in its last two paragraphs. Sounding like a prophet of old, Lincoln exclaimed that "American Slavery is one of those offences which, in the
providence of God, must needs come, but which, having continued
through His appointed time, He now wills to remove." The president
declared that God had given "to both North and South, this terrible
war, as the woe due to those by whom the offence [of slavery] came."
However, Lincoln hoped and prayed "that the mighty scourge of war
may speedily pass away." "Yet if God wills that it continue . . . until
every drop of blood drawn with the lash, shall be paid by another
drawn with the sword, . . . so still it must be said 'the judgments of the
Lord, are true and righteous altogether.'"[30]

Lincoln in the message's last paragraph changed to a softer tone,
much more characteristic of his temperament and spirit. His words
were designed for the moment, but they have echoed through the ages.
"With malice toward none; with charity for all; with firmness in the
right, as God gives us to see the right, let us strive on to finish the work
we are in; to bind up the nation's wounds; to care for him who shall
have borne the battle, and for his widow, and his orphan—to do all
which may achieve and cherish a just, and a lasting peace, among ourselves, and with all nations."[31] For Lincoln, who believed in the providence of God and the progress of America toward a higher temporal
order that would serve as a model for the world, these words expressed
achievable ideals and reflected his benevolent policy toward the way-
ward South.

The inauguration festivities and the press of office aspirants so exhausted Lincoln that he took to bed for several days. Mary Todd Lincoln, as well as others, feared for his health. She remarked to Elizabeth Keckley, "Poor Mr. Lincoln is looking so broken-hearted, so completely worn out, I fear that he will not get through the next four years." The war, however, was fast coming to an end, and Lincoln wanted to guide the Union effort to its final triumph. He wanted to insure that the conflict ended soon and on the terms that he had repeatedly expressed. When General Grant on March 20 invited him to visit his headquarters in Virginia, Lincoln seized the opportunity to be with the army at this important time and, not incidentally, escape the grinding toil in Washington. On March 23 the president left Washington on the *River Queen* amidst speculation that he was going to seek an end to the war. Gideon Welles wrote in his diary: "The President has gone to the front, partly to get rid of the throng that is pressing upon him, though there are speculations of a different character. . . . No doubt he is much worn down; besides he wishes the War terminated, and to this end, that severe terms shall not be exacted of the Rebels" by the military commanders.[32]

Arriving at City Point on March 24 with an entourage that included Mary and Tad, Lincoln rode out the next day to the scene of that morning's desperate effort by Lee's forces to break through the Union lines at Fort Stedman. He could see the wounded and dead still lying on the ground from Lee's failed assault and could hear the fighting nearby. During a cease-fire, Lincoln reviewed the troops along the line. A naval officer who accompanied the president to the scene of the battle heard him remark that he had seen enough of the horrors of war and hoped that this was the beginning of the end of the conflict.[33]

Two days later, General William Tecumseh Sherman arrived at City Point to map strategy for the final campaign against the Confederate armies. Fresh from his march through South Carolina and into North Carolina, Sherman was surprised upon his arrival to find Lincoln at Grant's headquarters and anxious to confer with his generals. On March 28 the three Union leaders met on board the *River Queen* at the City Point dock; Admiral David Dixon Porter also attended some of the conference. The president repeatedly urged the generals to end the fighting quickly and humanely. When Sherman predicted that one more major battle would be necessary, Lincoln exclaimed, "Must more blood be shed! Can not this last bloody battle be avoided?" Grant and Sherman explained that, though the Confederate forces were defeated, Lee would "make one more desperate effort" to prevent the encirclement of his army.[34]

During the conference, Sherman, who had briefly met the president four years earlier, asked Lincoln if he had plans for the disbandment of the rebel armies and the treatment of their leaders. The president replied that all he wanted was the end of the rebellion and the return of the men to their homes and work, "whereupon they would be guaranteed all their rights [in] a common country." Based on notes made the evening after the meeting, Admiral Porter reported Lincoln as saying: "Let them once surrender and reach their homes, they won't take up arms again. Let them all go, officers and all. I want submission, and no more bloodshed. Let them have their horses to plow with, and, if you like, their guns to shoot crows with. I want no one punished; treat them liberally all round. We want those people to return to their allegiance to the Union and submit to the laws. Again I say, give them the most liberal and honorable terms." Though Porter's recollected words of Lincoln might not have been exactly what he said, the president's statement conveyed clear instructions to Grant on the treatment of the defeated rebels. Two weeks later, at Appomattox Court House, the commanding general gave Lee the surrender terms that Lincoln wanted.[35]

At City Point, Lincoln also informed Grant and Sherman that "in his mind he was ready for the civil reorganization of affairs at the South as soon as the war was over." According to Sherman, "he distinctly authorized me to assure Governor [Zebulon B.] Vance and the people of North Carolina" that, once the war was over, in order "to avoid anarchy the State Government, with their civil functionaries, would be recognized by him."[36] Sherman's understanding of Lincoln's policy—or rather misunderstanding of it—became important when, after the president's death, the general offered political as well as military terms to the Confederate army in North Carolina. As he had instructed Grant earlier, Lincoln did not want his generals arranging a political settlement with the rebels. Sherman's extraordinary action was quickly reversed in Washington, followed by wild charges that Sherman was in league with the rebels.

When Grant's forces in early April smashed the Confederate defenses at Petersburg, occupied Richmond, and moved westward to force the surrender of Lee's army, Lincoln, still in Virginia, continued to press his generals to "let 'em [the rebels] up easy." Meeting General Grant at Petersburg on April 3, the day after its fall, Lincoln, according to a member of the commanding general's staff, "intimated very plainly, in a conversation that lasted nearly half an hour, that thoughts of leniency to the conquered were uppermost in his heart."[37]

On April 4, the president made a historic visit to the fallen Confederate capital, where he walked the streets of the smoldering city, received the cheers of the freed slaves, and visited the White House of the Confederacy. The next day, Lincoln met with Confederate Assistant Secretary of War John A. Campbell, a former U.S. Supreme Court justice and a participant in the Hampton Roads Conference. Also present in the meeting, which occurred on board the gunboat *Malvern,* were Union General Godfrey Weitzel and prominent local attorney Gustavus A. Myers. In the meeting, Lincoln repeated his peace terms—the restoration of the Union, emancipation, and the end of armed hostilities against the government. Then, according to Myers, who a few days later wrote a memorandum regarding the meeting, Lincoln "professed himself really desirous to see an end to the struggle, and he said that he hoped in the Providence of God that there never would be another." To facilitate an early ending of the war, the president told Campbell and Myers that "he was thinking over a plan by which the Virginia Legislature might be brought to hold [a] meeting" in Richmond "for the purpose of seeing whether they desired to take any action on behalf of the State in view of the existing state of affairs." The president said that, when he returned to City Point, he would write to Campbell and Myers on the matter. Asked whether the oath of allegiance was necessary to reestablish loyalty, Lincoln replied that "he had never attached much importance" to the oath; however, he would leave the matter to General Weitzel, commanding in Richmond, who agreed that no test should be required. Finally, Myers recorded, "the President declared his disposition to be lenient towards all persons, however prominent, who had taken part in the struggle" and that he was "disposed" to return confiscated property.[38]

After returning to City Point, Lincoln, as had been discussed at Richmond, put in writing to Campbell the "three things" that "are indispensable" to peace. In a separate dispatch, the president authorized General Weitzel to permit the "gentlemen who have acted as the Legislature of Virginia" to meet for the sole purpose of recalling Virginia troops from the rebel army. The president instructed Weitzel to "allow Judge Campbell to see [the message], but do not make it public." Lincoln informed Grant about his directive to Weitzel but indicated that "I do not think it very probable that anything will come of this, . . . since it seems that you are pretty effectually withdrawing the Virginia troops from opposition to the government."[39]

When Weitzel issued the call for the rebel legislators to return to Richmond, Lincoln's action immediately lost its confidentiality. A firestorm of protest among congressional Radicals greeted the president's decision. Even moderate or conservative Republicans expressed dismay. Most critics misconstrued Lincoln's purpose in the affair. They jumped to the wrong conclusion that the president had repudiated the rump Restored Government of Virginia (Union), headed by Francis H. Pierpont, which since 1861 had been recognized by both the president and Congress. In Richmond at this time, members of the Joint Committee on the Conduct of the War, chaired by Lincoln antagonist Benjamin F. Wade, "were all thunder-struck" by the president's directive to Weitzel. George W. Julian, a Radical member of the committee, recorded in his journal: "Curses loud and deep were uttered by more than one at this infamous proposition to treat with rebel leaders. I never before saw such force and fitness in Ben Wade's swearing. . . . This false magnanimity is to be our ruin after all." On the defensive, Lincoln insisted to members of his cabinet, to Governor Pierpont, and to others that he had no intention of recognizing the rebel legislators for any purpose other than recalling the state's troops. On April 12, three days after Appomattox, the president revoked his order permitting the Virginia legislature to assemble, explaining that General Grant "has since captured the Virginia troops," thus the reason for allowing it to meet "is no longer applicable." When the order was revoked, no more than 15 legislators had wandered back to Richmond.[40]

On April 5, the day after his return to City Point from Richmond, Lincoln gave further evidence of his almost obsessive desire to conciliate former Confederates and restore national harmony as soon as the armies laid down their arms. A cordial meeting with General Rufus

Barringer, who had been captured in Lee's retreat from Petersburg, demonstrated Lincoln's wish to let bygones be bygones even in the case of prominent rebels. Informed of the unnamed general's presence, Lincoln indicated to the post commander at City Point that he had never seen a live Confederate general. He asked if he could meet the prisoner, a request that was quickly granted. When they met, Lincoln mistook the Confederate officer for his brother, Daniel Moreau Barringer, with whom he had served in Congress in 1847–1849. After the general had corrected the mistake, the two men went to a nearby tent, where they had a long and friendly conversation. Lincoln reminisced about his service in Congress with the general's brother, whom he referred to as "my chum." The president and General Barringer, according to a witness to this extraordinary meeting, also discussed the merits of military and civil leaders, both North and South. Lincoln often illustrated his point "with some appropriate story, entirely new, full of humor and sometimes of pathos." Before they parted, Lincoln wrote out a note to Secretary of War Stanton directing him to make Barringer's "detention in Washington as comfortable as possible under the circumstances." Barringer never forgot the president's good will toward him or toward the South. After his return home, he wholeheartedly accepted the results of the war, affiliated with the Union Republican party, and worked for the true reintegration of North Carolina and its people into the nation. This course of action was what Lincoln had in mind for former Confederate leaders.[41]

After more than two weeks with the army in Virginia, Lincoln on April 9 returned home to Washington on the *River Queen*. The Marquis Adolphe de Chambrun, on board the vessel as part of Mrs. Lincoln's entourage, wrote his wife that the president's "only preoccupation" at this time "was to recall the Southern States into the Union as soon as possible." Chambrun indicated that when Lincoln "encountered opposition on this point, . . . he would exhibit signs of impatience . . . [and] nervous fatigue which he partially controlled but was unable to dissimulate entirely. On one point his mind was irrevocably made up. The policy of pardon, in regard to those who had taken a principal part in the rebellion, appeared to him an absolute necessity." When someone on the *River Queen* exclaimed that Jefferson Davis "must be hanged," Lincoln, according to the Marquis, calmly replied with a biblical admonition:

"Let us judge not that we be not judged." A remark by a member of the party that the sight of the notorious Libby prison rendered mercy impossible produced the same reply from the president.[42]

As the end of the war became imminent, the Republican press, with the exception of a few Radical newspapers like the *New York Evening Post,* provided important public support for Lincoln's magnanimous peace terms. However, they disagreed with him on pardons for Confederate leaders, insisting that high-ranking rebels should be punished or at least disfranchised. Like Lincoln, the Republican press indicated that the war must be pressed until the rebels had ceased their insurrection. These newspapers, including the *New York Tribune,* the *New York Times,* the *Washington Chronicle,* the *Chicago Tribune,* the *Boston Journal,* and the *Philadelphia Press,* contended that the majority of Southern whites had been dragooned into the rebellion and, after much suffering, were now anxious for the war to end and the restoration of the Union of their fathers.

The *New York Times* declared that "the great end and aim of our policy in dealing with the population of the revolted States ought to be the removal of all traces of the struggle from their memory"; the Lincoln "government has taken the ground that the object of this war is to put down the rebellion and preserve the Union," the *Times* reminded its readers. President Lincoln has assured the people of the South that remaining questions "must be heard and acted upon within the Union by the government of the Union, each section being duly represented and having precisely the weight to which it is entitled." He has repeatedly said that these questions, "so far as the action and influence of the Executive Department are concerned," will be "canvassed and decided in a liberal and conciliatory spirit." The *Philadelphia Press* declared that, though the "leading criminals" should not "retain all their rights as citizens," there should be no "judicial bloodshed," and, after the armies surrender, Lincoln should proclaim a general amnesty. "Our character as one of the most advanced Nations in the great March of Civilization," the *Press* righteously argued, required that the Union be magnanimous to the defeated rebels. Other Northern Republican or Union newspapers expressed a similar message.[43]

Radical Republicans, however, feared that under Lincoln's conditional terms the war would end and the South would be restored to the

Union without guarantees for the punishment and disfranchisement of rebel leaders, the confiscation of their property, the establishment of truly loyal governments in the South, and bona fide freedom for blacks, including the federal imposition of civil and political rights. The Marquis de Chambrun reported that, after the president's visit to Richmond, Senator Charles Sumner confronted Lincoln with the Radical demand that "an unconditional surrender of all the rebel armies" should be required, followed by martial law in the South and the imposition of "civil and political equality between the two races"; but Lincoln rejected this plan "with all his force."[44]

Some Radicals like Senator Benjamin F. Wade of Ohio, outraged by cascading reports of the suffering of Union prisoners in Confederate camps like Andersonville, called for retaliation against rebels held in the North and severe postwar punishment for those responsible for the mistreatment of Union prisoners. George Templeton Strong, an urbane New York Radical, let his passions get away from him when he bitterly confided to his diary: "I almost hope," he wrote, "that the war may last till it becomes a war of extermination. Southrons who could endure the knowledge that human creatures were undergoing this torture within their own borders, and who did not actively protest against it, deserve to be killed." However, some Radicals, like Senators Sumner and Henry Wilson of Massachusetts, deplored acts of revenge against Southerners, insisting that such methods were uncivilized. Lincoln agreed, and, though the moderate *New York Times* called on him to "bring the crimes of the rebels before the great tribunal of the opinion of the civilized world," he made no move to do so or to retaliate against Confederates who had mistreated Union prisoners. Radicals generally, as Congressman George W. Julian of Indiana acknowledged, knew that Lincoln, not they, was the master of Southern affairs and his conciliatory policy toward the defeated South would prevail—at least in the spring of 1865.[45]

On April 11, Lincoln, from the balcony of the White House, delivered his last speech. This famous address dealt with the issue of reconstruction once the war had ended. In essence the president laid down no new policy, though in defending the course of the Union government in Louisiana, he admitted that he would have preferred qualified black suffrage as a part of that state's constitution. The policy for each

Southern state, Lincoln declared, must be flexible while the "important principles"—emancipation and loyalty—"may, and must, be inflexible." In conclusion, he indicated that "it may be my duty to make some new announcement to the people of the South." The president probably had in mind a declaration extending temporary military control to states where no loyal governments existed, a purpose that became clearer when he met with his cabinet three days later. In that meeting, the cabinet reviewed a plan drawn up by Secretary of War Stanton for the establishment of military governments in two Southern states for the purpose of restoring law and order and initiating the restoration of civil rule. Lincoln asked Stanton to modify his plan and have a draft ready for discussion at a cabinet meeting on April 18. Lincoln also responded to a cabinet member's question about what should become of the heads of the rebel government. "I should not be sorry to have them out of the country," he answered; "but I should be for following them up pretty close to make sure of their going." All members of the cabinet agreed for the sake of amity and goodwill toward the defeated South that it was desirable to have as few judicial proceedings as possible involving rebel leaders.[46]

As fate would have it, the cabinet meeting scheduled for April 18 never occurred, and Lincoln never witnessed the actual end of the war. The outrage at his assassination would dramatically change the conciliatory mood in the North that Lincoln had carefully cultivated, if not created. The implications of this change would soon be felt in the struggle over reconstruction between his successor, the inept Andrew Johnson, who thought he was following Lincoln's policy, and the Republican majority in Congress, who now took a harder line toward defeated Confederates. In the end, the Northern public supported Congress and insisted on a far more stringent political settlement for the South than Lincoln ever envisioned.

# CHAPTER 8

# The Riddle of Death

## Robert V. Bruce

The earliest surviving fragments of Abraham Lincoln's writing are two copybook verses inscribed during his middle teens. One, though often quoted, was no more than commonplace doggerel among boys of that day. The other, though it has been almost ignored, struck a note that would reverberate throughout Lincoln's life:

> Time what an emty vapor tis and days how swift they are
> swift as an indian arrow fly on like a shooting star
> the present moment Just is here then slides away in haste
> that we can never say they're ours but only say they're past.[1]

Lincoln may have composed those lines; he was known as a versifier in those days, and the spelling and grammar are certainly original. In any case, he chose to write them down, and that fact alone ought to have interested his biographers. Considering that his lifelong favorite poem bore the title "Mortality," that he was noted as much for deep melancholy as for high humor, and that over the years his self-reported dreams, visions, and premonitions centered on death, the indifference of his biographers to that adolescent keynote seems stranger still. True, Lincoln's brooding over death has not escaped the notice of his biographers. Two of them, George Forgie and Dwight Anderson, have seized on that turn of mind, and from it have spun out far-fetched surmises about his political objectives. But the tendency itself has been simply accepted as given. This essay proposes to analyze its elements.

The first of those elements is the uncommon intensity and independence of Lincoln's response to the mystery of death. The word "independence" requires some understanding of what was conventional wisdom in Lincoln's day. An appropriate specimen of that is a letter written on February 8, 1842, by one Luke Bemis of Newmarket, New Hampshire, to Miss Elizabeth Lincoln of Hingham, Massachusetts, hometown of Abraham's ancestors. It exemplifies both the unpredictability of death in that day and the commonly held article of faith that made its familiar visitations bearable:

> Even while we were talking of that dear little girl on Sunday afternoon she was an angel in Heaven. On Thursday she was apparently as well as usual . . . on Friday morning she complained of being sick. . . . She has gone to join her Mother, Brother, and Sisters. Of five dear children but one is left on earth. . . . How soon we shall all be gathered together again God only knows.[2]

Five days before, Elizabeth's western namesake Abraham had written his closest friend, Joshua Speed, who was uneasy about the health of his bride-to-be, "The death scenes of those we love, are surely painful enough; but these we are prepared to, and expect to see. They happen to all, and all know they must happen."[3] And on the very day of Bemis's letter, Lincoln delivered a formal eulogy on the victim of a brief illness. Both occasions invited—indeed, almost demanded—conventional homilies. Yet in neither of those commentaries on death did Lincoln hold up the prospect of a reunion in heaven, something that Luke Bemis did as a matter of course. That nonconformity demonstrates how much more searchingly Lincoln approached the riddle of death than did most of his Springfield contemporaries.

Earlier, in his Indiana boyhood and adolescence, Lincoln's silence on the hereafter had been less out of keeping with the views of those around him. Not only was death more commonplace and unchallengeable then, but also the rural Indiana of Lincoln's youth had no hospitals and undertakers to hide the dying and the dead. With familiarity came a matter-of-fact acceptance of death, by violence and accident as well as disease, and a casual fatalism later exemplified by Lincoln himself when as a politician in his twenties he notified the *Sangamo Journal* that "if alive on the first Monday in November, I shall vote for Hugh L. White for President."[4] The young Lincoln's Indiana contemporaries in their letters and diaries made little of the idea of an afterlife, except in the most allusive and general way. They embraced no such elaborate imagery as then permeated the popular literature of the Eastern seaboard. What gave Midwestern frontier people comfort in the face of death was simply the thought of rest and a release from life's hardships.

But Lincoln did not share even that unquestioning resignation. Then, as later, he felt an extraordinary compulsion to question, to analyze, to comprehend the essence of what he saw and experienced. And he saw death in close-up. In a sense, he even sampled it and took the experience seriously enough to include it in a brief, third-person, autobiographical sketch more than 40 years later. "In his tenth year," wrote Lincoln of himself, "he was kicked by a horse, and apparently killed for a time."[5] That same year, death came in earnest to the Lincoln family. In the course of a fortnight, the deadly "milk sickness" killed the aunt and uncle of Abraham's mother Nancy, and then Nancy herself. As she lay dying, it was later recalled, she said, "I am going away from you, Abraham, and I shall not return."[6] That would have been the natural moment for her to speak of a heavenly reunion, but if she did, the fact has not come down to us.

Neither has any testimony that her nine-year-old son openly demonstrated grief beyond the usual for that time, place, and situation. Still, since he seemed not to be close to his father, he must have felt the loss keenly. Many years later he wrote to another bereaved child: "In this sad world of ours, sorrow comes to all; and to the young it comes with bitterest agony, because it takes them unawares. The older have learned to ever expect it. . . . I have had experience enough to know what I say. . . ."[7] Louis Warren has concluded that "Abraham idealized and even idolized [his mother's] memory," though Lincoln said little about her in later life.[8] His sister Sarah, two years older than he, tried to fill the mother's role in the year before their father remarried; and when she died in childbirth a few years later, Abraham's grief did impress those who saw it. "I never will forget that scene," recalled a relative of Sarah's husband. "He sat down in the door of the smoke house and buried his face in his hands. The tears slowly trickled down from between his bony fingers and his gaunt frame shook with sobs. We turned away."[9] Lincoln gave his stepmother all the affection of a natural son, as if she were his own mother come back after all; and perhaps an earlier, though temporary, transfer of the maternal image to his sister contributed to his later pain at her death.

Most striking and suggestive of all was the Ann Rutledge episode. The familiar story need not be rehearsed here, except to point out the one incontrovertible element in it: Lincoln's conspicuous display of grief at the girl's sudden death in 1835, a death like Nancy's and Sarah's. It may be that long-repressed grief at the loss of his mother had broken out again, to swell Lincoln's grief at the similar death of Ann. Perhaps it was more than coincidence that the name "Nancy" is a variant of "Ann."

Whatever its wellsprings, that grief startled Lincoln's friends and neighbors. And it was not his last such reaction to the death of others. Though he played a leading role in a war that took two-thirds of a million lives, the battle deaths of those close to him personally—Elmer Ellsworth, Edward Baker, Ben Helm—also brought him to tears. But it was not only the death of others that overwhelmed Lincoln. He was also evidently haunted at times by the thought of his own inescapable death. In 1839, he even injected that awareness rather oddly into a speech on the Sub-Treasury, in order, he said, to illustrate the soundness of reasoning from past experience:

> We all feel to know that we have to die. How? We have never died yet. We know it, because we know, or at least think we know, that of all the beings, just like ourselves, who have been coming into the world for six thousand years, not one is now living who was here two hundred years ago.[10]

This was the major premise of the classic syllogism. All men are mortal; Lincoln is a man; therefore Lincoln is mortal. When we weep for everyone, we weep for ourselves. This is not to say that a sense of his own mortality caused Lincoln's celebrated melancholy. That probably owed most to innate temperament and perhaps physiology. And Lincoln had burdens, setbacks, and worries enough otherwise to fill the bill. But the melancholy and the sense of personal mortality surely fed on each other.

The best evidence of Lincoln's feelings about his own mortality is in the songs, poetry, and drama that resonated with them in his own mind. We have seen the earliest known poem to strike a response in the boy; and in the last year of the president's life, his newspaper confidant, Noah Brooks, recorded that Lincoln liked "all songs which had for their theme the rapid flight of time, decay, and the recollection of early years."[11] One of his favorite songs in the war years was one called "Twenty Years Ago," with its lines:

> I've wandered to the village Tom,
> I've sat beneath the tree;
> Upon the schoolhouse playing ground
> Which sheltered you and me. . . .
> Some now are in the churchyard laid
> Some sleep beneath the sea,
> But few are left of our old class,
> Excepting you and me . . . [12]

And a favorite poem of those years, one that he sometimes repeated to his friends from memory, was Oliver Wendell Holmes's "The Last Leaf," with its reference to "the pruning knife of Time" and especially its stanza:

> The mossy marbles rest
> On the lips that he has prest
>     In their bloom,
> And the names he loved to hear
> Have been carved for many a year
>     On the tomb.

To the artist Francis Carpenter, Lincoln said of that particular stanza: "For pure pathos, in my judgment, there is nothing finer than those six lines in the English language!"[13]

With all due allowance for the taste of another day, praise like that tells us that the sentiment, not the style, struck home. The inference is still plainer in the case of the poem that possessed Lincoln's mind throughout his adult life. A New Salem physician introduced him to it in 1831, when Lincoln was 22. Though Lincoln knew neither the title of the poem nor its author's name until shortly before his own death, it was in fact called "Mortality," and was written by a young Scotsman named William Knox, who died in 1825 at 36. The burden of Knox's poem is that life is short and all must die:

Oh! Why should the spirit of mortal be proud?
Like a swift-fleeting meteor, a fast-flying cloud,
A flash of the lightning, a break of the wave,
He passeth from life to his rest in the grave.

Thirteen more stanzas follow, which, life indeed being short, I shall not quote in full. They merely repeat the basic theme with minor variations.

The hold this poem had on Lincoln's mind was extraordinary in both duration and intensity. It obviously spoke to his soul. He wrote in 1846: "I would give all I am worth, and go in debt, to be able to write so fine a piece as I think this is"—this from the subsequent author of the Gettysburg Address. In the summer of 1845, he met the poem "in a straggling form in a newspaper," as he put it, and carried the clipping in his pocket until he had it by heart.[14] His sister-in-law recalled that in his home during the 1850s he would fall into a deep, abstracted silence for 20 or 30 minutes at a time and then come out of it with a quotation from "Mortality," "The Last Leaf," or "The Burial of Sir John Moore." On the circuit in those years, a young lawyer later testified, he "would frequently lapse into reverie and remain lost in thought long after the rest of us had retired for the night, and more than once I remember waking up early in the morning to find him sitting before the fire, his mind apparently concentrated on some subject, and with the saddest expression I have ever seen in a human being's eyes."[15] In such moods, wrote the lawyer, Lincoln would often recite "Mortality." Years later in the White House one night of wind and rain, Lincoln remarked pensively that Knox's poem "is my almost constant companion; indeed, I may say it is continually present with me, as it crosses my mind whenever I have relief from anxiety."[16]

Perhaps inspired by Knox, Lincoln tried his hand at poetry in 1846. His own estimate of the result was rightly modest, but the last two verses of a section on revisiting childhood scenes are significant:

I hear the loved survivors tell
    How nought from death could save,
Till every sound appears a knell,
    And every spot a grave.
I range the fields with pensive tread,
    And pace the hollow rooms,
And feel (companion of the dead)
    I'm living in the tombs.[17]

He was then 37 years old.

In brooding over the death ordained for all men, Lincoln was, as earlier suggested, implicitly confronting his own. The dreams and premonitions he now and then spoke of make this explicit. His erstwhile junior partner wrote in 1885 that Lincoln had said to him more than once, "Billy, I feel as if I shall meet with some terrible end." "He felt this for years," Herndon added.[18] After Lincoln's assassination, this remark sounded like a prophecy of murder, and perhaps in Lincoln's own mind it had a connotation of violence. If so, the connotation may have been a symptom of Lincoln's terror at facing the end of the self in whatever form it might come. In 1864, he told both Noah Brooks and Francis Carpenter in vivid detail about an unsettling, indeed a haunting experience he had had in 1860, when he saw a double image of himself in a mirror, one image being distinctly paler than the other. What might have interested another man only as an odd optical effect gave Lincoln, as he told Brooks, "a little pang as if something uncomfortable had occurred." It was Mrs. Lincoln who suggested to him that it was an omen of his death in a second term as president, but her knowledge of his moods and foreboding may have unconsciously suggested that notion to her.[19] In his farewell to the people of Springfield some months later, he remarked, "I now leave, not knowing when, or whether ever, I may return."[20]

In the presidency his foreboding continued. He was a lifelong fatalist, as Billy Herndon often remarked, and not least on the subject of his possible assassination. He scorned elaborate protective measures in the conviction that what would come, would come. He would not, he said in July 1864, "be dying all the while."[21] But in that same month he told a reporter, "I feel a presentiment that I shall not outlast the Rebellion."[22] Most famous, because of what followed close upon them, are two dreams he recounted in the spring of 1865. In one he heard the sounds of mourning, went to the East Room, and found a catafalque with a shrouded corpse on it. "The President was killed by an assassin," said the mourners. In telling of the dream, he comforted his wife by pointing out that since he saw the corpse it must have been that of some other fellow.[23] But as a wrestler with the riddle of mortality, Lincoln had surely pondered the paradox of imagining one's own nonexistence. At his last cabinet meeting, he reported the other dream as one that had preceded nearly every great event of the war. In it, as Navy Secretary Gideon Welles recalled his words, "he seemed to be in some singular, indescribable vessel, and . . . was moving with great rapidity towards an indefinite shore."[24] That evening he went to Ford's Theatre for his long anticipated appointment with death.

"Moving with great rapidity towards an indefinite shore"—what could this have been but an image of mortality as he had conceived it since boyhood? It brings us to the second major element in this analysis: Lincoln's thought about what came *after death,* that "indefinite shore." As the phrase implies, there is evidence that not only in his youth but also throughout his life he had no clear, settled conviction of a literal afterlife, but at most an occasional flicker of hope. Thus he shared with the folk of his Indiana youth their vagueness about the aftermath of life, but not their matter-of-fact acceptance of death; whereas he shared with the larger, literate society of his day its emotional reaction to death, but not its refuge in an elaborately detailed and homelike heaven of reunion. In short, he rejected the chief defense of each against the terror of oblivion.

Those who argue otherwise depend for hard evidence on a single sentence in a letter that he wrote in 1851. Lincoln's father lay dying 70 miles away and wanted very much to see his son. Lincoln's uncommon dread of death may partially explain his refusal to come at that pathetic call. At any rate, he wrote: "Say to him that if we could meet now, it is doubtful whether it would not be more painful than pleasant; but that if it be his lot to go now, he will soon have a joyous meeting with many loved ones gone before; and where the rest of us, through the help of God, hope ere-long to join them."[25]

After Lincoln's death, Billy Herndon showed that letter to "several of Mr. Lincoln's old and dear friends." They "laughed at me," he wrote privately, "for my credulity in believing that Mr. Lincoln believed in immortality and heaven as stated in the letter; it was said to be merely a message of consolation from a dutiful son to his dying father."[26] The laughter of Lincoln's "old and dear friends" is eloquent testimony to his thinking, as he had given them to know it; and their explanation of the letter is entirely plausible. Lincoln was honest but he was also humane and in this case perhaps remorseful, certainly not one to tell a dying man a cruel and useless truth in preference to a comforting and harmless lie—if, indeed, it may be called a lie. In it Lincoln said of the afterlife what most believed, and what he himself did not know as a fact to be false. He merely chose not to express his personal doubt in those circumstances. Moreover, Lincoln was an experienced lawyer; and as a writer, his most striking characteristic was the almost scholastic precision of his language. He had a genius for saying precisely what he meant and no more, yet in such a way that at first impression it sounded like what his audience wanted to hear—as in his remarks about race in the debates with Douglas, or his letter to Greeley about emancipation. He could split hairs as well as rails. Given that turn of mind, it was probably no accident that his letter said not "I believe that," but rather "Say to him that" he will meet his loved ones in the hereafter.

The most direct and forthright comment by Lincoln on the notion of life after death was reported after more than half a century by Mrs. Samuel Hill in a newspaper interview. At New Salem she had asked the young Lincoln, "Do you really believe there isn't any future state?" Lincoln replied, as she remembered it, "Mrs. Hill, I'm afraid there isn't. It isn't a pleasant thing to think that when we die that is the last of us."[27] Historians are wary of recollections long after the fact, but even the lapse of 50 years could not have seriously distorted so simple and direct a statement. Lincoln's remark, of course, reflected only his thought at that moment in his youth. But that it remained unchanged through most of his life can be inferred from his consistent silence on the subject.

Except for his equivocal message to his dying father, he expressed no faith in life after death in any of his surviving letters, speeches, or even private memoranda to himself—and this at a time when allusions to posthumous socializing had become clichés almost as commonplace and unthinking as "Dear Sir" and "Yours truly." The definitive source for Lincoln's own writings, public and private, is his *Collected Works,* edited by Roy Basler in eight large volumes and two shorter supplements. A page by page search of them reveals nothing more on the subject of life after death than has been quoted here. Many of his spoken remarks, like that to Mrs. Hill, were published piecemeal by a cloud of witnesses in the decades after his death. Those recollected words were systematically compiled and published in 1996 by Don and Virginia Fehrenbacher. Also in that year Michael Burlingame edited and published the interviews with Lincoln's associates conducted by one of his White House secretaries, John G. Nicolay; and in 1998, Douglas Wilson and Rodney Davis brought out a complete edition of the letters, interviews, and statements about Lincoln assembled by his former law partner William Herndon. These three volumes total more than 1,500 pages. They and the *Collected Works* clearly show Lincoln's metamorphosis from agnosticism in his youth to belief during his middle years in the controlling power of some abstract force called Fate or Necessity, and at last, in the war years, to firm faith in an all-wise and all-powerful being whom he called God.

But however often or fervently Lincoln the president may have invoked the name of God, these recorded words express no faith in an afterlife. The word "Heaven" shows up on a few occasions. But it does so in a figurative or casual way, as in his first inaugural address, when he said to the secessionists, "*you* have no oath registered in Heaven to destroy the government."[28] Those sparse and glancing references to "Heaven" carry no more theological weight than the line in Lincoln's favorite passage from Hamlet: "O my offence is rank, it smells to heaven."

Consider Lincoln's best-known letters of consolation, wherein allusions to reunions in heaven might seem all but obligatory in that day. To the parents of Elmer Ellsworth he sent eloquent praise of their son's character and conduct in life, but as to the future could only say "May God give you that consolation which is beyond all earthly power."[29] Upon the gallant death of his old friend Colonel William McCullough, he wrote McCullough's young daughter: "I am anxious to afford some alleviation of your present distress"; but his consolation was simply that "you are sure to be happy again," and that "the memory of your dear Father, instead of an agony, will yet be a sad sweet feeling in your heart."[30] And less than four months before he himself died, his famous letter to the Widow Bixby on the reported deaths of her five sons in battle tendered "the consolation that may be found in the thanks of the Republic they died to save . . . the cherished memory of the loved and lost, and the solemn pride that must be yours, to have laid so costly a sacrifice upon the altar of Freedom."[31] But not a word about reunion in heaven. (Many years later John Hay reportedly said privately and without elaboration that he had drafted the Bixby letter. His claim, as variously reported, was strangely silent as to Lincoln's input, if any, except for one version that says Lincoln simply approved the letter without alteration. But as Lincoln's secretary and after-hours confidant, Hay knew much about Lincoln's views; so if he did draft the letter, it was presumably consistent with Lincoln's beliefs about death and the hereafter.)

It happens also that Lincoln's favorite poems, though dwelling on death, made no allusions to a busy, convivial heaven. The poem "Mortality" promised only "rest in the grave." "The Last Leaf" said nothing on the subject. In Poe's "The Raven," which Lincoln knew by heart, the narrator asked if he would meet the lost Lenore in the hereafter, to which the Raven not unexpectedly replied, "Nevermore."

The death of his son Willie in 1862 made Lincoln's will to believe in an afterlife almost desperate. Yet, though he humored his anguished wife in her flirtation with spiritualism, he never succumbed to the notion himself. Once he read a visitor the lines from Shakespeare's *King John*:

> And father cardinal, I have heard you say
> That we shall see and know our friends in heaven
> If that be true, I shall see my boy again.

But he added, the friend remembered, "Did you ever dream of a lost friend and feel you were holding sweet communion with that friend and yet have sad consciousness that it was not a reality?—just so I dream of my boy Willie."[32] The Reverend Francis Vinton asserted that in that anguished time he had plied Lincoln with biblical assurances that Willie lived in Paradise, and that Lincoln had thrown his arm around Vinton's neck, sobbed aloud on his breast, and cried out "Alive? Alive?"[33] But besides the fact that a Lincoln who embraced a visitor and sobbed on his breast was not the Lincoln known to anyone else of record, it may be noted that Lincoln's question was not an affirmation.

Why, with his obvious longing for it, did Lincoln withhold any explicit statement of faith in an afterlife his contemporaries took for granted? Though he admitted to being superstitious in small matters, he had an unusually questioning and analytical temperament, had practiced law for many years, and showed an admiring interest in the progress of science. To believe, he must have wanted evidence of an afterlife, and he could find none. Indeed, he had personal evidence to the contrary. Though he did not say so, he may have been mindful of that boyhood kick from a horse, when he was "apparently killed for a time," as he later wrote. Accounts of the incident vary, but they agree that when he came to after several hours he completed a remark that had been interrupted by the kick. Quasi-death had been total oblivion, without so much as a consciousness of time's passing.

If Lincoln found the annihilation of the self an intolerable prospect, and if he could not achieve faith in an afterlife, what other refuge might he have found? How might he have dealt with the presumption that the war he prosecuted consigned its dead to the oblivion he dreaded? Those questions lead to the third major element in this analysis.

We know ourselves, in large part, through the responses of others. To that extent they are the mirror of our being, the medium of our self-recognition and self-definition. If, then, our pale images should linger in that mirror after our physical deaths, we cannot help but feel that in some degree we would still live. Conversely, others, when absent or dead, live for us in our mental images of them. This reinforces our feeling that remembrance is survival. Such a feeling was strong in Abraham Lincoln. In Lincoln's three letters of consolation quoted earlier, the key word, the bedrock of consolation, is not "Heaven" but "memory."

To see memory as the essence of life came naturally to Lincoln. "Of the earth, earthy" though he seems in legend, he lived less through the physical senses than do most of us. Lincoln seemed to live most intensely through the process of thought, the expression of thought, and the exchange of thought with others. His definition of life was Cartesian: I think, therefore I exist.

And he carried this to a corollary: when my thoughts die, so shall I. Fully half of Lincoln's poem of 1846 on childhood scenes deals with a childhood friend who had gone mad:

> . . . an object more of dread,
> Than aught the grave contains—
> A human-form, with reason fled,
> While wretched life remains.

Allusion in these verses to "pangs that kill the mind," to "the funeral dirge of reason dead and gone," imply that to Lincoln mere physical functions and animal consciousness were no life at all.[34] Thus tending more than most to locate life in the mind rather than the body, Lincoln would more readily than most have turned to the idea of survival by proxy in the minds of others.

In 1841, at the time of Lincoln's most desperate bout with depression, he confided to Joshua Speed that "he had 'done nothing to make any human being remember that he had lived,' and that to connect his name with the events transpiring in his day and generation, and so impress himself upon them as to link his name with something that would redound to the interest of his fellow man, was what he desired to live for."[35] This self-revelation links his strong feelings about death and his doubts of an afterlife not only to his chronic melancholy but also to another conspicuous element of his character: his powerful, almost obsessive ambition. In that, as in his melancholy, the fear of oblivion may not have been the only or even the most important factor. But it does seem more than probable that it helped fuel the ambition which Herndon called "a little engine that knew no rest."[36]

In 1856 Lincoln made a private note with respect to his old rival Stephen Douglas:

> With *me*, the race of ambition has been a failure—a flat failure; with *him* it has been one of splendid success. His name fills the nation; and is not unknown, even in foreign lands. I affect no contempt for the high eminence he has reached. So reached, that the oppressed of my species, might have shared with me in the elevation, I would rather stand on that eminence, than wear the richest crown that ever pressed a monarch's brow.[37]

Publicly, in debating Douglas in 1858, he said: "I claim no extraordinary exemption from personal ambition. . . . But I protest I have not entered upon this hard contest solely, or even chiefly, for a mere personal object."[38] He lost the senatorial contest, but it gave him some comfort nevertheless. In a speech of 1859 he said: "Men will pass away—die—die, politically, and naturally; but the principle will live, and live forever."[39]

His elevation to the presidency gave Lincoln's mind still more ease in this respect. "Fellow-citizens," he said in 1862, "we cannot escape history. We of this Congress and this administration, will be remembered in spite of ourselves. No personal significance, or insignificance, can spare one or another of us. The fiery trial through which we pass, will light us down, in honor or dishonor, to the latest generation."[40] To Secretary of War Edwin M. Stanton he read aloud Fitz-Greene Halleck's poem "Marco Bozzaris," the theme of which is the victory of fame over death. The poet says to the hero:

For thou art Freedom's now, and Fame's
One of the few, the immortal names
That were not born to die.[41]

If Lincoln did not believe that those who died for the Union would afterward live in a blissful Valhalla, he could at least believe that, as he said at Gettysburg, they would live in everlasting memory. And he cherished that hope for himself as well. After the Emancipation Proclamation, Lincoln had seen Joshua Speed again and reminded him of their conversation of 1841, more than 20 years before. With "earnest emphasis," as Speed puts it, Lincoln then said, "I believe that in this measure my fondest hope will be realized."[42] He had at last achieved his best hope of life after death.

When Lincoln died in the Petersen house, it was given to Stanton to pronounce the epitaph that is best remembered. Stanton himself had a lifelong fear of death, expressing itself in more bizarre ways than did Lincoln's. This, as well as the great contest in which they were comrades, may have contributed to the closeness of the two men during the war. Many were the times when they could be seen side by side in a carriage, deep in conversation. One subject of those talks is suggested not only by "Marco Bozzaris" but also by the fact that, early in 1864, Lincoln wrote out a copy of Knox's poem "Mortality" for Mrs. Stanton. On that terrible night in the Petersen house, busy as he was, Stanton must have reflected on what Lincoln had said to him of death and its meaning. And in the hour of Lincoln's death, he made his comment.

What idea formed in Stanton's mind at that moment? Not a tribute to Lincoln's character or his achievements, not a paraphrase of Mark Antony on Brutus, not an estimate of Lincoln's place in heaven.

"Now," said Stanton, "he belongs to the ages."[43]

To sum up, this essay suggests a relationship between salient elements of Abraham Lincoln's thought and character. His analytical and introspective mind, his innate tendency toward melancholy, and perhaps the sudden death of his mother in his early boyhood, combined to make the riddle of mortality a focal point of his private philosophy. That intractable mystery of death gave form and substance to his lifelong bouts of depression, which in turn gave urgency and depth to his compensating humor. The haunting sense of human transience and ultimate helplessness—a sense in which all men are indeed equal—also deepened his compassion, forbearance, and ability to comprehend both the extent and the bounds of what is possible in the brevity of life. Most suggestive is his rejection of both the frontier's passive, unquestioning acceptance of familiar death and the larger society's emotional refuge in a posthumous resumption of familiar life. Lincoln's antidote for despair was the concept of immortality through remembrance, eternal consciousness by proxy in the mind of posterity. His desperate will to achieve this was a powerful force in his uncommonly absorbing ambition.

The elements of this conjecture are all plausible, and most are demonstrable. But since Lincoln, at least by medical definition, is dead, and since the nexus of these elements lay deep in his well-guarded mind, the total conjecture itself is forever beyond verification. Still, it gives us a more coherent way of thinking about what we cannot help thinking about anyway. This, after all, is the primary charge their calling lays upon historians.

But historians, more than any others who make a profession of studying mankind, are also charged with seeing the whole web of human life, even when tracing only a single strand in it. So it must be said that in any just portrait of Abraham Lincoln, his strong conscious-ness of mortality is a shadow that heightens the light; and that while it influenced his life and thought, it fell far short of accounting for all he was and did. On the contrary, if he had not been so central to the life of his own time, and so full of life and laughter himself, he could not have so fully achieved his fondest hope by living now and hereafter in our thoughts.

## CHAPTER 9

# Epilogue:
# Lincoln in "Modern" Art

## Gabor Boritt and Harold Holzer

I n 1984, the well-known photographer George Tice published an album of his camera studies entitled *Lincoln*. This collection of frank portraits of eroding statues throughout America was inspired, the author noted, by a visit to "the Lincoln Motel and Abe's Disco . . . in the heart of Newark." Not surprisingly, the book offered a generally grim view of surviving public art devoted to Abraham Lincoln: the famous Gutzon Borglum seated bronze in Newark was shown littered with graffiti; the replica of Thomas Ball's *Emancipation Group* in Boston was set against a depressing backdrop of tawdry billboards and commercial storefronts; and the statue that stood once at Wilkensburg, Pennsylvania, was not even visible—it had earlier been stolen, leaving only its forlorn base crumbling in an overgrown, vacant lot.

Tice had manipulated his camera to suggest that modern America had grown negligent and indifferent to Lincoln. He did also elicit a nonphotographic validation when he asked a North Carolina resident if she thought her town would agree to accept, and mount, a gift from Tice: a replica of the Augustus Saint-Gaudens Lincoln statue from Chicago, the twin of which stands in London's Parliament Square. "There would probably be opposition to it," came the blunt reply. "Probably" it would not be accepted. Perhaps things would change, the resident speculated, in about 25 years.[1]

Granting that Lincoln images had never thrived in the old Confederacy, this admission was nonetheless telling. All over the nation, public Lincoln art was fading from memory at the time, some of it literally oxidizing into a tarnished blur in public squares and parks around the country. And modern painting, increasingly abstract, seemed to regard the iconic image of Lincoln as a throwback to the most stolid representational art of the nineteenth century.

George Tice and the reluctant citizen of North Carolina would undoubtedly be surprised by the fact that public sculptures honoring Lincoln made an extraordinary return to favor in the last decade of the millennium, and it did not require the passing of a quarter century to inspire it. A new statue memorializing the second Lincoln-Douglas debate, for example, now graces the spot where the 1858 joint meeting took place in Freeport, Illinois. A Lincoln bronze cheerfully greets visitors to the town square at Gettysburg, Pennsylvania, just outside the house where the president stayed and probably put the finishing touches on the Address he delivered at the National Cemetery on November 19, 1863. A sculptural tribute to Lincoln's role in the Black Hawk War is planned for central Illinois.

Further research suggests that unlike sculptors, whose large, expensive efforts depend upon outside patronage, some painters never really abandoned Lincoln at all; for a time, it seems, only their audiences did, perhaps a reflection of declining interest in both the genre and the subject. But even in a world whose images are increasingly defined on the World-Wide Web, not on canvas, Lincoln art seems again to be thriving at all levels in both old and new forms.

One cannot easily find universal agreement among art historians about the advent of modern art. Some date it to the arrival of the Impressionists in France of the 1880s, others to the dawn of the twentieth century. For the purposes of this survey, the context might properly be defined by historical, not artistic, events. If the Civil War constituted the most convulsive event of an earlier America, then the Great Depression might be said also to have convulsed the society some 70 years later. Like the Civil War, the Depression, followed by World War II, inspired many artists, including the painters who labored under the auspices of the Works Progress Administration, to vivify American history and heroes in public buildings across the country.[2] Their work often included Lincoln.

With the United States—and democracy—threatened by ugly totalitarian forces, artists again turned to him. Once more they began exploring and interpreting the unique physiognomy that had appeared on so many canvases, engravings, lithographs, and statues in the era of the American Civil War. Thomas Hart Benton might view Lincoln as a highly stylized, totem-like figure invoking the storm clouds of war to end slavery. Norman Rockwell could stress the young Lincoln as role model for hard work and study. Horace Pippin would see the antislavery champion as a virtuous man. William H. Johnson would use him to remind America that his promise of liberty for blacks was violated daily. And Marsden Hartley would deconstruct the angles of Lincoln's face and rearrange them to stress an asymmetrical, powerful connection to the present.

A poet as well as an artist, Hartley saw Lincoln as an "American Ikon" [*sic*], and spoke vividly for many artists of his generation when he reminisced in verse about the challenges of crafting portraits of the hero:

I have walked up and down the
valleys
of his astounding face,
I have witnessed all the golgothas
I have climbed the steep declivities
of all his dreams
listened to the whickering of the wind
around them;
like a lilliput I have sat quietly
upon his haggard chin
look up at the breaking rain
falling from his furrowed lids . . .
I have scaled the sheer surface of his
dignities
watching the flaming horizon with calm.[3]

It was no accident that Hartley saw Lincoln with what the painter-poet's most recent biographer calls "geological grandeur," for like many artists of the period, he was influenced greatly by the work of Gutzon Borglum at Mount Rushmore.

On a somewhat smaller scale, sculptors from Paul Manship to Louis Slobodkin dotted American cities and towns with their own images of the hero. Lincoln loomed large in American culture, high and low, through World War II, and a few years beyond, on stage, on the screen, even in the time-tested art of World War, the recruitment poster.

Yet when, in the wake of war, artists created the first truly native style of painting, abstract expressionism, its major figures from Jackson Pollock forward seemed to forget the man whom the poet James Russell Lowell had called "the first American" in 1865.[4] Indeed, American history seemed to become something to escape from. The succession of movements that followed abstract expressionism only followed suit.

Andy Warhol may have been the best publicized and best known painter of recent decades, but he evidently did not create a Lincoln (although Leroy Nieman did). Even as the avant garde kept rebelling against the status quo, whatever it was, Lincoln and historical figures did not capture their attention. Jasper Johns's various flags may have come closest to touching the subject. The rebels rebelled against history and failed to see its potential for revolutionary inspiration. Neither nostalgic conservatives like Andrew Wyeth, one of the most admired painters in the United States during the last three decades of the twentieth century (whose father N. C. kept returning to Lincoln), nor Andrew's son, Jamie (who did a memorable John F. Kennedy) felt compelled to turn to the man who had, for so long, been the symbol of America. Such painters reflected the larger cultural ethos of the country. Indeed, among the great modern artists, it fell to a Spaniard, Salvador Dali, to create a memorable modern Lincoln—which he dedicated to Mark Rothko, the American modernist who did not paint the great president himself.

All modern artists live in a world where inspiration, the secrets of the heart and mind, mix with commercial realities. And commerce, reflecting culture, balked at the Civil War President. And yet, all along, outside the limelight, Lincoln continued to attract American artists of substantial talent and, by the 1990s, there appeared the beginnings of a new trend. Lincoln had never disappeared, of course. In a low-key way, he remained ubiquitous: on the copper penny, on the five-dollar bill, re-created with regularity for postage stamps, often sitting in judgment of his successors in political cartoons. But by the last decade of the century an ever larger number of talented artists turned to him, and three new statues were placed in public places, including the aforementioned one in Gettysburg by a major sculptor of the era, Seward Johnson. Lincoln's stovepipe hat seemed once again to grow very familiar, his bow tie askew in posters and prints, the beard decorating the dust jackets of best-selling books, the soft gray eyes penetrating the Internet.

If the renaissance seems particularly pronounced in the realm of public sculpture, the trend owes much to the momentum triggered by a general revival in the genre sparked by the appearance on the Mall in Washington of acclaimed sculptural tributes to the veterans of the Vietnam and Korean wars, the nearby sculpture garden memorializing Franklin D. (and Eleanor) Roosevelt, and the memorial to the African American soldiers of the Civil War. The controversy that surrounded placing the sculpture of the late black tennis star, Arthur Ashe, on the boulevard in Richmond that boasts equestrian statues of Confederate icons, brought further attention to public art. As the century drew to a close, proponents of a World War II memorial, as well as a new Martin Luther King statue, argued about the location of artworks that will almost certainly grow into important emotional touchstones in the nation's capital. After a long hiatus, nudged along by unprecedented prosperity, and a culture both strengthened and threatened by a huge influx of immigrants, the potent power of public art seems greater than ever.

At the dawn of a new millennium—and within sight of the bicentennial of Lincoln's birth in 2009—the age-old question, "what is art?," clearly remains unanswered, perhaps unanswerable. So, too, does the inquiry: "what is *Lincoln* art?" What *is* clear is that the boundaries of this art have expanded to embrace new forms and new uses. Presidents now routinely pose or speak with the face of Lincoln reassuringly supporting them, just as ordinary citizens can now pose at will with the life-sized, street-level Lincoln sculpture at Gettysburg. Lincoln remains a standard against which to measure modern leaders in the genre of political caricature. A nineteenth-century painter named Edward Dalton Marchant once referred to Lincoln as "the most difficult subject who ever taxed my skills as an artist."[5] He may remain so, but not for want of relentless trying, and a revival in large-scale memorializations for public places.

Back in the 1920s, a decidedly modern artist showed visitors to a corner of his Paris apartment, where he kept a large cardboard box "full of illustrations, photographs, engravings, and reproductions clipped from newspapers," the guest recalled. "All of them dealt with a single person—Abraham Lincoln. 'I've been collecting them since I was a child, Pablo Picasso said. 'I have thousands, thousands!' He held up one of Brady's photographs of Lincoln, and said with great feeling: 'There is the real American elegance!'"[6]

But if Picasso ever painted Lincoln himself, the artwork seems not to survive. The work of other twentieth-century painters does, however—along with that of folk artists, sculptors, engravers, lithographers, cartoonists, advertisers, and even the makeup artists who create faces for films and television. The ubiquity of their work has never before been systematically examined, much less appreciated. Nor has Lincoln's enduring "American elegance" been carefully explored.

The modern image of Abraham Lincoln does deserve study. However, these introductory words, and the portfolio that follows, do not pretend to be definitive. If Hartley or Benton had survived the test of time, much more recent work will not. All the same, we hope to extend the horizons of both Lincoln scholars and "buffs" and engage a broader public. What we offer, to some degree, is idiosyncratic and personal, emphasizing the most recent years to see how we look at Lincoln at the dawn of the new millennium. Thus it is perhaps subject to more than the usual revisions required for chapters in a book such as this. We are eager to hear dissenting opinions and discover additional examples of outstanding Lincoln art. We would be glad to hear from you at gboritt@gettysburg.edu and harold.holzer@metmuseum.org.

## Acknowledgments

The authors gratefully acknowledge the assistance and advice of many friends and colleagues and thank them for crucial support, particularly Don Pollard for photographing so many works of art, and also Ken Corbran, Judy Boritt, and Jake Boritt. We also thank the following people for valuable advice: at the Metropolitan Museum of Art, H. Barbara

Weinberg and Thayer Tolles; and at the Studio Museum of Harlem, Lowery Sims, director. And we gratefully acknowledge Jennifer Russell, deputy director of the Museum of Modern Art; Kristen L. Kertsos at the National Museum of American Art; Harry Henderson of Croton-on-Hudson, New York; Mamie Shuman of American Artistry of Dallas; Kim Bauer of the Illinois State Historical Library; Ame Willis Ivanov of Anchorage, Alaska; Corinne Russell at the Charleston (Illinois) Chamber of Commerce; and Randall R. Griffey at the Nelson-Atkins Museum of Art in Kansas City. At the Civil War Institute of Gettysburg College: Tina Fair Grim oversaw the difficult task of pulling together into one disk the work of two coauthors. History students Tim Parry and especially Jared Peatman, Gabor Boritt's research assistants, performed numerous chores with ingenuity, including tracking down difficult-to-find art. Others helping at the CWI are recognized in the acknowledgments to the book. We are indebted to many others, too. We are grateful to all.

# I. INCREASED DEVOTION?

## Paintings

# LINCOLN REASSEMBLED

Marsden Hartley (1877–1943) painted *Young Worshipper of the Truth* around 1939, the year of Lincoln's otherwise generally unnoted 130th birthday. The artist's nearly Cubist interpretation of Polycarp von Schneidau's 1854 daguerreotype[1] (see below) focused wholly on the individual elements of Lincoln's remarkable face: the large ears, the dreamy eyes, the prominent nose, and the full mouth, but Hartley's striking rearrangement of these elements combines for a startling, daring work of art. The political inspiration for the original photograph, which showed Lincoln holding an antislavery newspaper, was altogether forsaken in order to concentrate on the character traits Hartley vigorously portrays. Emerging from a black void, his unique, young Lincoln demands attention, just as we might imagine that Lincoln himself, grotesquely awkward, astonishingly tall, irredeemably homely, once somehow commanded attention in his lifetime. (Hartley: Sheldon Memorial Art Gallery, Nebraska Art Association, Nelle Cochran Woods Memorial; Von Schneidau: The Lincoln Museum, Fort Wayne, Indiana)

---

1. Lloyd Ostendorf, *Lincoln's Photographs: A Complete Album* (Dayton, Ohio: Rockywood Press, 1998), 18–19; Van Deren Coke, *The Painter and the Photograph* (Albuquerque: University of New Mexico Press, 1964), 32–33.

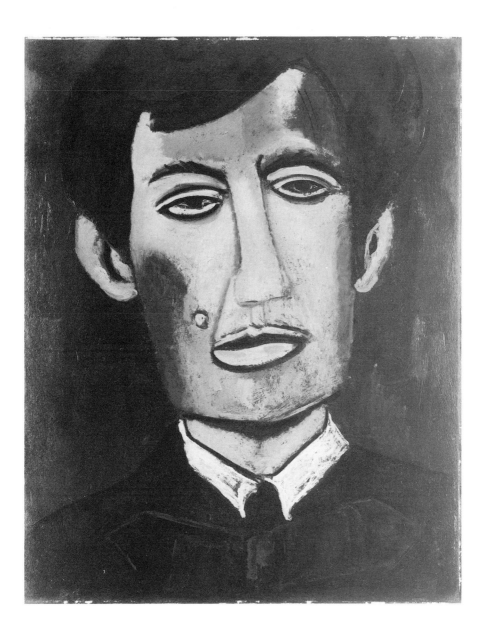

## MAN AND MONUMENTS

Marsden Hartley painted Lincoln against a symbolic backdrop only once—for the oil portrait *Weary of the Truth* (1940). The president's profile emerges from views of the United States Capitol and the Washington Monument. In life, his perseverance helped guarantee that the construction of the expensive Capitol dome go forward during the Civil War; its completion would demonstrate, Lincoln believed, faith in the "preservation of the Union."[1] But work on the Washington Monument stalled during the Rebellion, and the now-famous obelisk stood stunted and unfinished, an eyesore whose construction would not resume until the 1870s.[2] Perhaps this irony held no significance for Hartley. His Lincoln gazes beyond the Washington, D.C., skyline into the distance, inspired by, but not dependent upon, the example of the first president or the constraints of the legislative branch. Filling the foreground with his prominent ear and nose, thick beard and huge greatcoat, his high hat parallel to, and even more monumental than, the landmarks of the city, Hartley's Lincoln looks beyond the past and points to the future. (Yale University Art Gallery; gift of Donald Gallup)

---

1. John Eaton quoted in Don E. Fehrenbacher and Virginia Fehrenbacher, *Recollected Words of Lincoln* (Stanford: Stanford University Press, 1996), 147.
2. Harold Holzer, "'There is About it a Mantle of Pure Radiance:' The Washington Monument," *American History Illustrated* (December 1984), 34–40.

An 1862 photograph by the Brady studios (see below) served as the model for Hartley's portrait of the White House Lincoln, *Great Good Man* (1942). The subject has grown his famous beard, but in Hartley's hands it is intentionally exaggerated, and dominates the composition, suggesting wisdom along with benevolence. Lincoln's rugged face is at once simplified and analyzed, its hard lines flattened, heavily lidded eyes and facial mole widened, and even the contours of his lapels are eliminated in an effort to winnow down to basic truths. The resulting image owes a debt to photography, of course, but even photographic historian Van Deren Coke conceded that it was a brilliant "paraphrase."[1] Here an even greater debt—to Cézanne and Picasso—is much more in evidence.[2] So, too, perhaps, is the influence of Borglum's Lincoln at Mount Rushmore, creating a Lincoln, in art historian Randall R. Griffey's words, "primitive and common, but also powerful, important and larger than life."[3] (Hartley: Museum of Fine Arts, Boston. Reproduced with permission. ©1999 Museum of Fine Arts, Boston; Brady: The Lincoln Museum, Fort Wayne, Indiana)

1. Van Deren Coke, *The Painter and the Photograph*, 33.
2. *American Paintings in the Museum of Fine Arts*, Boston (2 vols., Boston: Museum of Fine Arts, 1969), 134.
3. Randall R. Griffey, "Marsden Hartley's Late Paintings: American Masculinity and National Identity" (unpublished doctoral dissertation, University of Kansas), 187, 190.

## ICON IN THE BACKGROUND

Palmer Hayden (1890–1973) often dreamed what he would later paint[1] and created two versions of *The Janitor Who Paints (The Janitor Paints a Picture)*, 1939. At one time the painting received criticism for caricaturing its subjects, but Hayden's work is a protest, depicting an artist friend, Cloyd L. Boykin, who was compelled to make his living as a janitor. The large clock suggests the unending demands made on the janitor, and the title is a reproach to the world.[2] The first version of the painting was softened with the portrait of Lincoln in the background, the portrait of a friend who symbolized the original promise of freedom. Perhaps Boykin in fact had such a painting in his home, as many African Americans, as well as whites, did in his time. (Painting reproduced from Alain Locke, *The Negro in Art: A Pictorial Record of the Negro Artist and the Negro Theme in Art* [Washington: Association of Negro Folk Education, 1940], 43). The second version of the painting, most likely completed many years later, survives in Washington's Smithsonian. X ray scanning shows that Hayden made the racial characteristics less exaggerated, painted over Lincoln, and made the protest all the harsher.[3]

---

1. Harry Henderson, who knew Hayden well, in telephone conversation with Gabor Boritt, February 11, 2000.
2. Romare Bearden and Harry Henderson, *A History of African-American Artists from 1792 to the Present* (New York: Pantheon, 1993), 100.
3. Mary Schmidt Campbell, David Driskell, David Levering Lewis, and Deborah Willis Ryan, *Harlem Renaissance Art of Black America* (New York: Studio Museum of Harlem and Abrams, 1987), 32–33, 43, 132–33, has the portrait as well as contrasting interpretations.

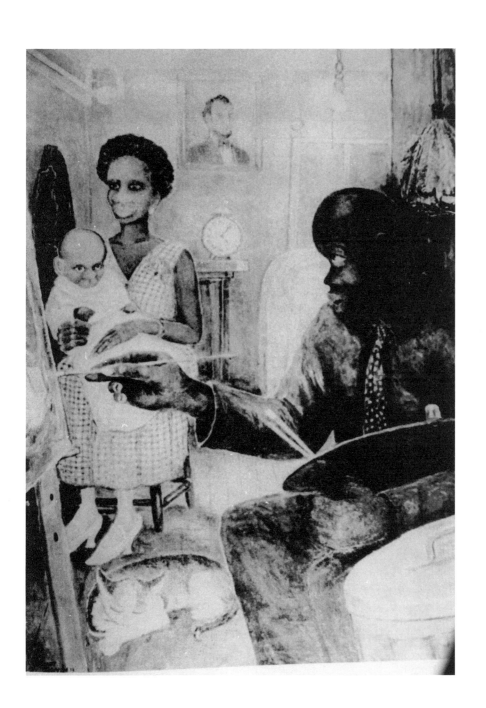

## THE REGIONALIST LIBERATOR

Lincoln University of Missouri, a school for African American students, commissioned Thomas Hart Benton (1889–1975) to paint this mural in 1955. Though it owes a debt to Thomas Ball's Emancipation Proclamation sculpture, which depicts an African American lifted from his knees by Abraham Lincoln,[1] Benton emphasized Lincoln's gigantic proportions, not the slave's subservience. Their linked arms, intentionally out of proportion as if to stress their common human experience, cut diagonally across the full canvas, dominating the background scenes of the long-ago Civil War, as well as references to both old and modern aspirations like education and good housing. Lincoln seems to be rising from a pedestal that is reminiscent of the view of a tree stump—was the tree itself felled by the young rail-splitter, or does the stump represent politics? Lincoln soars above the scene like a timeless totem, connecting the sacrifices of the past with the dreams of the future. (Lincoln University, ©T. H. and R. P. Benton Testamentary Trusts/Licensed by VAGA, New York, N.Y.)

---

1. Wayne Craven, *Sculpture in America* (rev. ed., New York: Cornwall Books, 1984), 260.

## TELLING HIS HEART[1]

As the world headed toward war, America witnessed a period of revived interest in historical art, even as its black community created its own historical narrative. African American Horace Pippin's short, sparkling career included seven historical paintings, all portraying antislavery heroes: three of John Brown and four of Lincoln. Pippin's simplicity cut to the heart of the Lincoln story by portraying a good man. In this view Pippin (1888–1946) was much like Hartley, who used that very phrase in a title. One of the paintings reproduced here (top), *Abe Lincoln, The Good Samaritan* (1943), carries both biblical and frontier connotations, as Pippin's Lincoln offers to help a child to split wood. In the other painting (bottom), General Grant looks on as *Abraham Lincoln, The Great Emancipator* (1942) pardons the sleeping sentry—a story that, as with so much touched by Lincoln, reached the heights of legend. For once, the kneeling man, about to rise to freedom, is not a black man. Pippin's "Great Emancipator" emancipates whites, too. As art historians Romare Bearden and Harry Henderson explained, whites also required emancipation, as expiation for the sin of slavery.[2] Or, as Lincoln had told an often reluctant public in 1862: "In giving freedom to the slave, we assure freedom to the free."[3] (*Samaritan:* Courtesy of the Pennsylvania Academy of Fine Arts, Philadelphia. Bequest of David J. Grossman in honor of Mr. and Mrs. Charles S. Grossman and Mr. and Mrs. Meyer Speiser; *Emancipator:* Museum of Modern Art, New York)

---

1. With acknowledgment for the caption title to Judith Stein, et al., *I Tell My Heart: The Art of Horace Pippin* (Philadelphia: Pennsylvania Academy of the Fine Arts, 1993).
2. Bearden and Henderson, *A History of African-American Artists*, 365.
3. "Annual Message to Congress, December 1, 1862," Basler, et al., eds., *Collected Works of Lincoln*, 5:537.

## LET MY PEOPLE GO

Those artists of Lincoln's era who portrayed the so-called Emancipation Moment depicted either imaginary scenes showing whites literally unshackling blacks, or councils of white leaders gathered around official tables reading, hearing, or signing the Proclamation.[1] The best-known of the latter type was Francis B. Carpenter's painting, *First Reading of the Emancipation Proclamation of President Lincoln* (1864), shown below in its engraved adaptation.[2] But when the African American artist William H. Johnson (1901–1970) created his own version, *Let Me Free* (top), Frederick Douglass had been "invited" to the symbolic table—as he had been to the White House in Lincoln's day and so honored. But in 1945, the Proclamation still sits there awaiting Lincoln's signature, as does the body of a murdered slave. Other casualties, executed in a mass hanging, loom in the background, along with a contraband fleeing from bondage.[3] With lynching still alive at the time, the painting's protest is poignant.

Long before historians had proposed the thesis of black self-liberation, Johnson (and others outside of the art world) suggested something of it. In this painting, Douglass is the symbolic equal of the president and a slave is shown freeing himself. Lincoln himself had some understanding of this possibility. In November 1863, soon after returning from Gettysburg, he told his secretary John Hay, apropos of the influx of black people into the Gulf States, that freedom would come even if secession succeeded. "The slaves, despairing of liberty through us would take the moment into their own hands, and no longer opposed by the government of the United States they would succeed."[4] (Carpenter: The Lincoln Museum; Johnson: The National Museum of American Art, Smithsonian Institution)

1. David Brion Davis, "The Emancipation Moment," in Gabor S. Boritt, ed., *Lincoln the War President: The Gettysburg Lectures* (New York: Oxford University Press, 1992), 10–12.
2. See Harold Holzer, Mark E. Neely, Jr., and Gabor S. Boritt, *The Lincoln Image: Abraham Lincoln and the Popular Print* (New York: Scribner, 1984), 110–23.
3. Richard J. Powell, *Homecoming: The Art and Life of William H. Johnson* (Washington: National Museum of American Art, 1992), 203.
4. Michael Burlingame and John R. Turner Ettlinger, eds., *Inside Lincoln's White House: The Complete Civil War Diary of John Hay* (Carbondale: Southern Illinois University Press, 1997), 117.

## FOUR SCORE AND SEVEN YEARS AGO

Johnson most likely created Lincoln sketches for a never-completed WPA (Works Progress Administration) mural around 1939–42.[1] These gouaches, pen and ink on paper, with the most developed version reproduced here, show the giant folk hero dominating the compositions—just as elsewhere the artist's rendering of John Brown created a giant of folklore more than of history. At Gettysburg, the nearly complete absence of black soldiers from the greatest battle of a war to which African Americans were central, has caused major moral problems for historians and artists both. Not for Johnson. As Adelyn Breeskin wrote, the painter carried a "yearning" to paint "his own people," and was also "able to retain a certain simplicity that was entirely sincere. . . ."[2] So Johnson simply put a black soldier next to Lincoln, guarding him at Gettysburg. Facts mattered not. He got to the heart of the story. (The National Museum of American Art, Smithsonian Institution)

---

1. Adelyn D. Breeskin, *William H. Johnson, 1901–1970* (Washington: Smithsonian Institution, 1971), 18.
2. Ibid., 152, 16, 18.

## HEAVEN-SENT

The Massachusetts-born N. C. Wyeth (1882–1945), star pupil of illustrator Howard Pyle, emulated his teacher's realistic style in a series of mural commissions for such buildings as the Missouri State Capitol, the Federal Reserve Bank of Boston, and hotels in Atlantic City and Utica. He may have been the illustrator who did most to give life to the visual style that came to characterize American cinema.[1] His Lincoln portraits graced an edition of *Poems of American Patriotism* and a young readers' *Anthology of Children's Literature.* There were also magazine illustrations, and this image for a 1939 Morrell & Co. calendar, *America in the Making.* Most of Wyeth's Lincolns are active—delivering the Second Inaugural, writing the Bixby letter, speaking at Gettysburg—but here, the artist presents a generically inspiring figure, emerging from a cloud perhaps representing civil war, but equal to the storm, and judging from the celestial background, heaven-sent. (University Museums, Iowa State University)

---

1. David Michaelis, *N. C. Wyeth: A Biography* (New York: Knopf, 1998).

## REALIST IN RENAISSANCE

In the 1960s, the reputation of Norman Rockwell (1894–1978) went into decline, his illustrations increasingly dismissed as poster-size equivalents of greeting cards. But by 1999, plans were announced for a major exhibition of his work, starting at the High Museum of Art in Atlanta, running coast to coast and in-between, and ending up at the Guggenheim Museum in New York. The cognescenti did an abrupt about-face and the artist returned to favor seemingly overnight (not that he ever lost his appeal for ordinary Americans, who throng the Rockwell Museum in Stockbridge, Massachusetts). Even the chief art critic of the *New York Times* hailed him for "microscopic versimilitude," noting that he was easily the most popular American artist of the century. For too long, the *Times* went on, he had been subjected to the snobbish belief "that good art should be difficult if not (better yet) discomforting."[1] Rockwell was a careful draftsman, a story-telling illustrator with a large dose of sentimentalism, "the very antithesis of what is modern about America," museum director Ned Rifkin wrote. Yet, he continued, Rockwell's "art is not a simple one—it only appears to be so."[2] During his long career, he turned often to the subject of Lincoln, with works clearly intended to extol Lincolnian virtues and inspire new generations. His Lincolns studied and worked hard, and were meant as examples to young boys. But they were also cleverly constructed. This 1963 canvas (left) of the railsplitter-reader took aim from an intentionally low perspective to emphasize Lincoln's soaring height, thereby suggesting his future dominance.[3] The artist had achieved the same effect with the 1962 portrait of the lawyer, *Lincoln for the Defense* (right). If Rockwell is back in fashion at the dawn of the twenty-first century, so are realistic portrayals of Lincoln. (Norman Rockwell Family Trust and *The Saturday Evening Post*, Feb. 10, 1962).

---

1. *New York Times,* Arts & Leisure Section, Nov. 7, 1999. Cf. Barbara Solomon, ibid., January 24, 2000: "It is almost comical. Here we are at the end of our daring century— the century that took the figure out of art, the plot out of fiction and the tune out of music—and do you know who the hottest artist is? Norman Rockwell."
2. Ned Rifkin, "Why Norman Rockwell, Why Now?" in Maureen Hart Hennessey and Anne Knutson, *Norman Rockwell: Pictures for the American People* (Atlanta: High Museum; Stockbridge, Mass.: Rockwell Museum; New York: Harry N. Abrams, 1999), 19, 20.
3. Though created as the logo for the Lincoln Mutual Savings Bank in Spokane, the work has never been used for commercial purposes. See Donald R. Stoltz, Marshall L. Stoltz, and William F. Earle, *The Advertising World of Norman Rockwell* (New York: Harrison House, 1985), 114–15.

## GOD AND SEX

Spanish surrealist Salvador Dali (1904–1989) looked upon the American as something of a saint. But the most important person in Dali's life was his wife Gala, the inspiration for countless works. In this print of a ca. 1975 painting, *Gala Contemplating the Mediterranean Sea—which at Twenty Meters becomes a portrait of Abraham Lincoln—Homage to Rothko,* beautiful Gala is nude before God. Dali himself is nude in the window in the lower left, though others see Gala in that figure, too. As ever, Dali is interested in the double image, and the double meaning. The female nude dominates the orginal painting that is housed in *Fundacion-Gala Salvador Dali,* in Figures, Spain, with a second smaller version in the *Minami* Art Museum in Tokyo. Gala looks out a cross-shaped window. Above her is the top view of Dali's 1951 painting, *Christ of St. John of the Cross.* Lincoln, like Dali (or Gala), is in a lower left window. When the viewer backs away from the print and squints, Lincoln's face appears and takes up the entire design—the face of a man close to God. (Boritt Collection, © 2000 Artist Rights Society, [ARS], New York)

## THE PORTRAIT AS LANDSCAPE

New York City artist Richard Wengenroth (b. 1928) began painting and drawing Lincoln, he recalls, "by exploring ways of using his remarkable face as a metaphor for the American landscape." He reinterprets many of the best-known Lincoln photographs in new ways and some of his images are as large as five-by-four feet. This example, an acrylic on paper, takes Mathew Brady's iconic "five-dollar bill" photographic portrait and creates with sharp angles a new understanding. A former chairman of the Baruch College Art Department, City University of New York, Wengenroth explains: "I have wound up with more than 50 different images which I intend as a total installation."[1] (Photo courtesy Richard Wengenroth)

--------

1. Richard Wengenroth to Harold Holzer, February 24, 1998.

## FOR CIVIL WAR BUFFS

Students of the Civil War tend to be passionate about their subject. They visit battlefields by the millions, buy books, videos, games, relics, and collect art that illustrates the past faithfully. These collectors tend to like the representation to be accurate to the last button of a uniform—and to be also romantic. If there is a Lincoln industry, as the field as a whole is sometimes called, there is certainly a Civil War industry, and numerous artists make their living portraying interesting and at times important military moments. The artists often create oil paintings, and then sell meticulously reproduced limited edition prints based on the oils. Perhaps none is as popular and successful as Mort Künstler (b. 1931), whose enterprise, run from Oyster Bay, New York, appears to blanket the land. Here he depicts *The Gettysburg Address*. The original of the painting, now in a private collection, had been displayed at the Gettysburg National Military Park.

# WYETH SCHOOL

Rea Redifer (b. 1933) was raised on a hardscrabble Indiana farm and made his home on the Brandywine in Pennsylvania. He studied painting at Chadds Ford under Carolyn Wyeth and settled there for good. Andrew Wyeth, too, put him through "a rough apprenticeship," Redifer recalled, "and the trouble with having such a mentor is that he is overwhelming. One spends the next twenty years letting go."[1] Redifer's work partakes of the nostalgia for which Wyeth is noted, and radiates a similar peace and a similar anxiety. He paints Lincoln again and again and sees both a heroic figure and a hard man who presided over America's bloodiest war. This 1988 portrait he called *The Candidate*. (Private Collection)

---

1. As quoted in Gabor S. Boritt, "The Art of Rea Redifer," *Blue & Gray* (October 1992), 57.

## NEWS FROM THE FRONT

Lincoln was portrayed from life in the White House by several artists—but always formally, rigidly confronting the viewer alongside such traditional, reassuring symbols of power as classical pillars of state. It took a modern artist, John Dyer (b. 1945), to portray the commander in chief informally, waiting anxiously in a White House sitting room for news from the battlefield, alongside such human accouterments as spectacles, a penknife, books, and letters. To accomplish in oil *News From the Front—1864,* the painter consulted the 1860 Leonard Wells Volk life mask of Lincoln and posed a live model with his exact measurements in vintage clothing. The original now hangs in the State Capitol of New York, whose last two governors, Mario Cuomo and George Pataki, have been ardent Lincoln admirers. The painting is now also a limited edition print. (Photo courtesy John Dyer)

## SOMETHING OLD, SOMETHING NEW

Not since Gutzon Borglum blasted away at Mount Rushmore has an artist actually created a Lincoln portrait in public. In 1999, artist Ron Sanders (b. 1966) set up his easel in an exhibition of period paintings at the Lincoln Museum in Fort Wayne, Indiana, and working six hours a day for a month, completed *To Preserve the Union*. It was auctioned off for $6,000 on October 16, 1999.[1] Sanders's debt to symbol-laden nineteenth-century portraiture is apparent: a sword hangs above Lincoln's desk, representing war, and a broken manacle lies at his feet, symbolizing emancipation. Lincoln clutches the Proclamation in his right hand, and it is bathed by sunlight from the doors behind him, outside of which, winter notwithstanding, the trees are green, suggesting a renewal of national life. Sanders's boldest treatment was draping Lincoln in the American flag, and placing the stars representing the states firmly in his grasp. Though the parquet floorboard planks are crossed, symbolizing rebellion, Sanders's Lincoln will not let go. Asked if he was saying something new with this work, the artist replied: "I am much more interested in saying something true."[2] (Photo © Ron Sanders, used by permission)

---

1. *Fort Wayne News-Sentinel*, September 18, 1999.
2. Ron Sanders to Harold Holzer, December 13, 1999.

## PASSION

Wendy Allen (b. 1955) only paints Lincoln. When she tried other avenues, landscapes for example, she was left empty. Lincoln speaks to her. It is a passion. "It's never easy to define, let alone explain, a passion," she writes from her Connecticut home. "For me his face is familiar and comforting as well as an implicit symbol of humanity, wisdom, and moral courage. And he remains within our grasp as someone we can all relate to—self-made, self-taught. Perhaps my work, that transforms the black-and-white sepia images of the past, can help people identify Lincoln more as a modern figure, still powerful and relevant, with much to teach us."[1] Allen's untitled Lincoln, like Hartley's *Young Worshipper of the Truth,* is based on Von Schneidau's 1854 daguerreotype: see page 154 (Private Collection)

---

1. Allen to Boritt, January 5, 2000.

## ILLUSTRATOR

Sam Fink (b. 1916) calls himself an illustrator at a time when illustrators often call themselves artists. His extraordinary book, *The Illustrated Gettysburg Address* (1994), inspired 15 watercolor paintings, exhibited in Gettysburg for the entire year of 2000. Each painting is a unique Lincoln image that also contains the 272 words of the Gettysburg Address in dazzling calligraphy. His Lincoln wears an American eagle on his head; he stands before a giant American flag; he hugs the Address, as a father or mother would hug a child—a Pieta—or as a religious Jew might hug the Torah. Here he rides a white horse, such as he probably never rode in life, with the Gettysburg Address next to him. Over the years the artist kept notebooks. When he decided to read into them, "because of age," as he mused, and after having done his series of paintings, he found many notations on Lincoln. "Somewhere along my route he became a friend. Remained so all my life. I've tried to draw him over and over again and once more. There is no end to his chiseled beauty. At times I thought I could go on and try to capture him forever and ever."[1] (Courtesy of Sam Fink)

---

1. As quoted in "Sam Fink of the Gettysburg Address." *Gallery Notes,* Gettysburg College, 1999–2000.

## LINCOLN MULTICULTURAL

Carl Beam's *Lincoln and Ravens,* a photo emulsion steel engraving, forms a part of *The Columbus Suite* that the artist began to create at the approach of the 1992 quincentenary of the European discovery of America. The suite shows the greatness and sadness that followed, the blessings and the horror. Beam (b. 1945) meditates on the cultural interaction that helped create the New World. In *Lincoln and Ravens,* we see at one level the chiseled beauty of Abraham Lincoln, as we do in Alaska's nineteenth-century Lincoln Totem Pole, also the child of Native American culture. But at the end of the twentieth century, Beam conjures up another history, too, with the raven, often an important symbol of both death and myths in traditional Native American religions. At the same time, we thus look at both the past and the future. (For further discussion of Beam's work, see the introduction of this book.) We also see here (below) the use of the work in a public space in Gettysburg, as Kweisi Mfume, president of the NAACP, speaks before *Lincoln and Ravens,* in 1999. (Beam: Gettysburg College; Mfume: *Gettysburg Times*).

## COMMISSIONED BY TELEVISION

"C-SPAN's 'Hail to the Chiefs'"—so a television critic somewhat sardonically greeted the cable channel's 41-week series of three-hour specials, *American Presidents: Life Portraits.*[1] To illustrate the series, the network commissioned artist Chas Fagan (b. 1967), a 1988 Yale graduate who has exhibited widely and provided seven covers for the *Weekly Standard.* It took Fagan three months of work to complete all 41 portraits. In a unique example of the impact of television on the formal visual arts, the series then inspired an exhibit of the portraits—including this frequently reproduced one of Lincoln—at Washington's Union Station from September 27 to October 8, 1999. By the time it was shown on air, used in promotional materials, and illustrated in newspaper reviews, Fagan's Lincoln may have become one of the most frequently seen modern Lincoln images. Such is the power of television and the Internet. C-SPAN also invited viewers to send in their own tributes to the presidents. Of 707 entries (66 of them on Lincoln), 280 were visual: paintings, sculpture, textile, or website projects.[2] (Photo courtesy of C-SPAN)

---

1. Walter Goodman in the *New York Times,* August 17, 1999.
2. Lea Anne Long of C-SPAN to Harold Holzer, January 5, 2000.

# II. ALTOGETHER FITTING AND SOMETIMES PROPER

Illustrations, Prints, Caricatures, Ephemera, and More: A Potpourri

PLAYBILL

The 1930s and 40s saw democracy under attack in the world. For the Americans of the Great Depression, the New Deal, and World War II, Lincoln came to represent their abiding faith in democracy. Carl Sandburg's four-volume biography, *Abraham Lincoln: The War Years* (1939) won the Pulitzer Prize in 1940. Robert Sherwood, who had fully imbibed Sandburg's earlier, two-volume *Abraham Lincoln: The Prairie Years* (1926), added an implied warning to Americans reluctant to face down fascism, and he, too, won a Pulitzer for his play *Abe Lincoln in Illinois* in 1939. Appropriately, Norman Rockwell drew the cover for the playbill. (Boritt Collection)

Norman Rockwell

# THE PLAYBILL

## FOR THE PLYMOUTH THEATRE

## A LINCOLN PORTRAIT

Composer Aaron Copland's *Lincoln Portrait, for Speaker and Orchestra* was first performed in Cincinnati in May 1942, and has been a staple of the American classical repertoire ever since. A blending of original and traditional music with Lincoln's own words, it has attracted countless celebrity narrators and has been frequently recorded. In the days before compact discs, record album covers were an art genre unto themselves, and exerted enormous influence on image and style (e.g., Frank Sinatra leaning against a streetlight, topcoat slung over shoulder in the 50s, or the Beatles in their Sergeant Pepper uniforms in the 60s). Jules Halfant's design for this 1975 Vanguard disc emphasized the plainer aspects of Copland's masterpiece through a folk-art Lincoln statue posed before a wooden fence painted to resemble an American flag, and guarded by a toy soldier. In truth the music boasted as much majesty as it did homespun. (Collection of Harold Holzer)

SRV • 348 SD

# COPLAND: A Lincoln Portrait
### CHARLTON HESTON, NARRATOR
**Quiet City/Our Town, MUSIC FROM THE FILM/An Outdoor Overture**

VANGUARD
EVERYMAN
CLASSICS

## MAURICE ABRAVANEL, conductor
## UTAH SYMPHONY ORCHESTRA

## MOVING PICTURES

Among the actors who have memorably played Lincoln on screen are Frank McGlynn, Jr., the living waxwork who cuddled with Shirley Temple in *The Littlest Rebel* (1935), and the talented Walter Huston, who tried valiantly to enliven D. W. Griffith's moribund *Abraham Lincoln* (1930). "Lincoln" has moved on screen ever since 1903, with a brief appearance in an Edison Company version of *Uncle Tom's Cabin.* Among the most memorable portrayals have been those of (from top to bottom): Henry Fonda in *Young Mr. Lincoln* (1939), Raymond Massey in *Abe Lincoln in Illinois* (1940), Hal Holbrook in *Sandburg's Lincoln* (1974–76), and Sam Waterston in *Gore Vidal's Lincoln* (1988).[1] The static images of the nineteenth century could not capture "he who smiled, spoke, laughed, charmed . . . moved," Lincoln's private secretary John G. Nicolay lamented.[2] The medium of moving pictures was invented too late to capture the real Lincoln and gives us only his imitators. Are these merely actors laden with makeup or are they, as Woodrow Wilson said of movies, "writing history with lightning"?[3] (Photos: Collection of Richard Sloan)

---

1. Frank Thompson, *Abraham Lincoln: Twentieth-Century Portrayals* (Dallas, Texas: Taylor Publishing, 1999), filmography, 190–285.

2. Frederick Hill Meserve and Carl Sandburg, *The Photographs of Abraham Lincoln* (New York: Harcourt, Brace, 1944), 6.

3. Wilson quoted in Jack Temple Kirby, *Media-Made Dixie: The South in the American Imagination* (Athens: University of Georgia Press, 1986), 4.

## WALT DISNEY PRESENTS

During the early days of the 2000 presidential campaign, a media pundit observed that one chronically stiff Democratic contender moved and gestured "like the animatronic Abe Lincoln at [Walt] Disney World's Epcot Center."[1] In his haste to tease, the writer perhaps forgot that the stilted but apparently irresistible allure of Disney's Audio-Animatronics Lincoln made it one of the most frequently visited pieces of Lincoln art of the twentieth century. Here the astonishingly lifelike, accurately garbed figure stands before the dome of the United States Capitol, a guardian and spokesman for liberty, and perfect for the Magic Kingdom Park's family-style tourists. (Boritt Collection, © Disney Enterprises, Inc.)

---

1. "Daddy's Secret Weapon," *New York Observer,* November 1, 1999.

ONE THAT ESCAPED DESTRUCTION: IKE'S ABE

Future President—and future Gettysburg resident—Dwight D. Eisenhower (1890–1969) learned to paint while serving as the head of Columbia University between 1948 and 1950. The brush, paint, and canvas allowed him some escape from the unending demands of office. Like his passion for golf, his painting became famous, but Ike understood that his talents did not lay in the arts. "I refuse to refer to my productions as paintings," he wrote in a 1967 autobiographical book. The "productions . . . are daubs, born of my love of color and my pleasure in experimenting, nothing else. I destroy two out of each three I start." Lincoln, he preserved.[1] (Dwight D. Eisenhower Library)

---

1. Dwight D. Eisenhower, *At Ease: Stories I Tell Friends* (New York: Doubleday, 1967), 341.

## CHRISTMAS CARD

Dayton's Lloyd Ostendorf (1921–2000) is perhaps best known as an historian of Civil War–era photographs and as a Lincoln collector. But he was also an artist, a onetime protégé of cartoonist Milton Caniff, and a creator of illustrated books, original commissioned works, limited-edition prints, and Christmas cards (this one was sent in 1988). In all his work, including his production of quarterly Lincoln covers for the *Lincoln Herald* (which he long served as art editor), Ostendorf was dedicated to filling in the gaps. Although he relied on the period photographs he knew so well, his pictures illustrate Lincoln incidents that have never been portrayed—one of his best known is a portrait of an excited Lincoln delivering his "Lost Speech." Without the artist's realistic interpretations, these scenes could only be imagined. Here, Ostendorf captures Lincoln and his wife Mary at Christmastime. (Lloyd Ostendorf)

ABE and MARY LINCOLN'S
FIRST CHRISTMAS TOGETHER, 1842.

## THE SMALLEST TRIBUTES

No portraits call for a more intimate response from their owners than do postage stamps—which, after all, until the advent of self-adhesive stamps in the late 1990s, required their users to lick them! Lincoln has been a fixture on American stamps since his death and was honored in centennial issues in 1909 and sesquicentennial stamps in 1959, as well as in the occasional commemorative. The artists of the 1980s were granted wider license to interpret within their minuscule formats. In the 1984 Lincoln-Washington tribute for the National Archives "What Is Past Is Prologue" series (top), the ghostly profile of George Washington, the founder of the Union, subtly emerges from the stronger, taller, more detailed profile of its savior in the design of Michael David Brown. There can be little doubt which icon has become the dominant one in the American consciousness. Designer Bradbury Thompson took even more liberties for "A Nation of Readers" (bottom). Celebrating Library Week, it seemed to urge fathers to read to their sons as Lincoln had. It is true that Lincoln read aloud to Tad whenever he could, but the photograph on which this image is based actually showed the president and his boy examining a sample photo album, not a book.[1] (Stamp Designs © 1984 U.S. Postal Service. Reproduced with permission. All rights reserved)

---

1. Francis B. Carpenter, *Six Months at the White House: The Story of a Picture* (New York: Hurd and Houghton, 1866), 93; Ostendorf, *Lincoln's Photographs,* 182–83.

BEFORE THE WORLD AT THE MILLENNIUM: A MOSAIC

Lincoln is the quintessential American, the nation's best face to itself and to the world. In the twentieth century, countless foreign countries issued postage stamps in his honor. As the century and the millennium turned, the most recent addition came from Africa, the Republic of Togo. A technological relative of Dali's Lincoln, it is based on an image created in 1996 by MIT student Robert Silvers (b. 1968), and contains more than 1300 tiny Civil War photographs that together, especially when viewed from a distance, combine to form the "Gettysburg" Lincoln. (Boritt Collection)

THE
**FACES OF** MILLENNIUM **OF FACES**

## MAN IN THE MOON

An 1861 illustrated patriotic envelope portrayed the newly inaugurated Lincoln as a shooting star—exploding in a fireball of red, white, and blue and illuminating the country during the dark hour of secession. More than a century and a quarter later, in 1993, illustrator Stephen Alcorn's woodcut for a young people's book of Lincoln writings depicted the Civil War leader as the man in the moon.[1] Newly murdered and martyred, Lincoln now lighted the way for a return to a free, unified land, and to peacetime labors. The artist (b. 1958) tells us that Lincoln's reputation will endure though—the crescent moon is waning. (Stephen Alcorn: www.alcorngallery.com)

---

1. See Milton Meltzer, ed., *Lincoln in His Own Words* (New York: Harcourt, Brace, 1993), 194.

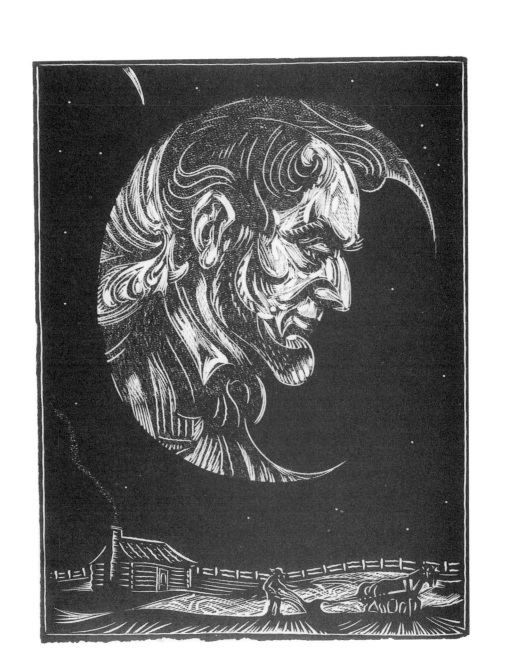

BEST-SELLER

David Herbert Donald's 1995 biography, *Lincoln,* was a runaway best-seller in both cloth and paperback editions, meaning hundreds of thousands of readers— and perhaps a million more browsers—saw this romanticized dust-jacket adaptation of Mathew Brady's 1864 "penny profile" photograph by illustrator Wendell Minor (b. 1944). The ubiquity of the book makes this one of the most familiar Lincoln images of the 1990s, a Lincoln gazing strongly into the future, an integral part of the American flag he defended and helped preserve. The golden medallion reproduced on the paperback edition is the symbol of the Lincoln Prize that Donald won. (Simon & Schuster)

DAVID
HERBERT
DONALD

LINCOLN

LINCOLN
PRIZE

LINCOLN

DAVID HERBERT DONALD
WINNER OF THE PULITZER PRIZE

SIMON &
SCHUSTER

## CHOCOLATE

The commercial uses of the Lincoln image appear to have no limit. The name identifies businesses ranging from one of the country's largest financial services companies to highways and alleyways with mom-and-pop stores. "Lincoln" was and is a good brand name. In Gettysburg, in Springfield, Illinois, and in many other historic places, indeed all over the land, businesses—and yes, scholars, too—ride on Abraham Lincoln. The chocolate pictured here, modeled after the penny, if created by Andy Warhol might qualify as pop art à la Campbell soup cans. As it is, the anonymous artisan/artist who created the design for Wal-Mart, Inc., would be forgotten once the chocolate was eaten—except for this book. (Boritt Collection)

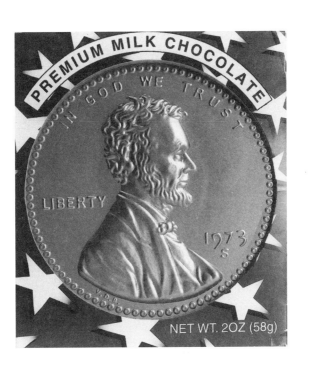

PREMIUM MILK CHOCOLATE

IN GOD WE TRUST

LIBERTY

1973
S

V.D.B.

NET WT. 2OZ (58g)

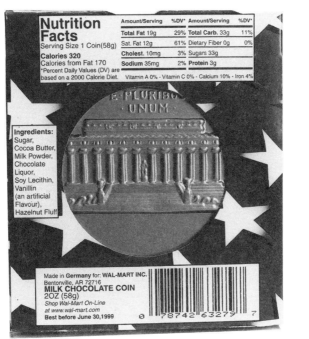

## Nutrition Facts
Serving Size 1 Coin(58g)

**Calories 320**
Calories from Fat 170
*Percent Daily Values (DV) are based on a 2000 Calorie Diet.

| Amount/Serving | %DV* | Amount/Serving | %DV* |
|---|---|---|---|
| **Total Fat** 19g | 29% | **Total Carb.** 33g | 11% |
| Sat. Fat 12g | 61% | Dietary Fiber 0g | 0% |
| **Cholest.** 10mg | 3% | Sugars 33g | |
| **Sodium** 35mg | 2% | **Protein** 3g | |

Vitamin A 0% - Vitamin C 0% - Calcium 10% - Iron 4%

E·PLURIBUS
·UNUM·

**Ingredients:**
Sugar,
Cocoa Butter,
Milk Powder,
Chocolate
Liquor,
Soy Lecithin,
Vanillin
(an artificial
Flavour),
Hazelnut Fluff

Made in **Germany** for: **WAL-MART INC.**
Bentonville, AR 72716
**MILK CHOCOLATE COIN**
2OZ (58g)
*Shop Wal-Mart On-Line*
at www.wal-mart.com
Best before June 30,1999

0  78742 63279  7

## AGWAY'S LINCOLN

The kitsch of American lawn ornaments is legendary. Agway, the chain store that caters to farmers and to the country's nostalgia for its agrarian past, and supplies gardening needs from seeds through fertilizers to trees and more, includes Abe Lincoln in its pantheon of lawn ornaments. (Collection of Harold Holzer)

COAL

Lincoln had combined a commitment to the workingmen with a commitment to the economic development of capitalism. He was convinced that over the long run all would benefit thereby. An appropriate symbol of this outlook is the statuette crafted in West Virginia from coal mined there. Here the statuette wears a necklace created from miniature pennies by Lois Einhorn, a published Lincoln scholar. (Boritt Collection)

## ADVERTISEMENT: EXHIBIT A

The sobriquet "Honest Abe" helped elect Lincoln to the presidency in 1860. The name carried substance and stuck with the martyred leader through historical memory. In the 1990s, when the Smithsonian Institution created a traveling exhibit to celebrate the sesquicentennial of its founding, one of the objects displayed was Lincoln's trademark stovepipe hat. A poster advertising the exhibit and reproduced in newspapers and magazines was calculated through its clever title to put a smile on viewers' faces. But in a democracy scandals have been ever associated with public life and politics. In dictatorships and the like scandals are not allowed to be noted. (Smithsonian)

# See the only cover-up ever associated with Abraham Lincoln.

**America's Smithsonian Traveling Exhibit at the New York Coliseum, June 11th–July 24th.**

You're looking at Abraham Lincoln's own top hat. The real thing. It's just one of the priceless treasures that are now on tour from the Smithsonian. Many have never been outside the Smithsonian Institution before. See everything from the Apollo 15 space suit to Dizzy Gillespie's trumpet. Visit soon. Missing a chance like this would truly be a scandal. Same-day tickets at the box office are FREE. For advance tickets ($3.50 service charge per ticket for phone orders), call **1-800-913-TOUR.**

SELF-TAUGHT

Lincoln lives and lives. In the hands of Onis Woodard (b. 1926) he is both a man of fable and a common man. An African-American woodcarver in Texas, Woodard's art comes down from his ancestors. He remembers his grandfather, a "whittler," sitting "under a shade tree," creating, and his grandson watching him "all the time." Woodard spent his life working at various jobs, but never gave up carving small objects. Not until 1991 did he sell his first piece. The catalpa, with its profusion of beautiful white blossoms and its soft wood, is his favorite; "a good, sharp pocket knife," his tool.[1] (Courtesy of William D. Bowman and Magdalena S. Sanchez)

---

1. Lynne Adele, *Spirited Journeys: Self-Taught Artists of the Twentieth Century* (Austin, Archer M. Huntington Art Gallery, University of Texas, 1997), 189; Onis Woodward in telephone conversation with Gabor Boritt, February 21, 2000.

## CARTOONIST MOURNING A MARTYR

World War II turned Bill Mauldin (b. 1921), the creator of "Willie and Joe," the Everyman GIs, into America's most popular cartoonist. After the war, his widely syndicated work reached millions of admirers. John F. Kennedy's assassination in 1963 inspired Mauldin to turn the Lincoln Memorial's Daniel Chester French sculpture into the nation's chief mourner.[1] (Reprinted with special permission from the *Chicago Sun Times, Inc.* © 1999; Boritt Collection)

---

1. *Lincoln Lore* 1515 (May 1964). See *Lincoln Lore* 839 (May 7, 1945) for announcement of contest.

For C. S. Britt
from a friend —
Mauldin

©1963 MAULDIN
Chicago Sun-Times

## DEPRESSED HERO

David Levine (b. 1926) has described himself as "a painter supported by a hobby—satirical drawings."[1] His drawings in the *New York Review of Books* hunt the essence of their subjects. Levine drew many of the major literary figures of his time in the United States and Europe, as well as some historical ones. Lincoln was an inevitable subject, and with each new drawing Levine reached a deeper dimension. Here the 1982 (top) and 1988 (bottom) versions are reproduced. His depictions were born out of what he saw as "a long line of depressed looking photographs of Lincoln." As Levine wrote in the late 1980s: "It also struck a note in me. I felt the complex feelings that I tried to put in the drawing. That is the contradictions that must have been tearing at Lincoln, both personal & political. I am not laying claim to knowledge in this area, just feelings."[2] (*The New York Review of Books*)

---

1. John Updike, *Pens and Needles: Literary Caricatures by David Levine* (New York: Dorset, 1969), book jacket.
2. Levine to Gabor S. Boritt, undated (ca. 1988).

## AMERICAN DEITIES

The caricaturist's Mt. Rushmore appeared on the cover of *The New Yorker* from the hands of Saul Steinberg (1914–1999) in the Bicentennial Year of 1976. A few months earlier he had already published what became perhaps the most famous sophisticated American cartoon of his generation, that much-copied, ironically parochial view of the United States: vantage point New York. It shows the spaces from the Hudson River to the Pacific as the equal of that between two Manhattan avenues, with distant places like Kansas City and China dwindling to insignificance. Though an immigrant, or perhaps because of it, "Steinberg found," in art critic Arthur Danto's words, "a way into the American head, and shows the American world to the American as an American." In this magazine cover, we have the native innocence presented admiringly. The deities sit for the feast: the Easter Bunny, Santa Claus, Abe Lincoln, Lady Liberty, Washington, and the Halloween Witch. The Thanksgiving turkey struts up front. To quote Danto again: "This is the group portrait of the Pantheon of a country that is serious about keeping its holidays, in the kindergarten and on the cover of *The New Yorker.* . . ."[1] The handwriting and 1990 date on the photo is by the artist. (©1976 Estate of Saul Steinberg/Artists Rights Society [ARS], New York)

---

1. Danto's introduction in Saul Steinberg, *The Discovery of America* (New York: Knopf, 1992), x, xvi.

Nov.29,1976     **THE**     Price 75 cents

# NEW YORKER

STEINBERG
Dec 1990

STEINBERG

## LONG ABRAHAMS

By entitling this Frank Bellew (1828–1888) cartoon (left) "Long Abraham Lincoln a Little Longer" to mark the reelection of the president in 1864, *Harper's Weekly* presaged the long life of this image. The cartoon continues to get longer as the decades roll by, morphing into Gahan Wilson's (b. 1930) long Abraham of 1978 (center), a tricky politician who beat the other tricksters of his trade. Robert Grossman (b. 1940) in turn crowned his long president with a Prussian helmet in 1991 (right) to illustrate an article that compared the "Saviour of the Union" with Bismarck, the creator of a united Germany. Both modern artists admire Lincoln. Grossman expressed their common feelings when he wrote: "I confess to feeling slightly guilty of blasphemy for showing America's genius-saint thus."[1] Both Wilson and Grossman appeared in the *New York Times,* in the *Book Review* and the daily paper respectively. (Boritt Collection)

---

1. Grossman to Boritt, February 11, 1992.

Long ABRAHAM LINCOLN a Little Longer.

## LINCOLN AND DOUGLAS à la DAUMIER

The grotesque figures of Daumier have few successors (among them some work by prominent cartoonist Pat Oliphant).[1] Beowulf Boritt's (1970–) sculpture harkens back to the French master of caricature whose work he saw in Paris as a boy.[2] Having grown up in Gettysburg, in the home of a "Lincoln scholar," the younger Boritt started doing Lincoln early, and has managed to steal time from a busy New York career to return to the subject repeatedly and in mature ways. His "Lincoln and Douglas," 1999, captures the Great Debaters' comically contrasting physiques combined with a late twentieth-century American skepticism about politics. (Courtesy of the Artist)

---

1. Wendy Wick Reaves, *Twenty-Five Years of Caricature: Oliphant's Presidents* (Kansas City and New York: Andrews and McMeel, 1990), includes sculptures of every president from Lyndon Johnson through George Bush. This book accompanied an exhibit at the National Portrait Gallery in Washington.

2. This work was selected for the portfolio after Gabor Boritt showed numerous photographs to Harold Holzer, and the latter picked it without knowing that the creator of this work was the son of his coauthor.

# III. CAN LONG ENDURE

## Sculpture

## LINCOLN ON A MOUNTAIN

Idaho-born sculptor Gutzon Borglum (1867–1941) had already fashioned a two-ton bust of Lincoln for the Capitol Rotunda when he conceived of a colossal monument honoring Lincoln, Washington, Jefferson, and Theodore Roosevelt, to be blasted and carved into a mountainside in western South Dakota, at Mount Rushmore. The original conception called for full-length figures, each 450 feet high. Even scaled back, it grew to be the largest sculpture created in America, prompting President Franklin D. Roosevelt to marvel: "I had seen the photographs and drawings . . . yet . . . had no conception of its magnitude, its permanent beauty, its importance."[1] Lincoln's portrait was unveiled in 1937. In 1959, film director Alfred Hitchcock made it the scene of the climax of *North by Northwest:* his heroes escape by climbing down the face of the monument. Hitchcock battled the National Park Service for permission to use the site, insisting that he wanted to show "the enemies of Democracy . . . defeated at the Shrine of Democracy itself."[2] But the sly master also considered having his leading man, Cary Grant, crawl briefly into Lincoln's nostril—and sneeze.[3] (Photo: The Lincoln Museum, Fort Wayne, Indiana)

1. Rex Allen Smith, *The Carvings of Mount Rushmore* (New York: Abbeville Press, 1985), 4; Wayne Craven, *Sculpture in America* (Newark: University of Delaware Press, 1968), 490–92.
2. Donald Spoto, *The Dark Side of Genius: The Life of Alfred Hitchcock* (New York: Ballantine Books, 1984), 443.
3. François Truffaut, *Hitchcock*, rev. ed. (New York: Simon and Schuster, 1985), 102.

## HOOSIER YOUTH

The Lincoln National Life Insurance Company of Fort Wayne, Indiana, deciding to create "one of the major monuments of the world" to honor the president for whom it was named, commissioned a statue from sculptor Paul Manship (1885–1966), son of a Confederate veteran, in the flush times of the 1920s, and paid him a breathtaking $75,000 in the Depression of the 1930s. The bronze, dedicated outside the corporate headquarters in late 1932, recalled the young Lincoln's 14 years in that state, not as a farmer, laborer, or rail-splitter, but "as a dreamer and a poet," clutching a book, leaning against a tree stump, absent-mindedly patting a dog. Some critics assailed it as overly theatrical, others praised it for its naturalness.[1] Still others who saw or read of its dedication might have recalled personally how far Lincoln had risen from his Indiana days: in 1932, Lincoln Life's Foundation investigated and found no fewer than 90 living Americans who could remember seeing Lincoln alive.[2] (Photo: The Lincoln Museum, Fort Wayne, Indiana)

---

1. Harry Rand, *Paul Manship* (Washington: Smithsonian Institution Press, 1989), 9, 95–96, 185.
2. Louis A. Warren, "'I Saw Lincoln,' They Testify," *Lincoln Lore* 180, 181 (September 19, 26, 1932).

## MARKING THE SPOT

The Lincoln Memorial Bridge spans the Wabash from Vincennes, Indiana, to Illinois—near the location where young Abraham Lincoln and his family crossed into the state of Illinois for the very first time in March 1830, their possessions loaded precariously into ox-drawn wagons, the icy river so high it flooded the road on the shore opposite. The sculpture *Lincoln Entering Illinois* by Nellie Verne Walker (1874–1973) has marked the spot since 1938, when it was erected in a 31-acre park in Lawrence County by the Illinois Daughters of the American Revolution. Walker, who studied under Lorado Taft, used no models for the work. But by conceiving of Lincoln as a full-figure bronze in profile, standing vividly apart from the family of travelers portrayed in bas-relief in limestone, she managed to portray the young man of destiny.[1] (Lawrence County, Illinois)

---

1. Durham, *He Belongs to the Ages,* 242; Mabel Kunkel, *Abraham Lincoln: Unforgettable American* (Charlotte, N.C.: The Delmar Co., 1976), 61; Louis A. Warren, "The Lincolns Crossing the Wabash," *Lincoln Lore* 480 (June 20, 1938). Warren was the principal speaker at the dedication of the statue.

# FATHER ABRAHAM

Clyde Du Vernet Hunt (1861–1941), created his sculpture in Paris and entitled it *The American Spirit*. When it was shown at the New York World's Fair in 1939, it moved a critic to observe that the sculptor had successfully captured Lincoln's "dominant characteristic . . . his love of humanity." Hunt died two years later, leaving the fate of the statue in doubt until, in 1949, the Bennington Museum arranged for the purchase and installation of the Vermont-born sculptor's three-ton bronze creation. The statuary has guarded the entrance to the museum ever since, slowly weathering to a pale green, something of a stylistic anachronism, but universal in concept because it does not represent the Great Emancipator liberating people of color. Few visitors realize that Hunt was inspired by the Buddhist conception of "Nirvana," and had previously sculpted a marble group with that title, whose elements of peace and hopefulness he incorporated into his Lincoln.[1] The kneeling woman symbolizes Faith; the nude boy, Hope. Lincoln is the incarnation of Charity. (The Bennington, Vermont, Historical Museum and Art Gallery)

---

1. Donald Charles Durman, *He Belongs to the Ages: The Statues of Abraham Lincoln* (Ann Arbor: Edwards Brothers, 1951), 269.

RAIL-BUILDER

Louis Slobodkin (b. 1903) entered the original version of this heroic sculpture in a competition at the 1939 World's Fair. Artists had been invited to submit their conceptions of "peace" and "unity." Albany, New York-born Slobodkin, trained as an architectural sculptor, submitted a statue of Lincoln as a builder of rails, rather than the traditional rail-splitter, seen here joining two fence rails that depend on each other for support. In Slobodkin's view, the design was a metaphor for unifying the warring sections of the country. Americans viewing it in 1939 may have also perceived a symbolic plea for world peace in the face of global war.[1] The statue won second prize, and though the original later disappeared, Slobodkin made this bronze copy for the Department of the Interior and retitled the result *Young Abe Lincoln*. The artist's attention to Lincoln's muscular physique added, whether intentionally or inadvertently, the additional message that "in unity there is strength." (Photo: F. Lauriston Bullard, *Lincoln in Marble and Bronze*, 1952.

---

1. Durham, *He Belongs to the Ages*, 246; F. Lauriston Bullard, *Lincoln in Marble and Bronze* (New Brunswick, N. J.: Rutgers University Press, 1952), 319.

248

# FIRST FAMILY

Unlike most prominent couples of their age, the Lincolns never posed together for photographers or artists, supposedly because Mary feared she would look ridiculously squat alongside her tall husband. Her reluctance left a void that has made it hard for later generations to imagine the couple together, although painters, printmakers, and illustrators did produce endless composites. The sole sculptural example originated when the city of Racine, Wisconsin, where the widowed Mary spent the summer of 1869, commissioned a sculpture of the Lincolns for the centennial of their 1842 marriage. It was dedicated a year late, in 1943, the work of Frederick C. Hibbard (b. 1881). The inscription on the base of this granite portrait describes it as "the first monument to be erected to a President of the United States and his wife."[1] The figure of Mary, for once, stands tall: seven feet high. (Photo: Steven K. Rogstad)

---

1. Bullard, *Lincoln in Marble and Bronze,* 322–325.

# FRONTIERSMAN

Vigorous, young, the rail-splitter: Avard Fairbank's bronze carries with him the robust dreams of democracy that stand tall and strong facing the future. Having studied in New York and Paris, lived in Italy, and taught sculpture at the University of Michigan, the artist is known, among other works, for his World War I *Doughboy* in Idaho. Fairbanks (1897–1997) did not think a somber-suited Lincoln would do in semitropical Hawaii. World War II had started for the United States at Pearl Harbor, and the casting of the sculpture barely beat the deadline of government restrictions on nonmilitary use of copper. But Americans could hardly do better than go forth to save the world with Lincoln on their side. The sculpture, the gift of a schoolteacher, was dedicated in 1944 in Ewa, on the island of Oahu.[1] (Photo: Bullard, *Lincoln in Marble and Bronze*)

---

1. Bullard, *Lincoln in Marble and Bronze*, 325–28.

## DYING COLOSSUS

At 62 feet, Bob Eglett's gigantic steel and fiberglass sculpture likely ranks as the largest full-length Lincoln. Commissioned by 20 Charleston, Illinois, business-men who pledged $1,000 each to finance it, the Eglett sculpture, built in St. Paul, Minnesota, was dedicated in 1969. But it never found a permanent home, and may thus also be the most well-traveled of heroic statues. The first choice, the nearby Coles County Fairgrounds, site of an 1858 Lincoln-Douglas debate, was rejected because soil tests revealed "unsuitable ground." The sec-ond choice, a small park inside Charleston proper, was rejected by the town. Finally, in 1978, amid rumors it would be dismantled, buried, or sold to nearby Lincoln, Illinois, the owners of a for-profit local campground east of Charleston bought the neglected statue and moved it there to lure customers. But the campground later closed down, and the statue is now inaccessible to the public, and deteriorating. Its great size has always attracted vandals, and at one time it was reported riddled with bullet holes—a sad decline for what townspeople call their "wandering giant."[1] (Charleston Area Chamber of Commerce)

---

1. Charleston Area Chamber of Commerce fact sheet; undated clipping in the Chamber of Commerce "Lincoln statue" file; Charleston *Town Crier,* October 9, 1976, May 27, 1978, November 13, 1978. See also illustration in *Talk* Magazine, February 2000: 146.

## WITHOUT VITRIOL

British war correspondent Edward Dicey once observed that Lincoln's mottled complexion looked as if it had been "scarred by vitriol."[1] Sculptor Leo Cherne (b. 1912) achieved the effect with his impressionistic bust, yet made Lincoln seem endearing and attractive as well—and perhaps sympathetically beleaguered. Modern beleaguered presidents Lyndon Johnson and Richard Nixon each owned copies of the statuette, and Nixon displayed it behind his desk in the Oval Office. This is Johnson's copy. (Lyndon Baines Johnson Library Collection)

---

1. Edward Dicey, "Washington During the War," *Macmillan's Magazine* 6 (May 1862), 16–17.

## MAN OF SORROWS

An admiring contemporary lauded sculptor Jo Davidson (1883–1952) as a "biographer in bronze," and the chronically caustic observer Dorothy Parker may actually have intended a compliment, as well as the usual gibe, when she dubbed him "the plastic historian."[1] Davidson became quite famous during his lifetime, and was widely praised for his portraits from life of Helen Keller and others.[2] So adept did he become at portraying his contemporaries that his historical sculptures tended to be forgotten. Yet alone among modern sculpted portraits of Lincoln, Davidson's depiction powerfully suggests the man burdened by the cares of the office—his face creased and timeworn, and his eyes downcast as if focusing on the unfathomable sorrows of the casualties of war. (Oklahoma City Art Museum; gift of Mr. and Mrs. S. N. Goldman)

---

1. Jo Davidson, *Between Sittings: An Informal Autobiography* (New York: Dial Press, 1951), 315.

2. See "Jo Davidson: Insightful Sculptor of the Heroes of his Time," *Washington Post,* 1 September 1978; also *Catalogue of the first retrospective exhibition of sculpture by Jo Davidson, November 26, 1947-February 1, 1948,* National Academy of Arts & Letters, New York; and *Jo Davidson: Portrait Sculpture* (Washington, DC: The National Portrait Gallery, 1978). None of the catalogues for Davidson exhibitions included illustrations of his Lincoln sculpture.

## PRESIDENTIAL TALISMAN

Ever since Richard M. Nixon first placed sculptor Leo Cherne's rugged little head of Lincoln behind his desk in the White House Oval Office, Lincoln images have served as the background talisman for countless televised presidential addresses to the nation—often, unfortunately, accenting the delivery of dire news during White House scandals. The comforting presence of Lincoln encourages presidents to endure criticism—Bill Clinton said so to Harold Holzer during a visit to the White House in 1998—but it is also used by modern presidents to confirm what historian Noble Cunningham has called "the heritage of the presidency in the building of the nation, and summoning of that heritage for its preservation . . . a heritage worthy of protecting" today.[1] Here, President Clinton signs a piece of legislation as this ca. 1958 bust by Robert Berks (b. 1922), which the president himself owns, looms behind him. Nearby is a replica of Jo Davidson's bust of Franklin D. Roosevelt. (White House Photograph)

---

1. Noble Cunningham, *Popular Images of the Presidency from Washington to Lincoln* (Columbia: University of Missouri Press, 1991), 128.

## LINCOLN MEETS HIS YOUNGEST ADVISOR

When President-elect Lincoln's train chugged into New York State en route to the 1861 inauguration, the first village at which it stopped was tiny Westfield. Here, Lincoln remembered, lived the little girl who had sent him the charming letter back in October, advising him that he "would look a great deal better"—and win more votes—if he grew whiskers.[1] Now, as he stepped out from the train to greet the well-wishers who had turned out to greet him, the luxuriantly bearded Lincoln scanned the crowd in search of his young correspondent. "If she is here, I would like to see her," he declared. "I think her name was Miss Barlly." Lincoln got the name wrong—it was in fact Grace Bedell—but when she was identified among the throng, Lincoln stepped off the train and, as the crowd parted, made his way toward the startled child and planted "several hearty kisses" on her cheek.[2] The moment of recognition—Lincoln extending his hand, Grace nearly frozen with shyness and surprise—was captured by local sculptor Don Sottile (b. 1946) for a larger-than-life bronze sculptural group erected in downtown Westfield in 1999. The site, where only a few years ago a vermin-infested, abandoned movie theatre blighted the town, is not far from the old railroad stop where Lincoln met Grace on the eve of the Civil War. (Photo: Don Sottile)

---

1. Basler, et al., eds., *Collected Works of Lincoln,* 4:130.
2. Ibid. 219.

# LINCOLN AT FREEPORT

Stephen A. Douglas stands and speaks, while Abraham Lincoln merely sits and listens, in Lily Tolpo's (b. 1917) life-size sculpture, erected on the site of the candidates' 1858 joint meeting at Freeport, Illinois. There is irony to the portrayal. Lincoln had been criticized, even by his own supporters, for being too passive at the opening debate six days earlier in Ottawa, and he opened the Freeport debate aggressively. Notwithstanding its Douglas-centered viewpoint, Tolpo's statue achieved recognition at the end of the century because a maquette copy sits in the background of C-SPAN's Washington studios, where it can often be glimpsed on television broadcasts. Tolpo's statue has all but eclipsed Leonard Crunelle's sculpture of *The Debater,* unveiled in Freeport's Taylor Park in 1929. (Photos by Steve Snyder, courtesy Rich Sokup, Lincoln-Douglas Society, Freeport, Illinois)

## ... AND AT OTTAWA

"Douglas and I, for the first time in this canvass, crossed swords here yester-day," Lincoln wrote after their initial debate at Ottawa, adding: "the fire flew some, and I am glad to know I am still alive."[1] Lincoln's mediocre performance there may have inhibited earlier efforts to memorialize that historic meeting. But in 1999, a few years after C-SPAN broadcast a live reenactment of the Ottawa debate, civic leaders commissioned sculptor Rebecca Childers Caleel (b. 1947) to make a heroic bronze for Washington Park Square, site of that first debate. Scheduled to be unveiled by the end of 2000, the maquettes suggest a calm Lincoln and a pugnacious Douglas. Perhaps this was close to the way the originals appeared in 1858, the Democrat as "a little bulldog," in the artist's words, "a little stomp-and-shouter . . . Lincoln more of a gentleman. He had dignity."[2] Caleel's Lincoln, based on the Volk life mask and period photographs, will be eleven feet high, the Douglas nine. (Photos by Paul E. Burd, courtesy Rebecca Childers Caleel)

---

1. Lincoln to Joseph O. Cunningham, Aug. 22, 1858, Basler, et al., eds., *Collected Works of Lincoln*, 3:37.
2. *Ottawa Daily Time*, October 22, 1999.

## ANOTHER AMERICAN DILEMMA

Militia captain Abraham Lincoln moves toward the same land to which the Sac leader Black Hawk tenaciously clings in sculptor Jeff Adams's maquette for his projected monumental sculpture honoring both men in Oregon, Illinois.

Both the pursued tribal leader and the future American president traveled through this Rock River Valley region during the Black Hawk War of 1832. The dual portrait, its sculptor explains, "pays tribute to the land they are both from, and to the changes to it that each of their tragic fates represent. They each pursued their convictions leading to their fates with dignity and integrity." *Paths of Conviction, Footsteps of Fate* would be the first sculpture ever to portray a Native American with Lincoln, whose own grandfather was killed by Indians "by stealth," as he bitterly remembered, though Lincoln proved less hostile to them than did many white leaders of his era. Sculptor Adams (b. 1960) appropriately shows the two leaders facing opposite directions.

The sculpture contrasts sharply, in style as well as substance, to Leonard Crunelle's 1930 *Captain Lincoln* in Dixon, Illinois. Crunelle, like the dominant culture of his time, saw only the white hero who helped bring peace to the American frontier. (Adams: Jeff Adams; Crunelle: Bullard, *Lincoln in Marble and Bronze*)

## CONTROLLED BY EVENTS

Decatur, Illinois, sculptor John McClarey (b. 1935) has created two bonded bronze versions of a statuette he calls *Freedom River*, each representing Lincoln as both "'a prime mover' and as one 'controlled by events' in the work of emancipation and Freedom"[1]—the latter an artistic bow to contemporary historical culture so eloquently reflected in historian David Herbert Donald's 1995 interpretation. In the original edition (top), McClarey's Lincoln seems to hold aloft the symbolic river of events; in the revised, more impressionistic version (bottom) he seems more a part of the river. In each, as the sculptor attests, "he remains visible as a central figure" in the drama, but with the river's "ultimate course . . . left for others to define." The bonded bronze statue of the second version has been given as the annual Richard N. Current Award of Achievement of The Lincoln Forum. (Photos: John McClarey, Don Pollard)

---

1. McClarey quoted in news release of The Lincoln Forum, November 19, 1999.

## GETTYSBURG

Gettysburg tree, Gettysburg clay, Gettysburg artist. Depending on the angle of the viewer's gaze, Lincoln is forbidding, tender, or slightly humorous. The chestnut and the soil were there when, in the midst of the bloodbath of the Civil War, the president came to the small Pennsylvania town where the greatest battle of the war had taken place. He reached deep inside himself to transfer his strength to his people so that they would be able to bear the terrible burden that seemed unbearable. So Roy Fender (b. 1936), a professor of art for many years at Western Maryland College, reached deep inside himself, and deep inside the wood and soil of Gettysburg, to conjure up from native materials Lincoln's elemental strength. (Courtesy of the Artist)

## MOODY, TEARFUL NIGHT

On April 14, 1865, Abraham Lincoln was the chief of the victorious United States and looked forward to peace, ready to face its endless heartaches. Only a few weeks before, in his Second Inaugural Address, he spoke of "malice towards none." That evening John Wilkes Booth altered history. Lincoln's limp body was taken from Ford's Theatre to the boarding house across the street by Dr. Charles A. Leale and four soldiers. This is the moment sculptor Richard Masloski (b. 1954) depicts with painful realism in his limited edition, 300-lb. bronze. On April 15, 1865, Lincoln was dead.

The upstate New York sculptor's road began when as a 20-year-old with a dead-end job he picked up a piece of clay and Lincoln's face came out of it. What Masloski calls "the quintessential American face" has stayed with him since. He has created a bronze bust of the careworn president, and also *Time to Rest,* showing Lincoln carrying the sleeping Tad on his shoulders. The self-taught sculptor has a credo. He works "for those People who mourn over the prevailing absence of People from much of today's Art; for those whose appetites are not filled with the Abstract. . . ." Masloski hopes "one-day" to see the sculptural group of *Moody, Tearful Night* "as a life-size monument."[1] (Photo: Thomas LaBarbera)

---

1. Chris Farlekas, "American Portraits in Bronze," *Times Herald Record* (Middletown, New York), Dec. 1, 1996; *The Americana Sculpture of Richard Masloski* (np, nd); Masloski to Boritt, December 31, 1996.

## WORK IN PROGRESS

J. Seward Johnson (b. 1930) brings modern sculpture down to earth. He re-creates Everyman. He is probably best known for fooling taxi drivers into stopping for his painted bronze figure of a man hailing a cab in New York; or for another of his figures being shot by a policeman in California. *Lincoln* meant a new departure for his art, a venture into history commissioned by the Gettysburg-based organization, The Lincoln Fellowship of Pennsylvania. Not surprisingly he created something of a whimsical sculpture. In this photograph he is taking a humorous break from his work in progress, incidentally showing how he creates his figures first and dresses them afterwards. (Boritt Collection)

For honor and
propriety.Tall
the best to you
Gabe.

## RETURN VISIT

People in Gettysburg talked for decades, probably longer, about a statue of their most famous visitor, to be placed in the center of the town. But the years rolled by, tourism multiplied, and Pennsylvania transportation authorities took a dim view of a monument that might become a major traffic hazard. Finally, in 1991, Seward Johnson's *Lincoln* was placed on the curb in front of the Wills House, where Lincoln stayed during his 1863 visit. His back is toward the square named after him, his arm pointing at the window of the room in which he probably completed the Gettysburg Address. Next to him stands the figure of a modern tourist—modeled after a newspaper reporter who walked into the Johnson studio. He wears a cable-knit sweater, wedding band, corduroy pants, sneakers, and his hand holds a common tourist copy of the Address. Lincoln stands his natural height, nearly 6'4", in a suit that is an exact replica of one he had worn, the hat, too, down to the label inside it, his boot sized to the outline of his feet as drawn by a Pennsylvania shoemaker. It is Lincoln with today's Everyman, down on earth where many modern Americans want their heroes. (Photo Jake Boritt)

# Notes

## Introduction

1. Randall C. Archibold, "Celebrating a Milestone for Freedom: Black Americans Honor Anniversary of Proclamation to End Slavery," *The New York Times,* January 1, 2000, Section B, 1, 4.
2. Priscilla C. Marsh, "An Eyeful for Mr. Lincoln," Nov. 15, 1999, Washington Post.com.
3. "Lincoln's Fraternal Democracy," in John L. Thomas, ed., *Abraham Lincoln and the American Political Tradition* (Amherst: University of Massachusetts Press, 1986), 11–30; Thomas Chamberlin, *History of the One Hundred and Fiftieth Regiment: Pennsylvania Volunteers. Second Regiment. Bucktail Brigade,* Philadelphia: McManus, 1895, 41; Roy P. Basler, Marion Dolores Pratt, and Lloyd A. Dunlap, asst. eds., *The Collected Works of Abraham Lincoln,* 9 vols., 2 suppl. vols. (New Brunswick, New Jersey: Rutgers University Press, 1953–55, 1974, 1990), 5: 484–85.
4. Owen to Boritt, Fall, 1999.
5. Basler, et al., eds., *The Collected Works of Abraham Lincoln,* 7:243.
6. Ibid., 6:328.
7. David Donald, ed., *Why the North Won the Civil War* (New York: Simon & Schuster, 1998), 111.
8. Ibid., 8:101.
9. Ibid., 7:394.
10. The discussion of Beam's work and the question of the Sioux is based on Amelia M. Trevelyan, "Seeing a New World: The Works of Carl Beam and Frederick Remington," Gallery Notes, Gettysburg College, 1993; David A. Nichols, *Lincoln and the Indians: Civil War Policy and Politics* (Columbia: University of Missouri Press, 1978); Hans L. Trefousse, "Commentary on 'Lincoln and the Indians,' " in Gabor S. Boritt, ed., Norman O. Forness, assoc. ed., *The Historian's Lincoln: Pseudohistory, Psychohistory, and History* (Urbana: University of Illinois Press, 1988), 170–74; Alvin M. Josephy, Jr., *The Civil War in the West* (New York: Knopf, 1991); Michael Clodfelter, *The Dakota War: The United States Army versus the Sioux, 1962–65*

(Jefferson, N.C.: McFarland, 1998); and David Herbert Donald, *Lincoln* (New York: Simon & Schuster, 1995), 392–95, 399. The quotations are from Donald.

11. Trevelyan, "Seeing a New World."

## One: The Voyage to Linconia

The following colleagues commented on "The Voyage": David Blight, Thavolia Glymph, Joseph P. Reidy, Edwin Redkey, and Michael Vorenberg. Earlier my siblings performed the same generous service: Judith Boritt and Adam Boritt. I am grateful to all.

1. Tammany Hall, Young Democratic Club, Resolution, March 1862, as cited in James M. McPherson, *The Negro's Civil War, How American Negroes Felt and Acted During the War for the Union* (New York: Pantheon Books, 1965), 77; Roy P. Basler, ed., Marion Dolores Pratt and Lloyd A. Dunlap, asst. eds., *The Collected Works of Abraham Lincoln,* 9 vols., 2 suppl. vols. (New Brunswick, N.J.: Rutgers University, 1953–55, 1974, 1990), 5:372; *Congressional Globe,* June 2, 1862, 37:3, 2504.

2. Basler, et al., eds., *Collected Works of Lincoln,* 3:371, 372.

3. Ibid., 3:29; 2:132.

4. Ibid., 501, 520.

5. Ibid., 3:145.

6. Ibid., 2:256; Douglas L. Wilson, *Honor's Voice: The Transformation of Abraham Lincoln* (New York: Knopf, 1998), 306.

7. Harold Holzer, ed., *The Lincoln-Douglas Debates* (New York: HarperCollins, 1993), 54–55. Words bracketed cite the *Chicago Times's* reports of audience reaction.

8. Basler, et al., eds., *Collected Works of Lincoln,* 2:255, 461.

9. Ibid., 2:541, 3:399

10. Ibid., 3:376, 4:24–5.

11. Ibid., 2:320, 404, 3:95, 469.

12. George M. Fredrickson, *Black Liberation: A Comparative History of Black Ideologies in the United States and South Africa* (New York: Oxford University Press, 1991), 61.

13. Lincoln the universalist would be given his most effective rebuttal in 1862 by another universalist, Frederick Douglass, who saw colonization through very different lenses. "If men may not live peaceably together . . . in the same land, they cannot so live on the same continent, and ultimately in the same world. . . . The same base and selfish lust for dominion which would drive us from this country would hunt us from the world." Philip S. Foner, ed., *The Life and Writings of Frederick Douglass,* 4 vols. (New York: International Press, 1950–55), 3:265. Lincoln most likely never saw Douglass's article.

14. Basler, et al., eds., *Collected Works of Lincoln,* 5:371–72; Michael Burlingame and John R. Turner Ettlinger, eds., *Inside Lincoln's White House: The Complete Civil War Diary of John Hay* (Carbondale: Southern Illinois University Press, 1997), 217. Hay declared colonization "a hideous & barbarous humbug." Cf. Michael Burlingame, ed., *Lincoln's Journalist: John Hay's Anonymous Writings for the Press, 1860–1864* (Carbondale: Southern Illinois University Press, 1998), 280. Giving July 1, 1864, as the absolute final date for Lincoln's abandonmnet of all colonization notions is the most conserative reading of the record. As historian Michael Vorenberg notes, Hay's diary entry allows for Lincoln reaching the very end much earlier which, for all practical purposes, he did. "Abraham Lincoln and the Politics of Black Colonization," *Journal of the Abraham Lincoln Association,* 14 (Summer, 1993), 42.

   The summary of Lincoln's views on colonization focuses on the central thread of his thinking. This thread, however, had minor variations. In a veiled fashion, he also admitted the injustice of the policy by tracing the need for it to white prejudice. About this prejudice, he told his black visitors in perhaps purposely muddled statement, "we all think and feel alike, I and you." Basler, et al., eds., *Collected Works of Lincoln,* 5:372. For a listing of the sources of Lincoln's statements about colonization, see the bibliographical note. It is not impossible, as historian Philip Paludan proposed, that for a time Lincoln saw some thriving colonies proving to skeptical whites the worth of black people, providing "the archetypical Republican success story," and so promoting equality at home. *The Presidency of Abraham Lincoln* (Lawrence: University of Kansas Press, 1994), 132.

15. Howard K. Beale, ed., *Diary of Gideon Welles, Secretary of Navy under Lincoln and Johnson,* 3 vols. (New York: Houghton Mifflin Co., 1960), 1:152; Basler, et al., eds., *Collected Works of Lincoln,* 5:48.

16. Basler, et al., eds., *Collected Works of Lincoln,* 2:132; 3:446; 5:535.

17. About the time of the visit of the African-American delegation to the White House, Lincoln used similar techniques in his famous reply to *New York Tribune* editor Horace Greeley's demand for emancipation in the "Prayer of Twenty Million." Lincoln seemed to address abolitionists, but his intended audience was their ever much larger number of opponents. He wrote: "My paramount object in this struggle *is* to save the Union, and is *not* either to save or destroy slavery. If I could save the Union without freeing *any* slave I would do it, and if I could save it by freeing *all* the slaves I would do it; and if I could save it by freeing some and leaving others alone I would also do that." Basler, et al., eds., *Collected Works of Lincoln,* 5:388. As far as it went, the statement carried truth, but it did not note that by this time Lincoln had firmly committed himself in the Cabinet to emancipation. In this light, the letter to Greeley becomes much less an oath of allegiance to the

Union than a strategem addressed to people whose support emancipation required, but who would oppose black freedom at any cost, except the cost of Union. Colonization was addressed to a like, or at least overlapping, constituency.

18. James Mitchell, *Report on Colonization and Emancipation* (Washington: 1862), 6.

19. Basler, et al., eds., *Collected Works of Lincoln*, 5:373, 374.

20. Ibid., 372, 375. This view is further supported, for example, in T. J. Barnet's report of another presidential interview to S. L. M. Barlow, November 30, 1862, S. L. M. Barlow Papers, Henry E. Huntington Library and Art Gallery; see also Adam S. Hill to S. H. Gay, August 21, 1862, S. H. Gay Papers, Columbia University Library; and the recollection of George W. Julian in Allen Thorndike Rice, ed., *Reminiscences of Abraham Lincoln* (New York: North American Publishing, 1888), 61–62.

21. Basler, et al., eds., *Collected Works of Lincoln*, 2:409; David [Herbert] Donald, ed., *Inside Lincoln's Cabinet: The Civil War Diaries of Salmon P. Chase* (New York; Longmans, 1954), 156; Francis P. Blair, Jr., *Destiny of the Races on this Continent* (Washington: 1859), 23. The younger Blair's notions were expounded, in some detail, directly to Lincoln in a letter by Francis Blair, Sr., November 16, 1861, with enclosures, Lincoln Papers.

22. Basler, et al., eds., *Collected Works of Lincoln*, 5:530–33; 8:55. Eight months earlier Lincoln drafted a harsh letter (which, as was not unusual for him in such cases, remained probably unsent) to Governor John A. Andrew who tried, self-righteously but falsely, to project an image that he was recruiting black settlers: "If . . . Massachusetts wishes to afford a permanent home within her borders, for all, or even a large number of colored persons who will come to her, I shall be only too glad to know it." Ibid., 7:191; see also 19, 192, 204, and Andrew to Lincoln, February 12, 1864, Lincoln Papers.

23. Basler, et al., eds., *Collected Works of Lincoln*, 2:409; 3:499; cf. Caleb B. Smith to Lincoln, May 9, 1862, Chiriqui Colonization Papers, Illinois State Historical Society.

24. Basler, et al., eds., *Collected Works of Lincoln*, 5:535; Blair to Lincoln, May 26, 1860; Usher to Lincoln, August 2, 1862, Lincoln Papers.

25. *Congressional Globe,* April 11, 1862, 37:2, 1634; Vorenberg, "Lincoln and the Politics of Black Colonization," 36.

26. He also used other, much less dramatic devices to minimize Northern fears of emancipation. He argued that blacks would offer less labor competition to whites if slavery were abolished and that, at any rate, they would desire to stay in the Southern clime (something the federal government seems to have encouraged blacks to do). See, for example, Basler, et al., eds., *Collected Works of Lincoln*, 5:373, 534–35.

27. Ibid., 2:262.

28. *Charles Sumner: His Complete Works,* 20 vols. (New York, 1969 reprint), 12:334; Donald, ed., *Diaries of Chase,* 112; *Congressional Globe,* June 2, 1862, 37:3, 2504. See also Gerritt Smith to Lincoln, December 6, 1861, and Chase to Lincoln, November 28, 1862, Lincoln Papers; Theodore Calvin Pease and J. G. Randall, eds., *The Diary of Orville Hickman Browning,* 2 vols. (Springfield, Ill.: Illinois State Historical Society, 1925–33), 1:577. Even as the colonization hoopla got into high gear, Lincoln decided to send the treaties needed to implement the policy to Sumner's Senate Foreign Relations Committee, where he had to know that they would die. Vorenberg, "Lincoln and the Politics of Black Colonization," 37–38. Douglass also described colonization as "an opiate," but in a different context. Foner, ed., *Life and Writings of Douglass,* 3:289.

29. Winthrop D. Jordan, *White Over Black, American Attitudes Toward the Negro, 1550–1812* (Baltimore: Penguin Books, 1969), 567.

30. Thomas P. Lowry, *Don't Shoot That Boy! Abraham Lincoln and Military Justice* (Mason City, Iowa.: Savas, 1999), 23. After the Civil War, some white intellectual circles substituted for the dead colonization idea the pseudo-Darwinian hope that blacks would follow in the footsteps of the dinosaurs. Black movements looking to Africa also grew.

31. Basler, et al., eds., *Collected Works of Lincoln,* 5:534; Benjamin Quarles, *Lincoln and the Negro* (New York: Oxford University Press, 1962), 123.

32. It was first suggested in 1862 by the Washington *National Republican.* Frederic Bancroft, "Schemes to Colonize Negroes in Central America," and "The Ile a Vache Experiment in Colonization," in Jacob E. Cooke, ed., *Frederic Bancroft, Historian* (Norman: University of Oklahoma Press, 1957), 212, 231.

33. McPherson, *The Negro's Civil War,* 77. Earlier J. G. Randall raised this very question without trying to answer it. *Lincoln and the South* (Baton Rouge: Louisiana State University Press, 1946), 90.

34. Basler, et al., eds., *Collected Works of Lincoln,* 7:23, 1:114, 5:503; Francis B. Carpenter, *Six Months at the White House with Abraham Lincoln: The Story of a Picture* (New York: Hurd, 1866), 90, 269; Joshua Speed to William Herndon, in Douglas L. Wilson and Rodney O. Davis, eds., *Herndon's Informants: Letters, Interviews and Statements about Abraham Lincoln* (Urbana: University of Illinois Press, 1998), 197. See also Chapter 2, p. 19, and Chapter 7, p. 141.

35. Basler, et al., eds., *Collected Works of Lincoln,* 7:281.

36. Forrest G. Wood, *Black Scare: The Racist Response to Emancipation and Reconstruction* (Berkeley: University of California Press, 1968), 33.

37. Pease and Randall, eds., *Diary of Browning,* 1:600; Basler, et al., eds., *Collected Works of Lincoln,* 5:374.

38. Speech delivered at the Cooper Union, June 1, 1865, Frederick Douglass Papers, Library of Congress, and *National Anti-Slavery Standard,* June 10, 1865. (This text is left out of the various editions of Douglass' works. I am indebted to Michael Burlingame for calling it to my attention); John W.

Blassingame, John R. McKivigan, Richard D. Carlson, Suzanne Selinger, Gerald W. Fulkerson, eds., *The Frederick Douglass Papers,* Series One: Speeches, Debates, and Interviews, Vol. 4: 1864–80 (New Haven: Yale University Press, 1991), 436–37.

39. Basler, et al., eds., *Collected Works of Lincoln,* 3:145, 6:410, 3:145, 7:243.
40. Quoted in Noah Andre Trudeau, *Like Men of War: Black Troops in the Civil War, 1862–1865* (Boston: Little, Brown, 1998), 423; "Lincoln in Richmond," *The Atlantic Monthly,* 15 (June, 1865), 754–755.


## Two: Young Man Lincoln

1. Abraham Lincoln, Farewell Address, Roy P. Basler, ed., Marion Dolores Pratt, and Lloyd A. Dunlap, asst. eds., *The Collected Works of Abraham Lincoln,* 9 vols., 2 suppl. vols. (New Brunswick, N. J.: Rutgers University Press, 1953–55, 1974, 1990), 4:190.
2. W. H. Auden, "New Year Letter," *The Collected Poetry of W. H. Auden* (New York: Random House, 1945), 274.
3. For a discussion of this subject and documentation for the incidents mentioned, see Douglas L. Wilson, *Honor's Voice: The Transformation of Abraham Lincoln* (New York: Alfred A. Knopf, 1998), 304–308. The quotation from Mentor Graham is from an 1860 interview with J. Q. Howard cited in his campaign biography, *The Life of Abraham Lincoln: with Extracts from his Speeches* (Columbus: Follet, Foster, 1860), 22.
4. Abraham Lincoln [hereafter AL] to Joshua F. Speed, March 27, 1842, *Collected Works* 1:282.
5. William H. Herndon and Jesse W. Weik, *Herndon's Life of Lincoln,* ed. Paul M. Angle (Cleveland: World Publishing, 1949), 352.
6. *Ibid.,* 352n.
7. AL to Joshua F. Speed, July 4, 1842, Basler, et al., eds., *Collected Works of Lincoln,* 1:289.
8. Herndon to Turman Bartlett, Aug. 16, 1887, quoted in Albert J. Beveridge, *Abraham Lincoln 1800–1858,* 2 vols. (Boston: Houghton Mifflin, 1928), 1:524. See Herndon's discussion of Lincoln's fatalism and evidence of his superstition in *Herndon's Life of Lincoln,* 352.
9. AL to John T. Stuart, Jan. 23, 1841, Basler, et al., eds. *Collected Works of Lincoln,* 1:229.
10. Joshua F. Speed to William H. Herndon, 7 Feb. 1866, Douglas L. Wilson and Rodney O. Davis, eds., *Herndon's Informants: Letters, Interviews, and Statements about Abraham Lincoln* (Urbana: University of Illinois Press, 1998), 197.
11. Ibid.
12. AL to Anson G. Henry, Nov. 19, 1858, Basler, et al., eds., *Collected Works of Lincoln,* 3:339.
13. "Address Before the Young Men's Lyceum of Springfield, Illinois," ibid., 1:115.

14. "Temperance Address," ibid., 279.
15. David Herbert Donald, *Lincoln* (New York: Simon & Schuster, 1995), 118.
16. AL to Andrew Johnston, April 18, 1846, Basler, et al., eds., *Collected Works of Lincoln*, 1:378.
17. Ibid., Sept. 6, 1846, 1:384–85.
18. Ibid., 385.
19. Quoted in Louis Menand, "William James & the Case of the Epileptic Patient," *New York Review of Books*, XLV:20 (Dec. 17, 1998): 81.
20. Ibid.

## Three: A Marriage

1. David Herbert Donald, *Lincoln* (New York: Simon & Schuster, 1995), 108.
2. Michael Burlingame, *The Inner World of Abraham Lincoln* (Urbana: University of Illinois Press, 1994), 268.
3. As quoted in Justin G. Turner and Linda Levitt Turner, *Mary Todd Lincoln: Her Life and Letters* (New York: Alfred A. Knopf, 1972), 293.
4. Douglas L. Wilson, *Honor's Voice: The Transformation of Abraham Lincoln* (New York: Alfred A. Knopf, 1998), 232.
5. Jean H. Baker, *Mary Todd Lincoln: A Biography* (New York: W. W. Norton & Co., 1987), xiii.
6. Douglas Wilson and Rodney Davis, eds., *Herndon's Informants: Letters, Interviews and Statements about Abraham Lincoln* (Urbana: University of Illinois Press, 1998), 604. Lincoln was clearly not as smitten by Rutledge as was his predecessor James Buchanan who, when his fiancee died, never married.
7. Ibid., 444, 623.
8. Turner and Turner, *Mary Todd Lincoln*, 296.
9. Wilson and Davis, eds., *Herndon's Informants*, 664.
10. Karen Lystra, *Searching the Heart: Women, Men and Romantic Love in 19th Century America* (New York: Oxford University Press, 1989), 28, 31, 57, 60, 102, 157–159, 180–183; Peter Gay, *The Tender Passion* (New York: Oxford University Press, 1986), 51–60.
11. Katherine Helm, *Mary, Wife of Lincoln* (New York: Harper and Brothers, 1928), 81.
12. Benjamin Franklin, *The Autobiography of Benjamin Franklin* (New York: St. Martin's Press, 1993), 78–79.
13. Alexis de Tocqueville, *Democracy in America* (New York: Harper Perennial, 1988), 592.
14. Turner and Turner, *Mary Todd Lincoln*, 21.
15. Quoted in E. Antonio Rotundo, *American Manhood: Transformations in Masculinity from the Revolution to the Modern Era* (New York: Basic Books, 1993), 112.

16. Roy P. Basler, ed., Marion Dolores Pratt, and Lloyd A. Dunlap, asst. eds., *The Collected Works of Abraham Lincoln*, 9 vols., 2 suppl. vols. (New Brunswick, New Jersey: Rutgers University Press, 1953–55, 1990), 1:78.

17. Ellen Rothman, *Hands and Hearts: A History of Courtship in America* (New York: Basic Books, 1984), 57.

18. Turner and Turner, *Mary Todd Lincoln*, 18; on breach of promise as an outmoded judicial procedure, Michael Grossberg, *Governing the Hearth: Law and Family in 19th Century America* (Chapel Hill: University of North Carolina Press, 1985), 35–38.

19. Quoted in Baker, *Mary Todd Lincoln*, 90; Wilson and Davis, eds., *Herndon's Informants*, 238, 623.

20. *Sangamon Journal*, September 9, 1842:16. The letters are also printed on August 5, and 24, 1842; Roy P. Basler, "The Authorship of the Rebecca Letters," *Abraham Lincoln Quarterly* 2 (June 1942): 80–90.

21. Andrew Cherlin, *Public and Private Families* (New York: McGraw Hill, 1999), 240–247; on Mary Todd and Abraham Lincoln courting inside, Wilson and Davis, eds., *Herndon's Informants*, 443.

22. John Gillis, *A World of Their Own Making: Myth, Ritual, and the Quest for Family Values* (Cambridge, Mass.: Harvard University Press, 1996), 135; also Stephanie Coontz, *The Social Origins of Private Life: The Social History of American Families, 1600–1900* (New York: Verso, 1988), 116; Rothman, *Hands and Hearts*, 60–63; John Modell, "Dating Becomes the Way of American Youth," *Essays on the Family and Historical Change*, ed. David Levine, et al. (Lubbock: Texas A & M University Press, 1983), 91–95.

23. Donald, *Lincoln*, 86; Charles Strozier, *Lincoln's Quest for Union: Public and Private Meanings* (New York: Basic Books, 1982), 43.

24. Kenneth Winkle, "Abraham Lincoln: Self-Made Man," forthcoming in the *Journal of the Abraham Lincoln Association*.

25. Rothman, *Hands and Hearts*, 60–63.

26. Rotundo, *American Manhood*, 115–136; Robert Griswold, *Family and Divorce in California, 1850–1890 Victorian Illusions and Every Day Realities* (Albany: State University of New York Press, 1982); Daniel Wise, *The Young Man's Counselor* (New York: Carlton and Porter, 1850), especially the chapters on energy and industry; Ronald Byars, "The Making of the Self-Made Man: The Development of Masculine Roles and Images in Ante-Bellum America" (Ph.D. diss., Michigan State University, 1979).

27. Basler, et al., eds., *Collected Works of Lincoln*, 1:305.

28. Wilson and Davis, eds., *Herndon's Informants*, 444, 665.

29. Jean H. Baker, *The Stevensons: Biography of an American Family* (New York: W. W. Norton & Co., 1993), 87–95, 103.

30. Helm, *Mary, Wife of Lincoln*, 93–94; Ruth Randall, *Mary Lincoln: Biography of a Marriage* (Boston: Little, Brown, 1953), 74.

31. Turner and Turner, *Mary Todd Lincoln*, 534.

32. Basler, et al., eds., *Collected Works of Lincoln*, 6:283, 371–372, 421, 434; 8:174; Randall, *Mary Lincoln*, 382.

33. Basler, et al., eds., *Collected Works of Lincoln*, 1:465, 477, 496. Evidently some of the Lincoln's private letters to each other were burned in a fire in Chicago after his assassination.

34. Turner and Turner, *Mary Todd Lincoln*, 34–36.

35. Elizabeth Keckley, *Behind the Scenes* (New York: Oxford University Press, 1988), 101–102; Turner and Turner, *Mary Todd Lincoln*, 113–114.

36. Linda Gordon, *Woman's Body, Woman's Right: A Social History of Birth Control* (New York: Viking, 1976), 49–62; Janet Brodie, *Contraception and Abortion in 19th Century America* (Ithaca, N. Y.: Cornell University Press, 1994), 205–224.

37. Brodie, *Contraception and Abortion*, 226; Ansley Coale and Melvin Zelnick, *New Estimates of Fertility and Population in the United States* (Princeton: Princeton University Press, 1963); Robert Wells, "Demographic Change and the Life Cycle of American Families," in Theodore Rabb and Robert Rotberg, eds., *The Family in History* (New York: Harper, 1971), 85–94.

38. Baker, *Mary Todd Lincoln*, 119–125; Wilson and Davis, eds., *Herndon's Informants*, 444.

39. Basler, et al., eds., *Collected Works of Lincoln*, 4:82; 1:391; Rufus Rockwell Wilson, ed., *Intimate Memories of Lincoln* (Elmira, N. Y.: Primavera Press, 1945), 135.

40. Turner and Turner, *Mary Todd Lincoln*, 50.

41. Glenna Matthews, *The Rise of Public Woman: Woman's Power and Woman's Place in the United States* (New York: Oxford University Press, 1992); Elizabeth Varon, *We Mean to Be Counted: White Women and Politics in Antebellum Virginia* (Chapel Hill: University of North Carolina Press, 1998), 116–119.

42. James Conkling to Merce, 21 September 1840, Conkling Papers; Basler, et al., eds., *Collected Works of Lincoln*, 1:299.

43. Henry Whitney, *Life on the Circuit*, 93.

44. Adam Badeau, *Grant In Peace: A Personal Memoir from Appomattox to Mt. McGregor* (Hartford: S. S. Scranton & Company, 1887), 356–362.

45. Wilson and Davis, eds., *Herndon's Informants*, 256.

46. Turner and Turner, *Mary Todd Lincoln*, 200.

47. Wilson and Davis, eds., *Herndon's Informants*, 485, Helm, *Mary, Wife of Lincoln*, 113.

48. William H. Ward, ed., *Abraham Lincoln: Reminiscences of Soldiers, Statesmen and Citizens* (New York: Thomas Crowell, 1895), 32.

## Four: Military Fantasies

1. General Orders No. 68, Headquarters Army of the Potomac, July 4, 1863, in U.S. War Department, *The War of the Rebellion: A Compilation of the Offi-*

*cial Records of the Union and Confederate Armies,* 128 vols. (Washington: GPO, 1880–1901), ser. 1, vol. 27, pt. 3, p. 519; Michael Burlingame and John R. Turner Ettlinger, eds., *Inside Lincoln's White House: The Complete Civil War Diary of John Hay* (Carbondale: University of Illinois Press, 1997), 62.

2. Abraham Lincoln to George G. Meade, July 14, 1863, in Roy P. Basler, ed., Marion Dolores Pratt, and Lloyd A. Dunlap, asst. eds., *The Collected Works of Abraham Lincoln,* 9 vols., 2 suppl. vols. (New Brunswick, N. J.: Rutgers University Press, 1953–55, 1990), 6:327–28; Burlingame and Ettlinger, eds., *Inside Lincoln's White House,* 63.

3. Theodore Calvin Pease and James G. Randall, eds., *The Diary of Orville Hickman Browning,* 2 vols. (Springfield, Ill.: Illinois State Historical Library, 1925), 1:523 (January 12, 1862); John G. Nicolay and John Hay, eds., *Complete Works of Abraham Lincoln,* 12 vols. (New York: Tandy, 1905), 7:141 n.1; Burlingame and Ettlinger, eds., *Inside Lincoln's White House,* 63.

4. AL to Mrs. Orville H. Browning, April 1, 1838, Basler, et al., eds., *Collected Works of Lincoln,* 1:118.

5. "Address Before the Young Men's Lyceum of Springfield, Illinois," January 27, 1838, ibid., 108–15, 112; Memorandum of Duel Instructions to Elias H. Merryman, [September 19, 1842], ibid., 300–301.

6. Speech at Peoria, Illinois, October 16, 1854, ibid., 2:247–83, 282.

7. Reply to Baltimore Committee, April 22, 1861, ibid., 4:341.

8. AL to Edwin M. Stanton, November 11, 1863, ibid., 7:11.

9. AL to Joseph Hooker, June 10, 1863, ibid., 6:257; Burlingame and Ettlinger, eds., *Inside Lincoln's White House,* 194.

10. AL to Ulysses S. Grant, July 13, 1863, Basler, et al., eds., *Collected Works of Lincoln,* 6:326.

11. AL to Henry W. Halleck, July 13, 1862, ibid., 5:322.

12. AL to William S. Rosecrans, March 17, 1863, ibid., 6:139; Speech to the Springfield Scott Club, August 14, 26, 1852, ibid., 2:135–57, 149–50.

13. Schuyler Colfax, *Life and Principles of Abraham Lincoln* (Philadelphia: Rodgers, 1865), 18; Sherman to Ellen Sherman, June 30, 1864, in Mills Lane, ed., *"War is Hell!": William T. Sherman's Personal Narrative of His March Through Georgia* (Savannah: Beehive, 1974), 59.

14. Sherman to John Sherman, December 31, 1864, in Rachel Sherman Thorndike, ed., *The Sherman Letters: Correspondence Between General and Senator Sherman From 1837 to 1891* (New York: Scribner, 1894), 241–42; McClellan to Mary Ellen McClellan, September 18, [1862], in Stephen W. Sears, ed., *The Civil War Papers of George B. McClellan: Selected Correspondence, 1860–1865* (New York: Ticknor & Fields, 1989), 469.

15. AL to Henry W. Halleck, January 1, 1863, Basler, et al., eds., *Collected Works of Lincoln,* 6:31; Burlingame and Ettlinger, eds., *Inside Lincoln's White House,* 62.

16. Second Inaugural Address, March 4, 1865, Basler, et al., eds., *Collected Works of Lincoln,* 8:332–33.

17. AL to Albert G. Hodges, April 4, 1864, ibid., 7:281–82.

18. Burlingame and Ettlinger, eds., *Inside Lincoln's White House*, 64–65.

## Five: Abraham Lincoln and Jefferson Davis as Commanders in Chief

1. The two documents can most readily be compared in *The Constitution of the United States of America . . . , To which is Appended, for its Historical Interest, The Constitution of the Confederate States of America* (Richmond: Virginia Commission on Constitutional Government, 1961).

2. David M. Potter, "Jefferson Davis and the Political Factors in Confederate Defeat," in David Herbert Donald, ed., *Why the North Won the Civil War* (New York: Simon & Schuster, 1996), 93–113.

3. See the excellent essay "The Military Systems of North and South" in *The Selected Essays of T. Harry Williams* (Baton Rouge: Louisiana State University Press, 1983), 149–72.

4. Emory M. Thomas, *The Confederate Nation, 1861–1865* (New York: Harper & Row, 1979), 160.

5. Ibid., 108–109.

6. With this reorganization went the setting up of Kirby Smith's Trans-Mississippi department and Beauregard's Department of South Carolina, Georgia, and Florida. Thomas Lawrence Connelly and Archer Jones, *The Politics of Command: Factions and Ideas in Confederate Strategy* (Baton Rouge: Louisiana State University Press, 1973), 124.

7. Douglas Southall Freeman, *Lee's Lieutenants: A Study in Command* (New York: Charles Scribner's Sons, 1944), 1:134–36.

8. David Donald, ed., *Inside Lincoln's Cabinet: The Civil War Diaries of Salmon P. Chase* (New York: Longmans, Green, 1954), 201–203.

9. Steven E. Woodworth, *Davis and Lee at War* (Lawrence: University of Kansas Press, 1995), 57–58.

10. Roy P. Basler, ed., Marion Dolores Pratt, and Lloyd A. Dunlap, asst. eds., *The Collected Works of Abraham Lincoln*, 9 vols., 2 suppl. vols. (New Brunswick, N. J.: Rutgers University Press, 1953–55, 1990), 6:139.

11. Linda Lasswell Crist and Mary Seaton Dix, eds., *The Papers of Jefferson Davis* (Baton Rouge: Louisiana State University Press, 1992), 7:305–306.

12. Basler, et al., eds., *Collected Works of Lincoln*, 6:329.

13. Donald, *Inside Lincoln's Cabinet*, 85.

14. John H. Cramer, *Lincoln Under Enemy Fire* (Baton Rouge: Louisiana State University Press, 1948).

15. Confederate Secretary of War George W. Randolph, in Clement Eaton, *A History of the Southern Confederacy* (New York: Macmillan, 1964), 49.

16. George William Bagby, editor of the *Southern Literary Messenger*, in Thomas, *Confederate Nation*, 142.

17. William Pitt Fessenden, in Francis Fessenden, *Life and Public Services of William Pitt Fessenden* (Boston: Houghton, Mifflin, 1907), 1:260.

18. Orestes Brownson to Charles Sumner, December 26, 1862, Sumner MSS., Houghton Library, Harvard University.

19. Charles Sumner, in Diary of Charles Francis Adams, March 16, 1861, Adams MSS., Massachusetts Historical Society.

20. Edward Younger, ed., *Inside the Confederate Government: The Diary of Robert Garlick Hill Kean* (New York: Oxford University Press, 1957), 101.

21. James D. Richardson, ed., *Messages and Papers of Jefferson Davis and the Confederacy, Including Diplomatic Correspondence, 1861–1865* (New York: Chelsea House, 1966), 1:215–16.

22. David Herbert Donald, *Lincoln* (New York: Simon & Schuster, 1995), 401–405.

23. Davis, *Papers*, 6:335, 340.

24. Lincoln, Basler, et al., eds., *Collected Works of Lincoln*, 6:78–79.

25. Michael Burlingame and John R. Turner Ettlinger, eds., *Inside Lincoln's White House: The Complete Civil War Diary of John Hay* (Carbondale: Southern Illinois University Press, 1997), p. 192.

26. Philip S. Paludan, *A Covenant with Death: The Constitution, Law, and Equality in the Civil War Era* (Urbana: University of Illinois Press, 1975); William Whitting, *The War Powers of the President, and the Legislative Powers of Congress in Relation to Rebellion, Treason and Slavery* (6th ed.; Boston: John L. Shorey, 1863), 11.

27. The best definition of the war powers under the Constitution remains J. G. Randall, *Constitutional Problems Under Lincoln* (Urbana: University of Illinois Press, 1951), 28–33.

28. David Herbert Donald, *Charles Sumner and the Rights of Man* (New York: Knopf, 1970), 16–17.

29. Conveniently reprinted in Frank Freidel, ed., *Union Pamphlets of the Civil War, 1861–1865* (Cambridge: Harvard University Press, 1967), 1:381–403.

30. *Lincoln Lore* 1634 (April 1974).

31. Francis B. Carpenter, *Six Months at the White House with Abraham Lincoln* (New York: Hurd and Houghton, 1866), 353.

32. Lincoln, Basler, et al., eds., *Collected Works of Lincoln*, 5:421.

33. Ibid., 4:322.

34. Ibid., 4:429.

35. Mark E. Neely, Jr., *The Fate of Liberty: Abraham Lincoln and Civil Liberties* (New York: Oxford University Press, 1991).

36. Richardson, ed., *The Messages and Papers of Jefferson Davis*, 1:185.

37. Ibid., 1:36. For an important differing interpretation of Davis's constitutional views, see Mark E. Neely, Jr., *Southern Rights: Political Prisoners and the Myth of Confederate Constitutionalism* (Charlottesville: University Press of Virginia, 1999), especially chapter 9.

38. Ibid., 1:122.

39. Ibid., 1:184.

## Six: The Constitution and Liberty

1. Abraham Lincoln to Alexander H. Stephens, December 22, 1860, in Roy P. Basler, ed., Marion Dolores Pratt, and Lloyd A. Dunlap, asst. eds., *The Collected Works of Abraham Lincoln*, 9 vols., 2 suppl. vols. (New Brunswick, N. J.: Rutgers University Press, 1953–55, 1990), 4:160–61; Alexander Stephens, *A Constitutional View of the Late War between the States* (Philadelphia: National Publishing, 1870), 2:447.

2. "Fragment on the Constitution and the Union," Basler, et al., eds., *Collected Works of Lincoln*, 4:168–69.

3. AL to James M. Brown, October 18, 1858, ibid., 3:327; "Speech in Independence Hall," February 22, 1861, ibid., 1861, ibid., 4:240; "Speech at Peoria, Illinois," October 16, 1854, ibid., 2:255.

4. Stephens, "Cornerstone Address" in Jon L. Wakelyn, ed., *Southern Pamphlets on Secession, November 1860-April 1861* (Chapel Hill: University of North Carolina Press, 1996), 405–406.

5. Leo de Alvarez, preface to Laurence Berns et al., eds., *Abraham Lincoln, the Gettysburg Address and American Constitutionalism* (Irving, Texas: University of Dallas Press, 1976), 1; Gottfried Dietze, in Merrill Peterson, ed., *Lincoln in American Memory* (New York: Oxford University Press, 1994), 333–34; Willmoore Kendall, "Equality: Commitment or Ideal?," *Intercollegiate Review* 24 (Spring 1989): 27–28; Dwight G. Anderson, "Quest for Immortality: A Theory of Abraham Lincoln's Political Psychology," in Gabor Boritt, ed., *The Historian's Lincoln: Pseudohistory, Psychohistory, and History* (Urbana: University of Illinois Press, 1988, 1994), 265, 267–69.

6. Peterson, *Lincoln in American Memory*, 299–300; Mark E. Neely, *The Fate of Liberty: Abraham Lincoln and Civil Liberties* (New York: Oxford University Press, 1991), 226–31; Garry Wills, *Lincoln at Gettysburg: The Words That Remade America* (New York: Simon & Schuster, 1992), 38–39, 145–46; Andrew McLaughlin, "Lincoln, the Constitution, and Democracy," in *Abraham Lincoln Association Papers* (Springfield, Illinois: Abraham Lincoln Association, 1937): 29–30; Howard Jones, *Abraham Lincoln and a New Birth of Freedom: The Union and Slavery in the Diplomacy of the Civil War* (Lincoln: University of Nebraska Press, 1999), 15; Phillip S. Paludan, *The Presidency of Abraham Lincoln* (Lawrence: University of Kansas Press, 1994), 18–19; Paludan, "Lincoln and the Rhetoric of Politics," in Lloyd Ambrosius, ed., *A Crisis of Republicanism: American Politics in the Civil War Era* (Lincoln: University of Nebraska Press, 1990), 77.

7. AL to Anton C. Hesing, Henry Wendt, Alexander Fisher, Committee, 30 June, 1858, Basler, et al., eds., *Collected Works of Lincoln*, 2:475.

8. Orestes Brownson, in Lawrence Kohl, ed., *The Politics of Individualism: Parties and the American Character in the Jacksonian Era* (New York: Oxford University Press, 1989), 109.

9. William Leggett, "Separation of Bank and State" [May 27, 1837] in L. W. White, ed., *Democratick Editorials: Essays in Jacksonian Political Economy by William Leggett* (Indianapolis, Ind.: Liberty Press, 1984), 142.

10. Daniel Feller, *The Jacksonian Promise: America, 1815–1840* (Baltimore: Johns Hopkins University Press, 1995), 33–52; Daniel Walker Howe, *The Political Culture of the American Whigs* (Chicago: University of Chicago Press, 1979), 23.

11. "Address before the Wisconsin State Agricultural Society, Milwaukee, Wisconsin," September 30, 1859, in Basler, et al., eds., *Collected Works of Lincoln,* 3:472–73; Gabor S. Boritt, *Lincoln and the Economics of the American Dream* (Memphis, Tenn.: Memphis State University Press, 1978), 790–91; Lucius E. Chittendon, in Don E. and Virginia Fehrenbacher, eds., *Recollected Words of Abraham Lincoln* (Stanford, Calif.: Stanford University Press, 1996), 99.

12. "On the Perpetuation of Our Political Institutions"; "Address before the Young Men's Lyceum of Springfield, Illinois"; "Speech in United States House of Representatives on Internal Improvements," June 20, 1848, Basler, et al., eds., *Collected Works of Lincoln,* 1:115, 488.

13. "Speech on the Sub-Treasury," ibid., 1:171–72; Paul Angle, *"Here Have I Lived": A History of Lincoln's Springfield* (Chicago: Abraham Lincoln Bookshop, 1971), 110–11; Boritt, *Lincoln and the Economics,* 65–71; Douglas L. Wilson, *Honor's Voice: The Transformation of Abraham Lincoln* (New York: Knopf, 1998), 200–201.

14. AL to William Herndon, February 15, 1848; "Eulogy on Henry Clay," July 6, 1852, Basler, et al., eds., *Collected Works of Lincoln,* 1:451, 2:130.

15. "Speech at Peoria, Illinois," October 16, 1854; "Eulogy on Henry Clay," ibid., 2:126, 248.

16. William H. Herndon, "Lincoln in Springfield," in *The Hidden Lincoln from the Letters and Papers of William H. Herndon* (New York: Viking, 1938), 423; "Speech at Peoria, Illinois," Basler, et al., eds., *Collected Works of Lincoln,* 2:274.

17. Joseph Gillespie to William H. Herndon, in Douglas L. Wilson and Rodney O. Davis, eds., *Herndon's Informants: Letters, Interviews, and Statements about Abraham Lincoln* (Urbana: University of Illinois Press, 1998), 183; "Temperance Address," February 22, 1842, Basler, et al., eds., *Collected Works of Lincoln,* 1:279.

18. "Fragment on Slavery," July 1, 1854; "Speech in Hartford, Connecticut" March 5, 1860, ibid., 2:222, 4:3.

19. Pauline Maier, *American Scripture: Making the Declaration of Independence* (New York: Knopf, 1997), 202; "Speech in New Haven, Connecticut," March 6, 1860, "Speech at Carlinville," August 31, 1858, "Speech in Peoria, Illinois,"

October 16, 1854, Basler, et al., eds., *Collected Works of Lincoln*, 2:276. 3:81, 4:16.

20. Paul Finkelman, *Slavery and the Founders: Race and Liberty in the Age of Jefferson* (Armonk, New York: M. E. Sharpe, 1996), 31–32.

21. Stephen A. Douglas, "Third Joint Debate at Jonesboro," in Harold Holzer, ed., *The Lincoln-Douglas Debates* (New York: HarperCollins, 1993), 150–52.

22. J. David Greenstone, *The Lincoln Persuasion: Remaking American Liberalism* (Princeton, N. J.: Princeton University Press, 1993), 241; Harold Hyman, *A More Perfect Union: The Impact of the Civil War and Reconstruction of the Constitution* (New York: Knopf, 1973), 59.

23. "Speech at Carlinville; Illinois," August 31, 1858, "Speech in Springfield, Illinois," October 16, 1854, Basler, et al., eds., *Collected Works of Lincoln*, 2:250, 3:79.

24. George Anastaplo, "Slavery and the Federal Convention of 1787," in *Abraham Lincoln: A Constitutional Biography* (Lanham, Md.: Rowman and Littlefield, 1999), 61, 68; "Speech at Elwood, Kansas," November 30, 1859, Basler, et al., eds., *Collected Works of Lincoln*, 3:496.

25. "Fifth Joint Debate at Galesburg," in Holzer, ed., *Lincoln-Douglas Debates*, 263; "Speech in Indianapolis," September 19, 1859, "Speech at Springfield, Illinois," October 4, 1854, "Speech at Elwood, Kansas," Basler, et al., eds., *Collected Works of Lincoln*, 2:245, 3:465, 496.

26. "Speech in Chicago, Illinois," July 10, 1858, "Speech at Springfield," October 4, 1854, ibid., 2:245, 492. This is not, of course, the exact wording of the Declaration; it is actually closer to the wording which appears in the Illinois state constitution, which declared that "all men are born equally free and independent." See *The Public and General Statute Laws of the State of Illinois* (Chicago: Stephen F. Gale, 1839), p. 33, and *A Compilation of the Statues of the State of Illinois* (Chicago: Keen & Lee, 1856), p. 65.

27. AL to Joshua F. Speed, August 24, 1855, "Speech in Springfield, Illinois," October 30, 1858, AL to Salmon P. Chase, June 9, 1859, ibid., 3:320, 334, 384.

28. "Speech at Springfield, Illinois," June 26, 1857, ibid., 2:401; "Sixth Joint Debate at Quincy," in Holzer, ed., *Lincoln-Douglas Debates*, 291.

29. "Speech at Kalamazoo, Michigan," August 27, 1856, "Speech in Buffalo, New York," February 18, 1861, "Speech at Pittsburgh, Pennsylvania," February 15, 1861, Basler, et al., eds., *Collected Works of Lincoln*, 2:366, 4:214, 221.

30. "First Inaugural Address—Final Text," March 4, 1861, ibid., 4:267, 270.

31. "Message to Congress in Special Session," July 4, 1861, "First Inaugural Address—Final Text," ibid., 4:268, 430.

32. George Ellis Moore, *A Banner in the Hills: West Virginia's Statehood* (New York: Appleton-Century-Crofts, 1963), pp. 20–22; Harold M. Hyman, *A More Perfect Union: The Impact of the Civil War and Reconstruction on the*

*Constitution* (New York: Knopf, 1973), p. 296; "Opinion on the Admission of West Virginia into the Union," December 31, 1862, Basler et al, eds., *Collected Works of Lincoln,* 6:26–28.

33. Paludan, *Presidency of Abraham Lincoln,* 109.

34. AL to Simon Cameron, July 17, 1861; to Edward Bates, June 15, 1862; "Reply to Emancipation Memorial Presented by Chicago Christians of All Denominations," September 13, 1862; to Orville H. Browning, September 22, 1861, Basler, et al., eds., *Collected Works of Lincoln,* 4:451, 532; 5:271, 421.

35. AL to Salmon P. Chase, September 2, 1863, ibid., 6:429; Don E. Fehrenbacher, "Lincoln and the Constitution," in *Lincoln in Text and Context: Collected Essays* (Stanford, Calif.: Stanford University Press, 1987), 127.

36. "Preliminary Emancipation Proclamation," September 22, 1862; AL to Salmon P. Chase, September 2, 1863, Basler, et al., eds., *Collected Works of Lincoln,* 5:433–34, 6:428; Stephens, *Constitutional View,* 2:610; Neely, *The Fate of Liberty,* 218.

37. Gideon Welles, "Administration of Abraham Lincoln, I," in Albert Mordell, ed., *Selected Essays by Gideon Welles: Lincoln's Administration* (New York: Twayne, 1960), 72–73; Sandel, *Democracy's Discontent: American in Search of the National Public Philosophy* (Cambridge, Mass.: Harvard University Press, 1994), 24–25.

## Seven: Toward Appomattox

1. James M. McPherson, *Abraham Lincoln and the Second American Revolution* (New York: Oxford University, 1991), 91. See also McPherson's *Battle Cry of Freedom: The Civil War Era* (New York: Oxford University Press, 1988), 824.

2. John Y. Simon, "Grant, Lincoln, and Unconditional Surrender," in Gabor Boritt, ed., *Lincoln's Generals* (New York: Oxford University Press, 1995), 197; Mark Grimsley, *The Hard Hand of War: Union Military Policy toward Southern Civilians, 1861–1865* (New York: Cambridge University Press, 1995), 210; Phillip S. Paludan, *"A People's Contest": The Union and the Civil War, 1861–1865* (New York: Harper, 1988), 296–97.

3. *Savannah Republican,* as quoted in *New York World,* November 10, 1864; entry for November 17, 1864, Frank E. Vandiver, ed., *The Civil War Diary of General Josiah Gorgas* (University: University of Alabama Press, 1947), 150; entry for November 15, 1864, John B. Jones, *A Rebel War Clerk's Diary,* ed. Earl Schenck Miers (New York: Sagamore, 1958), 448.

4. *New York World,* November 7, 8 (Fillmore quotation) 1864. See also the *Washington National Intelligencer,* September 20, 1864.

5. This quotation is taken from probably the last letter that Lincoln wrote. Abraham Lincoln to James H. Van Alen, April 14, 1865, Roy P. Basler, ed., Marion Dolores Pratt, and Lloyd A. Dunlap, asst. eds., *The Collected Works of Abraham*

*Lincoln*, 9 vols., 2 suppl. vols. (New Brunswick, N. J.: Rutgers University Press, 1953–55, 1990), 8:413.

6. "Last Public Address," April 11, 1865, ibid., 403.

7. Entry for November 25, 1864, *Diary of Gideon Welles, Secretary of Navy under Lincoln and Johnson*, 3 vols. (Boston: Houghton, Mifflin, 1911), 2:179.

8. "Annual Message to Congress," December 6, 1864, Basler, et al., eds., *Collected Works of Lincoln*, 8:145–46, 150–52.

9. Ibid., 152.

10. Don E. Fehrenbacher and Virginia Fehrenbacher, eds., *Recollected Words of Abraham Lincoln* (Stanford, Calif.: Stanford University Press, 1996), 182; Marquis Adolphe de Chambrun, *Impressions of Lincoln and the Civil War: A Foreigner's Account* (New York: Random House, 1952), 85.

11. *Harper's Weekly*, 8 (December 24, 1864): 818; *Washington Daily Morning Chronicle*, January 11, 1865; *Boston Journal*, December 7, 1864; *Boston Daily Advertiser*, December 7, 1864.

12. *Washington Daily Morning Chronicle*, January 4, 1865; Larry E. Nelson, *Bullets, Ballots, and Rhetoric: Confederate Policy for the United States Presidential Contest of 1864* (Tuscaloosa: University of Alabama Press, 1980), 164–65; *Boston Journal*, February 16, 1865.

13. *New York World*, January 23, 1865; Garret Davis's resolutions can be found in the *Sacramento Union*, January 12, 1865; James A. Rawley, *Abraham Lincoln and A Nation Worth Fighting For* (Wheeling, Ill.: Harlan Davidson, 1996), 204.

14. *New Orleans Tribune*, December 21, 1864; *Boston Commonwealth*, December 10, 1864.

15. Horace Greeley to Francis P. Blair, Sr., December 15, 1865, Blair Family Papers, Manuscript Division, Library of Congress, Washington, microfilm reel 17. The *Washington Daily Morning Chronicle*, issues of December 1864 and January 1865, was especially active in reporting widespread Southern disaffection and a desire to end the war before total ruin occurred.

16. Pass for Francis P. Blair, Sr., December 28, 1864, Basler, et al., eds., *Collected Works of Lincoln*, 8:188–89n; John G. Nicolay and John Hay, *Abraham Lincoln: A History*, 10 vols. (New York: Century, 1890), 10:96; memorandum of interview with Jefferson Davis [January 12, 1865], Abraham Lincoln Papers, Manuscript Division, Library of Congress, Washington, microfilm.

17. AL to Francis P. Blair, Sr., January 18, 1865, Basler, et al., eds., *Collected Works of Lincoln*, 8:220–21; *New York Herald*, January 23, 1865.

18. AL to Major Thomas T. Eckert, January 30, 1865, Basler, et al., eds., *Collected Works of Lincoln*, 8:277.

19. AL to William H. Seward, January 31, 1865, ibid., 250–51. Seward did not arrive at Fort Monroe until the next evening, February 1.

20. AL to the House of Representatives, February 10, 1865, ibid., 280–81. This dispatch was sent to Secretary of War Edwin M. Stanton and seen by Lincoln before mid-morning on February 2. Ibid., 282.

21. AL to U.S. Grant, February 2, 1865, ibid.; *New York Herald,* February 4, 1865.

22. William C. Harris, "Hampton Road Peace Conference," *Journal of the Abraham Lincoln Association* (Winter 2000): 52; For the acceptance of the veracity of Stephens's account regarding the five-year prospective ratification of the Thirteenth Amendment by the South, see Ludwell H. Johnson, "Lincoln's Solution to the Problem of Peace Terms, 1864–1865," *Journal of Southern History* 34 (November 1968): 58–82. David Donald in his biography of Lincoln repeats Stephens's account without critical comment on its accuracy. David Herbert Donald, *Lincoln* (New York: Simon & Schuster, 1995), 558.

23. Harris, "Hampton Roads Peace Conference," 49, 54.

24. AL to the Senate and House of Representatives [February 5, 1865], Basler, et al., eds., *Collected Works of Lincoln,* 8:260–61.

25. Years later, Secretary of Interior John P. Usher remembered that Lincoln seemed surprised at the cabinet's opposition to his proposal and, with feeling, remarked that if the bonds to compensate slaveholders could shorten the war by one hundred days, the amount would be repaid to the government. "But you are all opposed to me, and I will not send the message to Congress," Usher recalled Lincoln as saying. Nicolay and Hay, *Abraham Lincoln,* 10:136; entry for February 6, 1865, *Welles Diary,* 2:237.

26. Gabor Boritt, "War Opponent and War President," in *Lincoln, the War President: The Gettysburg Lectures* (New York: Oxford University Press, 1992), 199–200; Fehrenbacher, ed., *Recollected Words of Lincoln,* 458.

27. Gideon Welles, in Albert Mordell, ed., *Selected Essays by Gideon Welles: Civil War and Reconstruction* (New York: Twayne, 1959), 182–83; Alexander K. McClure, *Abraham Lincoln and Men of War-Times: Some Personal Recollections of War and Politics During the Lincoln Administration* (Philadelphia: The Times Publishing, 1892), 225. For Lincoln's fear of anarchy and concern that the war would result in "a violent and remorseless revolutionary struggle," see his 1861 Inaugural Address and his Annual Message to Congress, December 3, 1861, Basler, et al., eds., *Collected Works of Lincoln,* 4:268, 5:49. See also AL to William Rosecrans, ibid., 6:108, and AL to Governor Thomas C. Fletcher, February 20, 27, 1865, ibid., 8:308, 319.

28. Harris, "Hampton Roads Peace Conference," 52; *New York Tribune,* February 7, 1865.

29. U.S. Grant to Edwin M. Stanton, March 2, 1865; Stanton to Grant, March 4, 1865, Basler, et al., eds., *Collected Works of Lincoln,* 8:331n., 330–31; Ward Hill Lamon, *Recollections of Abraham Lincoln, 1847–1865* (Chicago: McClurg, 1895), 245–46.

30. Second Inaugural Address, March 4, 1865, ibid., 333.

31. Ibid.

32. Elizabeth Keckley, *Behind the Scenes. Or, Thirty Years a Slave, and Four Years in the White House* (New York: Oxford University Press, 1988), 157; entry for March 23, 1865, *Welles Diary*, 2:264.

33. John S. Barnes, "With Lincoln from Washington to Richmond in 1865," *Appleton's Magazine* 9 (May 1907): 521.

34. William Tecumseh Sherman to Isaac N. Arnold, November 28, 1872, Isaac Newton Arnold Papers, Chicago Historical Society, Chicago. This source was kindly given to me by Mark Bradley, who is studying Sherman and the ending of the war in North Carolina.

35. Fehrenbacher, ed., *Recollected Words of Lincoln*, 365; David Dixon Porter, *Incidents and Anecdotes of the Civil War* (New York: Appleton, 1885), 314. See also William Tecumseh Sherman to Isaac N. Arnold, November 28, 1872, Arnold Papers. Brooks Simpson in his fine study, *Let Us Have Peace: Ulysses S. Grant and the Politics of War and Reconstruction, 1861–1868* (Chapel Hill: University of North Carolina Press, 1991), 84, writes that, though Grant "was sure that Lincoln would endorse" his agreement at Appomattox, "he made it at his own discretion." In view of Lincoln's long discussions— and admonitions—with Grant on the subject of a generous peace, I believe that the general in chief's terms to Lee were carefully based on the president's instructions.

36. *Memoirs of General William T. Sherman*, rev. ed. (2 vols., New York: Appleton 1913), 2:327.

37. Horace Porter, *Campaigning with Grant* (New York: Century, 1906), 451.

38. Godfrey Weitzel, Louis H. Manarin, ed., *Richmond Occupied* (Richmond: Civil War Centennial Committee, 1965), 56–57; C. G. Chamberlayne, ed., "Abraham Lincoln in Richmond," Memorandum of Gustavus A. Myers, April 1865, *Virginia Magazine of History and Biography* 41 (October 1933): 320–22; John A. Campbell to Horace Greeley, April 26, 1865, Campbell Family Papers, Duke University Library, Durham; North Carolina.

39. AL to John A. Campbell [April 5, 1865]; AL to Godfrey Weitzel, April 6, 1865, Basler, et al., eds., *Collected Works of Lincoln*, 8:386–87, 389; AL to Ulysses S. Grant, April 5, 1865, ibid., 388.

40. AL to John A. Campbell [April 5, 1865]; AL to Godfrey Weitzel, April 6, 1865, ibid., 386–87, 389; "George W. Julian's Journal—Assassination of Lincoln," *Indiana Magazine of History*, 11 (December 1915), 333; *Welles Diary*, 2:279–80; Charles H. Ambler, *Francis H. Pierpont: Union Governor of Virginia and Father of West Virginia* (Chapel Hill: University of North Carolina Press, 1937), 255–57; AL to Godfrey Weitzel, April 12, 1865, Basler, et al., eds., *Collected Works of Lincoln*, 8:406–407; *New York Herald*, April 14, 1865.

41. William C. Harris, "Lincoln Meets a Confederate General," *Lincoln Herald* 100 (Spring 1998): 5–8.

42. Chambrun, *Impressions of Lincoln,* 84–85.

43. *New York Times,* February 24, March 31, April 7, 1865; *Philadelphia Press,* 13 April 1865. See also the *New York Tribune,* February 23, March 22, 24, 1865; *Chicago Tribune,* March 18, 1865; *Washington Chronicle,* April 4, 1865.

44. Chambrun wrote this account in 1874, apparently based on notes that he took on the trip to City Point. He often was in the company of Sumner, who also was a member of Mrs. Lincoln's entourage, during the senator's stay in Virginia and also the voyage back to Washington on the *River Queen.* Marquis de Chambrun, "Personal Recollections of Charles Sumner," *Scribner's Magazine* 13 (January 9, 1893): 156.

45. *Congressional Globe,* 38th Cong., 2d Sess. (January 30, 1865): 495; *St. Louis Missouri Democrat* (Radical Republican newspaper), February 10, 1865; Zachariah Chandler to his wife, January 16, 27, 1865, Zachariah Chandler Papers, Manuscript Division, Library of Congress, Washington, D.C., microfilm; entry for March 29, 1865, *The Diary of George Templeton Strong,* edited by Allan Nevins and Milton Halsey Thomas and abridged by Thomas J. Pressly (Seattle: University of Washington Press, 1988), 282; *Boston Daily Advertiser,* February 2, 4, 1865; *New York Times,* January 22, 1865; George W. Julian, *Political Recollections, 1840 to 1872* (Chicago: Jansen, McClurg, 1884), 255–56.

46. Basler, et al., eds., *Collected Works of Lincoln,* 8:399–405; entry for April 14, 1865, *Welles Diary,* 2:281–82; Mordell, ed., *Selected Essays by Gideon Welles,* 190–93; Frederick W. Seward, *Seward at Washington as Senator and Secretary of State: A Memoir of His Life, with Selections from His Letters, 1861–1872* (New York: Derby and Miller, 1891), 274. Frederick Seward attended the cabinet meeting in place of his injured father. Outside of Lincoln's circle, some Republicans wanted to "hang Jeff Davis on a sour apple tree," as the saying went. Entry for April 11, 1865, *Strong Diary,* 293.

## Eight: The Riddle of Death

1. Roy P. Basler, ed., Marion Dolores Pratt, and Lloyd A. Dunlap, asst. eds., *The Collected Works of Abraham Lincoln,* 9 vols., 2 suppl. vols. (New Brunswick, New Jersey: Rutgers University Press, 1953–55, 1990), 1:1.

2. Luke Bemis to Elizabeth Lincoln, February 8, 1842, in author's possession.

3. Basler, et al., eds., *Collected Works of Lincoln,* 1:267–69.

4. Ibid., 48.

5. Ibid., 4:62.

6. Louis A, Warren, *Lincoln's Youth: Indiana Years* (New York: Appleton, Century, Crofts, 1959), 54.

7. Basler, et al., eds., *Collected Works of Lincoln,* 6:16–17.

8. Warren, *Lincoln's Youth,* 55–59.

9. Ibid., 173–75; Albert J. Beveridge, *Abraham Lincoln, 1809–1858,* 2 vols. (Boston: Houghton Mifflin, 1928), 1:49.

10. Basler, et al., eds., *Collected Works of Lincoln,* 1:165–66.

11. David J. Harkness and R. Gerald McMurtry, *Lincoln's Favorite Poets* (Knoxville: University of Tennessee Press, 1959), 14.

12. Kenneth A. Bernard, *Lincoln and the Music of the Civil War* (Caldwell, Idaho: Caxton, 1966), 120.

13. Francis B. Carpenter, *Six Months at the White House with Abraham Lincoln* (New York: Hurd & Houghton, 1866), 58–59.

14. Basler, et al., eds., *Collected Works of Lincoln,* 1:378.

15. Maurice Boyd, *William Knox and Abraham Lincoln: the Story of a Poetic Legacy* (Denver: Sage Books, 1966), 58–59.

16. Allen Thorndyke Rice, ed., *Reminiscences of Abraham Lincoln by Distinguished Men of His Time* (New York: North American Review), 268.

17. Basler, et al., eds., *Collected Works of Lincoln,* 1:378–79.

18. Emmanuel Hertz, ed., *The Hidden Lincoln: From the Letters and Papers of William H. Herndon* (New York: Viking, 1938), 110–11.

19. Noah Brooks, *Washington in Lincoln's Time* (New York: Rinehart, 1958), 199.

20. Basler, et al., eds., *Collected Works of Lincoln,* 4:190.

21. Benjamin P. Thomas and Harold Hyman, *Stanton: The Life and Times of Lincoln's Secretary of War* (New York: Knopf, 1962), 393.

22. Carpenter, *Six Months,* 264.

23. Ward Hill Lamon, *Recollections of Abraham Lincoln, 1847–1865* (Chicago: McClurg, 1895), 114–17.

24. Howard K. Beale and Alan W. Brownsword, eds., *Diary of Gideon Welles,* 3 vols. (New York: Norton, 1962), 2:282–83.

25. Basler, et al., eds., *Collected Works of Lincoln,* 2:96–97.

26. Hertz, *Hidden Lincoln,* 87.

27. Douglas L. Wilson, *Honor's Voice: The Transformation of Abraham Lincoln* (New York: Knopf, 1998), 11–12.

28. Wayne C. Temple, *Abraham Lincoln From Skeptic to Prophet* (Mahomet, Ill. Mayhaven, 1995), 136.

29. Basler, et al., eds., *Collected Works of Lincoln,* 4:385–86.

30. Ibid., 6:16–17.

31. Ibid., 8:116–17.

32. Carpenter, *Six Months,* 115–17.

33. Ibid., 117–19.

34. Basler, et al., eds., *Collected Works of Lincoln,* 1:368–70.

35. William H. Herndon and Jesse W. Weik, *Herndon's Lincoln,* 3 vols. (Chicago: Belford, Clarke, 1889), 3:524–25.

*Press, 1860–1864* (Carbondale, 1998); Theodore Calvin Pease and J. G. Randall, eds., *The Diary of Orville Hickman Browning,* 2 vols. (Springfield, Ill., 1925–33), 1:478, 512, 612; David Donald, ed., *Inside Lincoln's Cabinet, The Civil War Diaries of Salmon P. Chase* (New York, 1954), 95, 98–99, 152, 156–57, 160; Howard K. Beale, ed., *Diary of Gideon Welles, Secretary of Navy under Lincoln and Johnson,* 3 vols. (New York, 1960), 1:123, 150–53, 162, 543; Lucius E. Chittenden, *Recollections of President Lincoln and His Administration* (New York, 1891), 337–40; Charles A. Barker, ed., *Memoirs of Elisha Oscar Crosby: Reminiscences of California and Guatemala, 1849–1864* (San Marino, Cal., 1945), 87f; John Eaton, *Grant, Lincoln, and the Freedman: Reminiscences . . .* (New York, 1907), 91–92; Earl Schenck Miers, et al., eds., *Lincoln Day By Day, A Chronology, 1809–1865,* 3 vols. (Washington, 1960), *passim,* especially 2:188; 3:34, 134, 134, 136, 159, 172, 218.

The secondary literature on the subject is also substantial. In addition to the standard biographies, see Charles H. Wesley, "Lincoln's Plans for Colonizing Emancipated Negroes," *Journal of Negro History* 4 (1919): 7–21; N. A. N. Gleven, "Some Plans for Colonizing Liberated Negro Slaves in Hispanic America," *Journal of Negro History* 11 (1926): 35–49; Warren A. Beck, "Lincoln and Negro Colonization," *Abraham Lincoln Quarterly* 6 (1950): 162–83; Paul Scheips, "Lincoln and the Chiriqui Colonization Project," *Journal of Negro History* 38 (1952): 418–53; Frederic Bancroft, "Schemes to Colonize Negroes in Central America," and "The Ile a Vache Experiment in Colonization," Jacob E. Cooke, ed., *Frederic Bancroft: Historian* (Norman, Ok., 1957), 228–58; Walter A. Payne, "Lincoln's Caribbean Colonization Plan," *Pacific Historian* 7 (1963): 65–72; George R. Planck, "Abraham Lincoln and Black Colonization: Theory and Practice," *Lincoln Herald* 72 (Summer 1970): 61–77; Thomas Schoonover, "Was Black Colonization an Expansionist Policy of the Lincoln Administration?" Paper presented at the Eighty-seventh meeting of the American Historical Association, 1972; Jason H. Silverman, "'In Isles Beyond the Main': Abraham Lincoln's Philosophy of Black Colonization," *Lincoln Herald* 80 (Fall 1978). Michael Vorenberg, "Abraham Lincoln and the Politics of Black Colonization," *Journal of the Abraham Lincoln Association* 14 (Summer 1993): 22–45, is the best survey. In the monographic literature see Benjamin Quarles, *Lincoln and the Negro* (New York, 1962), 108–23 *et passim.*

George M. Fredrickson, "A Man But Not a Brother: Abraham Lincoln and Racial Equality," *Journal of Southern History* 61 (1975): 39–58 *passim,* contended that Lincoln was a deeply committed colonizationist to his death. The psychological complexity and political sophistication of Lincoln's stance escaped Fredrickson. His *The Black Image in the White Mind, The Debate on Afro-American Character and Destiny, 1817–1914* (New York, 1971), provides an able analysis of its subject. However, Fredrickson's view that Lincoln's few references to climate, pp. 150–51 (which some claimed would force blacks to migrate southward), was central to his argument for colonization, misses the larger context of his thought, which denied the efficacy of natural limits of any sort. William W. Freehling in a provocative chapter in *The Reinterpretation of American History: Slavery and the Civil War* (New York, 1994), argued that colonization was "one reason the secessionist South considered president-elect Lincoln an immediate menace to slavery," p. 155, because it pointed to the loss of the institution in the border states and therefore the loss of the "Southern" loyalty of that region. The most insightful brief comments on the subject are Don E. Fehrenbacher, "Only His Stepchildren: Lincoln and the Negro," *Civil War History* 20 (1974): 307–308.

Benjamin Butler's recollections about how in 1865 he instructed Lincoln about the impossibility of colonization has misled many scholars. Butler, *Autobiography and Personal Reminiscences of Major-General Benjamin F. Butler: Butler's Book* (Boston, 1892), 903–905, 578. See Mark E. Neely, Jr., "Abraham Lincoln and Black Colonization: Benjamin Butler's Spurious Testimony," *Civil War History* 25 (1979): 77–83.

A substantial literature deals with the subject of colonization. P. J. Staudenraus, *The African Colonization Movement, 1816–1865* (New York, 1961) remains the best study of the American Colonization Society and also considers opposition to colonization. Henry Mayer, *All on Fire: William Lloyd Garrison and the Abolition of Slavery* (New York, 1998), looks at the most influential opponent of colonization. The best study of the outlook of free blacks, including their reaction to colonization, is James Oliver Horton and Louise E. Horton, *In Hope of Liberty: Culture, Community, and Protest among Northern Free Blacks, 1700–1860* (New York, 1997). David W. Blight, *Frederick Douglass' Civil War: Keeping Faith in Jubilee* (Baton Rouge, 1989), covers well the Civil War period. Edwin S. Redkey, *Black Exodus: Black Nationalist and Back-to-Africa Movements, 1890–1910* (New Haven, Conn., 1969), considers the persistence of colonization as an ideology among both black and white Americans after emancipation.

See also Victor Ullman, *Martin R. Delany: The Beginnings of Black Nationalism* (Boston, 1971); Sheldon H. Harris, *Paul Cuffee: Black America and the African Return* (New York, 1972); Floyd John Miller, *The Search for a Black Nationality: Black Emigration and Colonization, 1787–1863* (Urbana, 1975); Cyril E. Griffith, *The African Dream: Martin R. Delany and the Emergence of Pan-African Thought* (University Park, Penn., 1975); Wilson J. Moses, *Golden Age of Black Nationalism 1850–1925* (Hamden, Conn., 1978); David M. Dean, *Defender of the Race: James Theodore Holly, Black Nationalist and Bishop* (Boston, 1979); Sylvia M. Jacobs, ed., *Black Americans and the Missionary Movement in Africa* (Westport, Conn., 1982); Kwando Mbiassi Kinshasa, *Emigration vs. Assimilation: The Debate in the African American Press, 1827–1861* (Jefferson, N.C., 1988); Nell Irvin Painter, "Martin R. Delany: Elitism and Black Nationalism," in Leone Litwack and August Meier, eds., *Black Leaders of the Nineteenth Century* (Urbana, 1988); Wilson J. Moses, *Alexander Crummell: A Study of Civilization and Discontent* (New York, 1989); Paul Gilroy, *The Black Atlantic: Modernity and Double Consciousness* (Cambridge, Mass., 1993); Sidney J. Lemelle and Robin D. G. Kelley, *Imagining Home: Class, Culture, and Nationalism in the African Diaspora* (New York, 1994); George M. Fredrickson, *Black Liberation: A Comparative History of Black Ideologies in the United States and South Africa* (New York, 1995); Robert E. Desrochers, Jr., "'Not Fade Away': The Narrative of Venture Smith, an African American in the Early Republic," *Journal of American History* 84 (1997): 40–66; W. Jeffrey Bolster, *Black Jacks: African American Seaman in the Age of Sail* (Cambridge, 1997). Some of the above books illustrate the scholarly community's desire to give black aspirations and the African diaspora respectful consideration and so go beyond looking at colonization as a racist plot or as an alternative to abolition, e.g., David M. Steifford, "The American Colonization Society: An Application of Republican Ideology to Early Antebellum Reform," *Journal of Southern History* 45 (May 1979): 201–20. A substantial literature of primary documents also exists in print.

The reaction of the black community toward Lincoln's colonization propaganda deserves detailed study. In addition to work mentioned above, see James M. McPherson's pioneering *The Negro's Civil War, How American Negroes Felt and Acted During the War for the Union* (New York, 1965), 77–97, and "Abolitionist and Negro Opposition to Colonization During the Civil War," *Phylon* 26 (1965): 391–99. It should be noted that Samuel C. Pomeroy wrote to Lincoln on April 16, 1863, that 14,000 people applied to him for emigration (Papers of the Chiriqui Improvement Company, Illinois State Historical Library). Vorenberg, "Lincoln and Colonization," 42, characterizes this letter as bitter, "demanding to know whether he [Lincoln] ever intended to honor his promise of colonizing blacks."

Lincoln and Emancipation is also ripe for fresh work. But see John Hope Franklin, *The Emancipation Proclamation* (New York, 1963); Ira Berlin, Thavoila Glymph, Steven F. Miller, Joseph P. Reidy, Leslie S. Rowland, and Julie Saville, eds., *Freedom: A Documentary History of Emancipation, 1861–1867* (4 vols. to date; 1982—); Eric Foner, *Nothing but Freedom: Emancipation and Its Legacy* (Baton Rouge, 1983); and LaWanda Cox, *Lincoln and Black Freedom: A Study in Presidential Leadership* (Columbia, S. C., 1981), which remains a classic. Recent work that emphasizes, primarily from the perspectives of social history, black contributions to the ending of slavery, is surveyed by Peter Kolchin, "Slavery and Freedom in the Civil War South," in James M. McPherson and William J. Cooper, eds., *Writing the Civil War: The Quest to Understand* (Columbia, 1998), 145–50. This essay also considers the debate over the relative roles of African Americans and Lincoln on the road to Emancipation. The clearest statement of opposing views are McPherson, "Who Freed the Slaves?" in *Drawn with the Sword: Reflections on the American Civil War* (New York, 1996), 192–207, and Berlin's above cited essay with the identical title of "Who Freed the Slaves?"

Two works that should not be forgotten are V. Jacque Voegeli, *Free But Not Equal, The Midwest and the Negro During the Civil War* (Chicago, 1967) and Eugene H. Berwanger, *The Frontier Against Slavery: Western Anti-Negro Prejudice and the Slavery Extension Controversy* (Urbana, 1967).

The subject of Lincoln and race is touched upon in many of the above works. For a review of literature, see Arthur Zilversmit, "Lincoln and the Problem of Race: A Decade of Interpretations," *Papers of the Abraham Lincoln Association* 2 (1980): 22–25. See also David Lightner, "Abraham Lincoln and the Ideal of Equality," *Journal of the Illinois State Historical Society* 75 (Winter 1982): 289–308; Stephen B. Oates, *Abraham Lincoln: The Man Behind the Myth* (New York, 1984), 21–30; Richard E. Hart, "Springfield's African Americans as a Part of Lincoln's Community," *Journal of the Abraham Lincoln Association* 20 (Winter 1999): 35–54; and Hans L. Trefousse, "Lincoln and Race Relations," in Charles M. Hubbard, ed., *Lincoln and His Contemporaries* (Macon, Ga., 1999), 87–99.

For documentary collections, see Trefousse, *Lincoln's Decision for Emancipation* (Philadelphia, 1975); Arthur Zilversmit, *Lincoln on Black and White* (Malabar, Fla., 1983); Brooks Simpson, *Think Anew, Act Anew: Abraham Lincoln on Slavery, Freedom, and Union* (Wheeling, Ill., 1998); Michael Johnson, *Abraham Lincoln, Slavery, and the Civil War: Selected Writings and Speeches* (New York, 2000).

Some new light might be shed on Lincoln's feelings about race when Thomas P. Lowry and Beverly Lowry complete their examination of Lincoln's pardons. There might be a slight suggestion that in cases of rape, the president was harsher on blacks than on other people. Lincoln's pardons for the Sioux after the 1862 Minnesota uprising might be looked at in this context as well. Conversely, further examination is needed for his 1864 meeting with Frederick Douglass at a time when it appeared that the president would not be relected. Deeply worried about blacks remaining in slavery in a victorious Confederacy, Lincoln appeared to advocate greater slave resistance and their escape to the North.

Though white racists tend to hate Lincoln, some, from the early twentieth century to the present, have claimed him as the champion of white supremacy who wished to deport blacks from the United States. Thomas Dixon's novel *The Clansman* (New York, 1905), which grew into D.W. Griffith's film *The Birth of a Nation*, epitomized this orientation. Ironically, a like view, though never entirely absent from the black community, came to be increasingly adopted from the 1960s forward as part of the Civil Rights movement. Words of love that, for example, as Ralph Ellison wrote, seemed to be written less and less. In his posthumously published *Juneteenth* (New York, 1999), a black jazzman turned preacher thinks dreamily before the Lincoln Memorial:

> *Now I understand: That look, that's us! It's not in the features but in what that look, those eyes, have to say about what it means to be a man who tries to live and struggle against all the troubles of the world with but the naked heart and mind, and who finds them more necessary than all the power of wealth of great armies. Yes, that look and what put it there made him one of us. It wasn't in . . . his skin-tone that they tried to ease him into, but in that look in his eyes and his struggle against the things which put it there and saddened his features. It's in that, in being the kind of man he made himself to be that he's one of us.*
> *. . . "Ain't that him, Revern? Ain't that Father Abraham?" . . .*
> And too full to speak, he smiled; and in silent confirmation he was nodding his head, thinking. *Yes, with all I know about him and his contradictions, yes. And with all I know about men and the world, yes. And with all I know about white men and politicians of all colors and guises, yes. And with all I know about the things you had to do to be yourself—yes!*

Long before Ellison's book at last saw light, the pictures of Lincoln that used to be in black homes, that spoke of kinship and the promise of freedom, started to come down. As Negro History Week became Black History Month, it was forgotten that Carter Woodson, who started it all, timed it to tie black history to the birthdays of both Lincoln and Frederick Douglass.

The clearest expression of a hostile African-American view came from Lerone Bennett, Jr.: "Was Abe Lincoln a White Supremacist?" *Ebony* (Feb. 1968): 35–42. The article declared that Lincoln "is not the light . . . he is in fact standing in the light, hiding our way." Thirty-two years later Bennett enlarged his quest into a 650-page sensationalist magnum opus: *Forced Into Glory: Abraham Lincoln's White Dream* (Chicago, 2000). The book argued that racism was "the center and circumference" of Lincoln's "being," and that he was "one of the major supporters of slavery in the United States, a champion of 'ethnic cleansing.'" The Great Emancipator transformed into the Racist-in-Chief. Of course black resentment of white expectations of gratitude for an emanci-pation that a century and more later still did not bring full equality is understandable. Some may also find it heartening to see African Americans standing confidently, inde-pendent of the white Emancipator images. But as history, *Forced Into Glory* brings to mind Lincoln's comment about "a specious and fantastic arrangement of words, by which a man can prove a horse chestnut to be a chestnut horse." Basler, et al., eds., *Collected Works of Lincoln*, 3:16.

If Bennett distorts history, he also partakes of larger trends in American culture. For a penetrating look at the changing picture of Lincoln, see Merrill D. Peterson, *Lincoln in American Memory* (New York, 1994). Black disengagement from Lincoln was part of the drive for autonomy, a desire to stand on one's own feet. And it defined those feet in terms of color, just as much the United States did. One might see more here, an African-American effort to point to a less than democratic past and to act as the con-science of the nation. In any event, black disengagement paralleled the country's disen-chantment, indeed that of no small part of the world, with "great men." After all, many of the twentieth century's most influential leaders turned out to be monsters like Lenin, Stalin, Mao, Hitler, and lesser men of that ilk. Though few tried to picture Lincoln in those terms, the monsters also took their toll on the reputations of decent leaders. American democracy grew both more sophisticated and more jaded. Lincoln pictures came down from white homes, too.

Of course Lincoln is a symbol as well. So long as Americans were in a nation-build-ing stage, they could hardly find a better one than "the Savior of the Union." In a time of growing indifference to the nation state, such heros are needed less. Multiculturalism in some senses stands opposed to the notion of an inclusive American identity that Lin-coln espoused. Unity rather than diversity was his goal. What he did with Emancipa-tion, in the broadest sense of the term, is what he believed the Declaration of Indepen-dence did: "declare the *right* so that the *enforcement* of it might follow as fast as circumstances should permit . . . augmenting the happiness and value of life to all peo-ple of all colors everywhere." (Basler, et al., eds., *Collected Works of Lincoln*, 2:406). But perhaps for now America's common dreams are fading, leaving less room for the common hero. In any case, postmodern culture has modest use for history, especially for an understanding of the past via ideas.

The drive for racial equality also led toward a fight for gender equality, perhaps the most important social movement of recent decades, one that hoped to escape from the shadow of patriarchs and, at its extreme, derided dead white males. Social history grew important and made major contributions to our understanding of the past. History from the bottom up. Inhospitable to "kings and queens and great men," it tended to minimize the significance of particular events and individuals, seeing the story of hu-manity in terms of long-range processes and dominant structures. "Have Social Histori-ans Lost the Civil War?" asked Maris A. Vinovskis with a memorable *double-entendre* in *The Journal of American History* 76 (June 1989): 34–58. He answered yes. Social historians lost Lincoln, too. Yet, surely, they are starting to find him.

And here we have *The Lincoln Enigma*. At its heart is the belief that a giant in the earth, or a crucial moment, weighs more in the scales of history than lifeless ages. The Civil War produced such a giant and such moment. Within it, Lincoln's history and that of African Americans are forever intertwined. In 1962 Quarles confidently asserted that

"Lincoln became Lincoln," because of black people (Preface of *Lincoln and the Negro*). At the dawn of the millennium, Lincoln still remains important for Americans, including African Americans. If early in the twentieth century W. E. B. Du Bois could be critical of Lincoln but concluded that "I love him not because he was perfect but because he was not and yet triumphed," ["Again Lincoln," *The Crisis* 24 (Sept. 1922): 200], at the end of the century the hostile Bennett had to add that he studied Lincoln "to save my life" (Preface of *Forced Into Glory*).

The history of the black response to Lincoln deserves further careful study. In addition to works noted above, see John David Smith, "Black Images of Lincoln in the Age of Jim Crow, *A Lincoln Lore* 1681 (March 1978); Edna Greene Medford, "'Something More Than the Mere Union to Fight For: African Americans Respond to Lincoln's Wartime Policies," in Hubbard, ed., *Lincoln and His Contemporaries*, 101–20; Medford, "'Beckoning Them to the Dreamed of Promise of Freedom': African-Americans and Lincoln's Proclamation of Emancipation," in John Y. Simon, Harold Holzer, and William D. Pederson, eds., *The Lincoln Forum: Abraham Lincoln, Gettysburg and the Civil War* (Mason City, Iowa, 1999), 47–63. For a sociologist's look at memory, see Barry Schwartz, "Collective Memory and History: How Abraham Lincoln Became a Symbol of Racial Equality," *The Sociological Quarterly* 38 (Summer 1997): 469–96, and his forthcoming *Abraham Lincoln and the Forge of National Memory* (Chicago, 2000). See also William H. Wiggins, *O Freedom! African-American Emancipation Celebrations* (Knoxville, 1987). Over the years among the black voices of love, strong voices of skepticism and dissent have existed and deserve to be heard further. But Benjamin Quarles's conclusion, that Lincoln first rose to be the great American hero among African Americans, will stand.

The scene in Richmond, April 1865, described by Thomas Morris Chester, might be recalled again. "As if upon the wings of lightning" the news spread that Lincoln "had come." Black people, "feeling themselves free to act like men," thronged to greet him. They went "wild with enthusiasm. Old men thanked God in a very boisterous manner, and old women shouted upon the pavement as high as they had ever done at a religious revival." When Lincoln "bowed his thanks for the prolonged exultation" the people's voices seemed to reach for heaven. R. J. M. Blackett, ed., *Thomas Morris Chester, Black Civil War Correspondent: His Dispatches from Virginia* (Baton Rouge, 1989), 294–95. And it might be argued, as another reporter did, describing Lincoln's bow to one old black man who had bowed to him, "but it was a bow which upset forms, laws, customs, and ceremonies of centuries." "Lincoln in Richmond," *The Atlantic Monthly* 15 (June 1865): 754–55.

## Two: Young Man Lincoln

For a subject that is prominently featured in one of the best known and best loved American legends, the substantive literature focusing on Lincoln's young manhood is surprisingly modest. There has been, of course, an almost unending avalanche of literature whose aim is mainly inspirational, but this body of material has little to offer in the way of historical accuracy or depth of insight. The story of Abraham Lincoln's rise to greatness from poverty and obscurity is so well known as to be part of our national identity, but it is known only in outline. The details of that rise and their range of meanings in human terms are just beginning to be worked out.

The first book on the subject, William M. Thayer's *The Pioneer Boy and How He Be-came President* (Boston, 1863), is a fictionalized genre piece, yet it still commands attention because Thayer's material came directly from people who had known the president, the names of whom were supplied by Lincoln himself. Ward Hill Lamon's *The Life of Abraham Lincoln* (Boston, 1872) and William H. Herndon and Jesse W. Weik's *Herndon's Lincoln: The True Story of a Great Life* (New York, 1889) both draw on letters and interviews gathered by Herndon from people who knew Lincoln in his early years. Herndon's own depiction is especially important, for he was a friend and an observer of Lincoln's development from 1837 on. The letters and interviews he gathered from others are used selectively and with altered texts in his biography, but they are presented accurately and in their entirety in Douglas L. Wilson and Rodney O. Davis, eds., *Herndon's Informants: Letters, Interviews, and Statements about Abraham Lincoln* (Urbana, 1998).

There are two excellent studies of Lincoln's relationship to his father: John Y. Simon, "House Divided: Lincoln and His Father," The Tenth Annual R. Gerald Mc-Murtry Lecture (Fort Wayne, 1987) and Rodney O. Davis, "Abraham Lincoln: Son and Father," The Edgar S. and Ruth W. Burkardt Lecture Series (Galesburg, Ill., 1997). Lincoln's young manhood began in Indiana, where he lived from age 7 to age 21, and this period of his development is most in need of study. Still useful for basic information in this period are three older works: J. T. Hobson, *Footprints of Abraham Lincoln* (Dayton, 1909); J. Edward Murr, "Lincoln in Indiana," *Indiana Magazine of History* 13:4 (1917), 14:1 & 2 (1918); and Bess V. Ehrmann, *The Missing Chapter in the Life of Abraham Lincoln* (Chicago, 1938).

A book that can be recommended for its sources but not its text is Francis Van Natter, *Lincoln's Boyhood: A Chronicle of his Indiana Years* (Washington, 1963). The most comprehensive coverage of these important years thus far is Louis A. Warren's *Lincoln's Youth: Indiana Years* (New York, 1959), though Warren's treatment of the young Lincoln's development is not searching, and it leaves some promising sources and avenues unexplored.

For Lincoln's early Illinois years in New Salem, Thomas P. Reep's compilation of portraits and traditional stories, *Lincoln at New Salem* (n.p.: The Old Salem League, 1927), is an important source. Inspiring less confidence but more colorful are the recollections of Lincoln and his New Salem neighbors in T. G. Onstot, *Pioneers of Menard and Mason Counties* (Forest City, Ill., 1902). Benjamin Thomas's *Lincoln's New Salem* (Chicago, 1954 [1934]) is an authoritative treatment that, despite being somewhat dated, is still the best overview of the brief life of the village.

Ida M. Tarbell's little book, *The Early Life of Abraham Lincoln* (New York, 1896), based on her articles for *McClure's* magazine, was the first carefully researched book on this topic and is still evocative, not least because it is so well illustrated. The first volume of Albert J. Beveridge's *Abraham Lincoln: 1809–1858* (Boston, 1928) is by far the most detailed treatment of Lincoln's early life and continues to be useful. John Evangelist Walsh's *The Shadows Rise: Abraham Lincoln and the Ann Rutledge Legend* (Urbana, 1993) is the first full-length exploration of an important episode in Lincoln's early life that had long been labeled a myth.

A groundbreaking work on Lincoln's psychological development, which pays close attention to this period, is Charles B. Strozier's influential book, *Lincoln's Quest for Union: Public and Private Meanings* (New York, 1982). Michael Burlingame's *The*

*Inner World of Abraham Lincoln* (Urbana, 1994) is a provocative investigation of Lincoln's psychology and particularly his emotional life, and the documentation for his discussion of these topics is especially full and useful. David Herbert Donald's *Lincoln* (New York, 1995), is distinctive among major biographies for being a source of many insights on the young Lincoln's development.

"Young Man Lincoln" expands on ideas and information concerning Abraham Lincoln's formative years laid out in Douglas L. Wilson, *Honor's Voice: The Transformation of Abraham Lincoln* (New York, 1998). It attempts to show the difficulties Lincoln encountered—educational, vocational, and particularly emotional—that have heretofore been neglected in the accounts of his legendary rise. What Lincoln's poems on his Indiana childhood tell us about him is the subject of Douglas L. Wilson, "Abraham Lincoln and the 'Spirit of Mortal,'" in *Lincoln Before Washington: New Perspectives on the Illinois Years* (Urbana, 1997), and the same author's "The Literary Lincoln" (forthcoming). For a revealing treatment of the young William James's experience with madness, referred to in this essay, see Louis Menand, "William James & the Case of the Epileptic Patient," *New York Review of Books* 45:20 (Dec. 17, 1998), 81–93.

## Three: A Marriage

The Lincoln marriage has long fascinated scholars because it is an avenue toward understanding a president whom nobody knew very well, except his wife. Today's scholars are interested in the marriage for additional reasons: because it is a well-documented union between two middle-class Americans and because, while any president is exceptional, the marriage tells us about nineteenth-century rituals of courting, matrimony, sex, and child-raising. Thus, anyone who would understand the Lincolns' marriage must place it in the context of other American marriages of the time.

There are several useful studies of American marriage that do so. They include Ellen Rothman, *Hands and Hearts: A History of Courtship in America* (New York, 1984); Karen Lystra, *Searching the Heart: Women, Men and Romantic Love in 19th Century America* (New York, 1989); and E. Antonio Rotundo, *American Manhood: Transformations in Masculinity from the Revolution to the Modern Era* (New York, 1993).

Also evocative on the changing sex roles resulting from the impact of economic and social change in the 1840s and 1850s is Ronald Byars, *The Making of the Self-Made Man: The Development of Masculine Roles and Images in Ante-Bellum America* (Ann Arbor, 1979). Michael Grossberg's *Governing the Hearth: Law and the Family in 19th Century America* (Chapel Hill, 1985) places the change to smaller companionate families within the context of American family law.

Along with these studies of American marriage, Andrew Cherlin's *Public and Private Families* (New York, 1999), is indispensable for an understanding of the changes in American marriage. Stephanie Coontz has written a comprehensive study of the family in *The Social Origins of Private Life: A History of American Families* (London, 1988). And no serious student of the new concept of marriage based on "love" should overlook Peter Gay's *The Tender Passion* (New York, 1986), which is part of his larger study of the bourgeois experience in the nineteenth century.

For the specifics of the Lincoln marriage, the president's law partner William Herndon stamped the interpretation of the marriage with, first, an address he gave in 1866 shortly after Lincoln's assassination in which he claimed that Ann Rutledge was Lincoln's only love, and then in his biography of Lincoln. See William Herndon and Jesse Weik, *Herndon's Lincoln: The True Story of a Great Life* (Chicago, 1890). Later scholars have relied on this interpretation for most of their assessments of the relationship. The contemporary counterpoint of Herndon is a brief biography of Mary Lincoln written by her niece Katherine Helm, who relied on the memories of her mother Emilie Todd Helm in a charming anecdotal recollection entitled *The True Story of Mary, Wife of Lincoln* (New York, 1928). Another sympathetic account of the marriage appears in Ruth Randall's *Mary Lincoln: Biography of a Marriage* (Boston, 1953).

In recent years other sympathetic accounts of Mary Lincoln have encouraged a revision of the older interpretations. In 1987, Jean Baker published a biography of Mary Lincoln that tried to move beyond the story of Mrs. Lincoln and present a positive assessment of the marriage and the contribution of Mary Lincoln to her husband's life and career. See Jean H. Baker, *Mary Todd Lincoln: A Biography* (New York, 1987). But in the historiography of a relationship whose evaluation seems to depend on the gender of the historian, see recent negative assessments of the Lincoln marriage that focus on Mary Lincoln as its villain: Michael Burlingame, *The Inner World of Abraham Lincoln* (Urbana, 1994) and Douglas Wilson, *Honor's Voice: The Transformation of Abraham Lincoln* (New York, 1998).

Hearsay about Lincoln's private life continues unabated. Wilson's "Keeping Lincoln's Secret," *Atlantic Monthly* (May 2000): 78–80, discusses some of the "secret and private things" in Caroline Dall's letters about evidence she had read in Herndon's records of Lincoln's private life. They involved, according to the shocked Dall, his "profligacy and debauchery" before and after his marriage. There was also material on Mary Lincoln's supposed infidelity. But as Wilson's sensitive piece shows, this thirdhand testimony has disappeared. Did it ever exist? And who were the authors? There is no outside corroboration. What is available is Dall's thirdhand report on Herndon's secondhand reports. Wilson concludes that the compromising stories that Herndon apparently collected did nothing to change his view of Lincoln, and "it seems unlikely that they (will) do much to change ours." At this stage, they do not change my view of the Lincoln marriage.

## Four: Military Fantasies

No battle in American history has been subjected to as much scrutiny as Gettysburg. Scholars have labored mightily to produce long and detailed microhistories devoted to portions of the battle: a 601-page volume describing the events on the second day, for example, followed by another 507-page book on the Union right flank (Harry W. Pfanz, *Gettysburg: The Second Day* in 1987 and *Gettysburg: Culp's Hill and Cemetery Hill* in 1994, both University of North Carolina Press). The history of Pickett's Charge is such a growth industry that there is now a history of its history (Carol Reardon, *Pickett's Charge in History and Memory*, Chapel Hill, 1997). The battle of Gettysburg even has its own magazine.

Among the many controversies that arose during and after the battle, Meade's pursuit of Lee has come in for more than its share, and then some, of this ocean of ink. The reader who wishes to explore this issue in more detail could not do better than to start with Edwin B. Coddington, *The Gettysburg Campaign: A Study in Command* (New York, 1968), which remains the standard military history of the campaign as a whole.

Among the works specifically devoted to the pursuit are Gabor S. Boritt, "'Unfinished Work': Lincoln, Meade, and Gettysburg," in Gabor S. Boritt, ed., *Lincoln's Generals* (New York, 1994), which takes the side of Meade's critics; and Frank Williams, "'We had only to stretch forth our hands': Abraham Lincoln and George Gordon Meade," *North & South* 2 (1999), 81–120, which claims that Lincoln was duped by Halleck and others into underestimating the obstacles that led Meade not to attack Lee after July 3. Gary Gallagher, ed., *The Third Day at Gettysburg and Beyond* (Chapel Hill, 1994), contains essays that examine other aspects of the aftermath of the fighting.

For the motivation behind Lincoln's interest in taking an active part in the war, Douglas Wilson, *Honor's Voice: The Transformation of Abraham Lincoln* (New York, 1998), is a sensitive interpretation of the role of honor as one of the mainsprings of Lincoln's character. Bertram Wyatt-Brown discusses the importance of honor and the duel in the culture of the 1830s in "Andrew Jackson's Honor," *Journal of the Early American Republic* 17 (1997), 1–36. Mark E. Neely, Jr., "Wilderness and the Cult of Manliness: Hooker, Lincoln, and Defeat," in Gabor S. Boritt, ed., *Lincoln's Generals* (New York, 1994), connects the concept of courage, as part of the expected behavior of mid-nineteenth century males, to Lincoln's behavior as commander in chief. Neely perceptively quotes Lincoln's April 28, 1864 comment, recorded by John Hay, "Often I who am not a specially brave man have had to sustain the sinking courage of these professional fighters in critical times." Less persuasive is Neely's argument that Lincoln's interest in presenting a courageous front was the unlikely result of a "freak accident" (the 1861 Scotch cap incident) rather than a lifelong concern. For the tactical problem of defeating entrenched troops, which Lincoln would have faced had he taken the field, see Grady McWhiney and Perry D. Jamieson, *Attack and Die: Civil War Military Tactics and the Southern Heritage* (University, Ala., 1982, and Edward Hagerman, *The American Civil War and the Origins of Modern Warfare: Ideas, Organization, and Field Command* (Bloomington, 1988).

How successful Lincoln was as a military leader has been a matter of debate since 1861. G. F. R. Henderson, *Life of Stonewall Jackson*, 2 vols. (London, 1898), expresses the views of early critics of Lincoln's military record. Favorable revision of that record began with Arthur L. Conger, "President Lincoln as War Statesman," *Wisconsin Historical Society Proceedings* (1917), 106–40; followed by Colin R. Ballard, *The Military Genius of Abraham Lincoln* (London, 1926); and Sir Frederick Maurice, *Statesmen and Soldiers of the Civil War: A Study of the Conduct of War* (Boston, 1926). T. Harry Williams, *Lincoln and His Generals* (New York, 1952), takes the "Lincoln as military genius" argument to its height, in both style and content. Merrill D. Peterson, *Lincoln in American Memory* (New York, 1994), discusses the historiography of Lincoln's military reputation. Richard N. Current, "The Military Genius," chapter 6 in *The Lincoln Nobody Knows* (New York, 1958), summarizes the points made by both sides and accurately observes: "Since the points at issue are matters of judgment rather than of fact, it [the debate] will probably go on forever."

### Five: Abraham Lincoln and Jefferson Davis as Commanders in Chief

The best source for the literature on this subject is Mark E. Neely, Jr., "Abraham Lincoln vs. Jefferson Davis: Comparing Presidential Leadership in the Civil War" in James M. McPherson and William J. Cooper, eds., *Writing the Civil War: The Quest to Un-*

*derstand* (Columbia, S.C., 1998), 96–111. Neely notes "the gross imbalance between the amounts of scholarship on the two figures" (p. 97). Since the Lincoln literature is covered in the bibliographical notes of the other chapters, here only work on Davis or work that compares the two presidents needs to be noted.

The definitive collection of Davis's writing is a work in progress and has reached the middle of the presidential years: Lynda Lasswell Crist, ed., *The Papers of Jefferson Davis* (10 vols, Baton Rouge, 1999). Until this set is complete, earlier collections that cover the entire span of Davis's life remain useful: Dunbar Rowland, ed., *Jefferson Davis, Constitutionalist, His Letters, Papers, Speeches* (10 vols, Jackson, MS, 1923). Davis tells his own version of history in *The Rise and Fall of the Confederate Government* (2 vols, New York, 1881). See also Varina H. Davis, *Jefferson Davis: Ex-President of the Confederate States of America: A Memoir By His Wife* (2 vols, New York, 1890).

*Jefferson Davis, American* (New York, 2000) by William J. Cooper, Jr., is the definitive biography, which replaces the severely dated earlier studies. There are, however, valuable insights in Frank E. Vandiver's Harmsworth Inaugural Lecture, *Jefferson Davis and the Confederate State* (1964), in Clement Eaton, *Jefferson Davis* (New York, 1977), and William C. Davis, *Jefferson Davis: The Man and His Hour* (New York, 1991), all of which emphasize the Confederate leader's growth and see him as a modernizer. A contrasting view can be found in Paul D. Escott, *After Secession: Jefferson Davis and the Failure of Confederate Nationalism* (Baton Rouge, 1978). Important work that sheds light on Davis includes George C. Rable, *The Confederate Republic: A Revolution Against Politics* (Chapel Hill, 1994) and Mark E. Neely, Jr., *Southern Rights* (Charlottesville, 1999).

The temptation to compare the presidents of the USA and CSA has been overpowering, if not always enlightening, and has attracted some notable scholars. Ignoring partisan ventures, the following works might be noted in chronological order:

Russell Hoover Quynn, *The Constitutions of Abraham Lincoln and Jefferson Davis, A Historical and Biographical Study in Contrasts* (New York, 1959); Irving Werstein, *Abraham Lincoln versus Jefferson Davis* (New York, 1959); David Potter, "Jefferson Davis and the Political Factors in Confederate Defeat," in David Donald, ed., *Why The North Won the Civil War* (Baton Rouge, 1960); David Lindsey, *A. Lincoln/Jefferson Davis: The House Divided* (Cleveland, 1960); William and Bruce Catton, *Two Roads to Sumter* (New York, 1963); Edward M. Coffman, *Lincoln and Davis, A Question of Education* (Wisconsin, 1968); T. Harry Williams, *Two War Leaders: Lincoln and Davis* (Springfield, 1972); Holman Hamilton, *The Three Kentucky Presidents* (Lexington, KY, 1978); Ludwell H. Johnson, "Jefferson Davis and Abraham Lincoln: Nothing Succeeds Like Success," *Civil War History*, 27 (March 1981), 49–63; James Jansinski, "Oaths Registered in Heaven: Rhetorical and Historical Legitimacy in the Inaugural Addresses of Jefferson Davis and Abraham Lincoln" in Kathleen J. Turner, ed., *Doing Rhetorical History: Concepts and Cases* (Tuscaloosa, AL, 1998); Bruce Chadwick, *The Two American Presidents: A Dual Biography of Abraham Lincoln and Jefferson Davis* (Secaucus, 1999).

For a comparison of the visual images of the two presidents see Harold Holzer, "The Mirror Images of Civil War Memory: Abraham Lincoln and Jefferson Davis in Popular Prints" in *Lincoln Seen and Heard* (Lawrence, 2000), 73–102.

## Six: The Constitution and Liberty

The earliest writing on Lincoln and the Constitution, by Sydney George Fisher, William A. Dunning, and James Ford Rhodes a century ago, focused on specific constitutional problems during the Lincoln administration, such as the suspension of the writ of habeas corpus. It made no effort to review Lincoln's thinking on the Constitution as a whole. The largest generalization made about Lincoln and the Constitution, introduced during the war by opposition Democrats and given academic respectability by Lincoln biographer James Garfield Randall in *Constitutional Problems Under Lincoln* (1926; rept. Urbana, 1951), was that Lincoln had used the military powers that came to him as commander in chief during the war to make himself into a "dictator." This had became so much a matter of unexamined consensus by the time Randall wrote that the only question seemed to be whether his assumption of dictatorial powers was good or bad. And this has been reflected, without much reexamination, in books as different as Edmund Wilson's *Patriotic Gore: Studies in the Literature of the American Civil War* (New York, 1962) and Dwight Anderson's psychobiography, *Abraham Lincoln: The Quest for Immortality* (New York, 1982).

Those of a neo-Confederate bent, such as political scientists Willmore Kendall and George Carey in *The Basic Symbols of the American Political Tradition* (Baton Rouge, 1970) and American literature specialist Melvin E. Bradford in "Against Lincoln: An Address at Gettysburg" in Gabor Boritt's *The Historian's Lincoln: Pseudohistory, Psychohistory, and History* (Urbana, 1988) also delight in denouncing Lincoln as a "dictator." In the cases of Kendall and Bradford, however, the "dictatorship" charge receives a slightly different spin: not that Lincoln turned dictator to undermine the Constitution, but that he undermined the Constitution for the purpose of exalting a radical and untrammeled egalitarianism. Oddly, this egalitarian subversion, which conservatives like Kendall and Bradford condemned, was precisely what liberals concluded was worthy of praise. Garry Wills's *Lincoln at Gettysburg: The Words That Remade America* (New York, 1991), echoing Thurgood Marshall's dictum that "the Union survived the Civil War, the Constitution did not," cast Lincoln as a clever subverter of the Constitution who used the Gettysburg Address to install the Declaration of Independence as the principal document of American politics. Like the "dictatorship" question, the only difference seemed to be whether Lincoln's egalitarian subversion was right or wrong.

And yet there was something suspiciously ahistorical in the kind of grand, sweeping, almost conspiratorial results Wills, Kendall, and Bradford imputed to Lincoln—a man who had never actually written any sustained treatise on constitutional law and never articulated any great theory about his wartime powers, apart from insisting that he had them. Far from inaugurating any new era in the history of the Constitution, most of Lincoln's own declarations on the Constitution stressed his continuity with the founders. Harry Jaffa gave this classical form when, in *The Crisis of the House Divided* (New York, 1959), he used Lincoln's "apple of gold" analogy to underscore that Lincoln saw the Constitution and the Declaration—the procedural document about liberty and the moral document about equality—as complimentary rather than contradictory. For Lincoln (as Jaffa explained), the Constitution was the *formal* cause of American nationhood, while the Declaration was its *final* cause.

This argument has been echoed by a number of commentators who have tried to see Lincoln's presidential actions in the long view of his comments on the Constitution from the 1830s onward, and of the Constitution itself. In a series of forceful essays, gathered together in *Abraham Lincoln, Constitutionalism, and Equal Rights in the Civil War Era* (New York, 1998), Herman Belz insisted that Lincoln was "closer in outlook to the fixed constitutionalism of the Founding Fathers than to the pragmatic liberalism of the twentieth century." Mark Neely, in his chapter "Lincoln and the Constitution" in *The Fate of Liberty: Abraham Lincoln and Civil Liberties* (New York, 1991) insisted almost to extremes that Lincoln had too little interest in ideology to become what Belz called "a revolutionary constitutional innovator," and sharply diminished the apparent novelty of Lincoln's extra-constitutional actions as president. Similarly, Don E. Fehrenbacher insisted that even if Lincoln's presidency explored some new constitutional territory in terms of presidential powers, most of that exploration was unintentional. "The Civil War may have had revolutionary effects," Fehrenbacher remarked in "Lincoln and the Constitution" in *Lincoln in Text and Context: Collected Essays* (Stanford, 1987), "but it was begun and prosecuted for conservative purposes." Among historians at least, the old wisdom on Lincoln as a "dictator" seems to have died out. "Lincoln was never a military dictator even by mid-nineteenth-century standards, much less by those of the mid-twentieth century," observed Harold Hyman in the most comprehensive survey of the Civil War's impact on the constitution and law, *A More Perfect Union: The Impact of the Civil War and Reconstruction on the Constitution* (New York, 1973). And Philip Paludan, in what now must stand as the best political history of the Lincoln administration, *The Presidency of Abraham Lincoln* (Lawrence, 1994), argues that Lincoln's egalitarianism, based as it was on economic opportunism, was integrally linked to "the proper operation of existing institutions," and especially the Constitution.

From being the tyrannical demon of Copperhead imaginations that he was during the war, and then the democratic dictator of Wilsonian equality that he was for Randall and the generation of the Progressives, Lincoln has now emerged as a tempered conservative who struggled to save the Constitution and equality in an upside-down emergency that threatened them both. As George Anastaplo asks in his recent essay collection, *Abraham Lincoln: A Constitutional Biography* (Lanham, 1999), "Has not Lincoln been, among American politicians, *the* Constitutionalist?"

## Seven: Toward Appomattox

Any study of the Civil War, including its last months, should begin with James M. McPherson's superlative *Battle Cry of Freedom: The Civil War Era* (New York, 1988). Though somewhat dated, an extremely well-written account of the last year of the war is Allan Nevins's *War for the Union: The Organized War to Victory, 1864–1865* (New York, 1971). The best single-volume military history of the conflict, including the final campaigns, is Herman Hattaway and Archer Jones, *How the North Won: A Military History of the Civil War* (Urbana, 1983). No narrative of the last months of the war in Virginia surpasses Bruce Catton's *A Stillness at Appomattox* (New York, 1953). Noah Andre Trudeau, *Out of the Storm: The End of the Civil War, April-June 1865* (Boston, 1994), provides a fine chronological account of this eventful period.

The literature on Abraham Lincoln is vast. However, the classic multivolume work of James G. Randall on the Lincoln presidency and the events associated with it (completed by Richard N. Current in 1955), had the effect of discouraging historians from attempting studies of this great president's administration. See especially volume 4, *Lincoln the President: Last Full Measure* (New York, 1955). Since the 1980s, Civil War scholars have renewed their interest in the Lincoln presidency. The best general history of his wartime administration is Phillip S. Paludan, *The Presidency of Abraham Lincoln* (Lawrence, 1994). Don E. and Virginia Fehrenbacher have provided readers with a fascinating compilation of Lincoln sayings and stories as reported by contemporaries and brilliantly evaluated for their credibility by the authors. No one seeking insights into Lincoln's presidency should miss consulting this book (*Recollected Words of Abraham Lincoln* [Stanford, 1996]).

Recent biographies of Lincoln are a rich source of information on the final months of his presidency and the ending of the war. The best biography is David Donald's prize-winning *Lincoln* (New York, 1996), although Benjamin P. Thomas's *Abraham Lincoln: A Biography* (New York, 1952) still has appeal. Though not biographical, Mark E. Neely, Jr.'s, *The Fate of Liberty: Abraham Lincoln and Civil Liberties* (New York, 1991), a Pulitzer Prize winner, should be consulted for important constitutional issues during Lincoln's presidency.

Specific studies of politics and policies during the war are useful in understanding Lincoln's efforts on behalf of the peace. David E. Long, *The Jewel of Liberty: Abraham Lincoln's Re-election and the End of Slavery* (Mechanicsburg, Penn., 1994), is a fine account of the 1864 presidential election that foretold the success of Lincoln's objectives in the war and challenges the traditional view that the differences between Lincoln and McClellan were miniscule. Of course, the issue of reconstruction, with its corollary peace terms for the South, received increased attention after Lincoln's reelection. Herman Belz, *Reconstructing the Union: Theory and Policy During the Civil War* (Ithaca, 1969), provides a detailed account of the maneuvering, especially in Congress, over reconstruction policy. See also Brooks D. Simpson, *The Reconstruction Presidents* (Lawrence, 1998), for a fine overview of reconstruction policies at the highest level. Kenneth P. Stampp in *The Era of Reconstruction, 1865–1877* (New York, 1965), a popular synthesis of reconstruction history, found a narrow political purpose in Lincoln's generous terms for the defeated South. According to Stampp, Lincoln wanted to bring Southern Whigs into a national postwar conservative coalition with the Republican party.

Reflecting the intense interest in race relations and civil rights among late-twentieth century historians, LaWanda Cox and other scholars have sought to demonstrate that Lincoln by 1865 was moving toward a more radical reconstruction policy (see especially Cox, *Lincoln and Black Freedom: A Study in Presidential Leadership* [Columbia, S.C., 1981]). James M. McPherson, *Abraham Lincoln and the Second American Revolution* (New York, 1991), argues that Lincoln had come to insist on the unconditional surrender of the Confederacy followed by a revolutionary settlement for the South. Eric Foner develops a similar argument in his *Reconstruction: America's Unfinished Revolution, 1863–1877* (New York, 1988). He asserts that Lincoln's reelection, which reaffirmed his emancipation policy, guaranteed Union military success, and ensured a social revolution in the South, made inevitable the unconditional surrender of the Confederate forces. From the Confederate perspective, Charles W. Sanders, Jr., in "Jefferson Davis and the Hampton Roads Peace Conference: 'To secure peace to the two countries,'" *Journal of Southern History* 63 (November 1997): 803–26, also concludes that Lincoln's peace terms after the 1864 election required the unconditional surrender of the Confederate States.

William C. Harris's *With Charity for All: Lincoln and the Restoration of the Union* (Lexington, 1997) challenges the interpretation that Lincoln had changed his conciliatory policy toward the South. In his "The Hampton Roads Peace Conference: A Final Test of Lincoln's Presidential Leadership," *Journal of the Abraham Lincoln Association* 21 (Winter 2000): 31–62, Harris contends that Lincoln, despite Republican concern, two months before Appomattox still insisted only on the fundamental Union and emancipation objectives in the war. On the other hand, James A. Rawley in *Abraham Lincoln and A Nation Worth Fighting For* (Wheeling, Ill., 1996), while ignoring the unconditional surrender thesis, concludes that at the time of his death Lincoln intended on making major changes in his mild policy toward the South.

## Eight: The Riddle of Death

Abraham Lincoln's thoughts about God, death, and remembrance are fully recorded in his own writings and speeches, and in his spoken comments as recounted by those who heard them. That he lacked faith in an afterlife, however, must be surmised from his consistent silence on the subject whenever an affirmation might have been expected. But the cumulation of those significant silences makes the surmise persuasive.

Lincoln's public and private writings are definitively presented in the eight thick volumes and two shorter supplements of *The Collected Works of Abraham Lincoln* (New Brunswick, 1953, 1974, 1990), edited by Roy P. Basler et al. His spoken words, excerpted from a multitude of published recollections by contemporaries, have lately been compiled, evaluated, and published in *Recollected Words of Abraham Lincoln* (Stanford, 1996), edited by Don E. and Virginia Fehrenbacher. Compilations of testimony by those who knew Lincoln have recently been edited and published in Douglas L. Wilson and Rodney O. Davis, *Herndon's Informants: Letters, Interviews, and Statements About Abraham Lincoln* (Chicago, 1998) and Michael Burlingame, *An Oral History of Abraham Lincoln: John G. Nicolay's Interviews and Essays* (Carbondale, 1996).

There are many one-volume biographies of Lincoln, among the better ones being those by Benjamin P. Thomas and David H. Donald. Lincoln's formative years, important for this essay, are well covered in Louis A. Warren, *Lincoln's Youth: Indiana Years, Seven to Twenty-one, 1816–1830* (New York, 1959), and Albert J. Beveridge, *Abraham Lincoln, 1809–1858* (2 vols., Boston, 1928). Firsthand accounts of special pertinence to this essay are Noah Brooks, *Washington in Lincoln's Time* (New York, 1958); Francis B. Carpenter, *Six Months at the White House with Abraham Lincoln* (New York, 1866), and William H. Herndon and Jesse W. Weik, *Herndon's Lincoln: The True Story of a Great Life* (3 vols., Chicago, 1889). Michael Burlingame, *The Inner World of Abraham Lincoln* (Urbana, 1994), is a fresh, candid, and sometimes provocative study of Lincoln's character. Charles B. Strozier, *Lincoln's Quest for Union: Public and Private Meanings* (New York, 1982), analyzes psychological factors in Lincoln's life. Lincoln's religious views are examined in William J. Wolf, *The Almost Chosen People: A Study of the Religion of Abraham Lincoln* (Garden City, 1959), and Wayne C. Temple, *Abraham Lincoln From Skeptic to Prophet* (Mahomet, 1995).

The history of popular views of death, memorials, and afterlife is provided by Philippe Aries, *The Hour of Our Death* (New York, 1981); Colleen McDannell and Bernhard Lang, *Heaven: A History* (New Haven, 1988); Richard Morris, *Sinners, Lovers, and Heroes: An Essay on Memorializing in Three American Cultures* (Albany, 1997); Gary Landerman, *The Sacred Remains: American Attitudes Toward Death, 1799–1883* (New Haven, 1996); and Lewis O. Saum, *The Popular Mood of Pre–Civil War America* (Westport, 1980).

## Nine: Lincoln in "Modern" Art

The literature on the modern portraits of Abraham Lincoln—indeed, of the portraits of Lincoln in any age—remains scant.

Of the few titles, studies of Lincoln sculpture have been the most abundant. Donald Charles Durman, for example, contributed a pioneer attempt to catalogue the known Lincoln statuary through 1943 with the privately printed study *He Belongs to the Ages: The Statues of Abraham Lincoln* (Ann Arbor, 1951). Another useful book is F. Lauriston Bullard, *Lincoln in Marble and Bronze* (New Brunswick, 1952), which contains particularly good material on mid-twentieth-century Lincoln statues.

Franklin B. Mead had earlier combined a rather cursory survey of 26 existing Lincoln statues with a paean to Paul Manship's 1932 sculpture for the Lincoln National Life building in downtown Fort Wayne with *Heroic Statues in Bronze of Abraham Lincoln: Introducing the Hoosier Youth of Paul Manship* (Fort Wayne, Ind., 1932). Another essential study is Harry Rand, *Paul Manship* (Washington, 1922). Also helpful: Kim Bauer, *The Lincoln Legacy in Little-Known Illinois Sculpture*, on the Internet at www.prairie.org/detours/lincoln.

Rex Allen Smith's useful and entertaining *The Carving of Mount Rushmore* (New York, 1985), is the definitive study of the monument, replacing Willadene Price's catalogue, *Gutzon Borglum: The Man who Carved a Mountain* (n.p., 1961). The best book about the sculptor of the Lincoln Memorial is Michael Richman, *Daniel Chester French: An American Sculptor* (New York, 1976). Other sculptors are considered in Steven Rogstad, *Companionship in Granite* (Racine, 1998); Lois Kuhn Harris, *The World of Jo Davidson* (Philadelphia, rev. ed., 1958) and *Celebrating the Familiar: The Sculpture of Seward Johnson* (New York, 1987). The publication *Lincoln Lore* has long been a dependable source of information on new sculpture, e.g., "New Lincoln Statue in Mexico" by Angel Terrac in Juarez, *Lincoln Lore* 1515 (1964), 3.

One cannot deny the exhaustive research that informs Mabel Kunkel's sprawling book, *Abraham Lincoln: Unforgettable American* (Charlotte, 1976), an attempt, as the author put it in her dedication, to prove David C. Mearns's contention that "the proof of [Lincoln's] hold upon the minds and hearts of men is all around us." In a work that the junior high school teacher first undertook in preparation for an assembly program for her students, Kunkel amassed data on no fewer than 112 statues and countless "other ways and places in which Mr. Lincoln is remembered."

The authors of this chapter have also noted with appreciation the blunt—sometimes disturbing—view of public Lincoln sculpture seen through the unflinching lens of a modern photographer in George Tice, *Lincoln* (New Brunswick, 1984). And important new works on public memory and the post–Civil War American monument movement have arrived with Kathryn Allamong Jacob (photographs by Edward Harlan Remsberg), *Testament to Union: Public Monuments in Washington, D.C.* (Baltimore, 1998); Kirk Savage, *Standing Soldiers, Kneeling Slaves: Race, War, and Monument in Nineteenth-Century America* (Princeton, 1997); Harriet F. Sennie, *Contemporary Public Sculpture: Tradition, Transformation and Controversy* (New York, 1992); and, in a work dedicated to a single early twentieth-century sculptor, but offering useful commentary on the entire genre, Frederick C. Moffat, *Errant Bronzes; George Grey Barnard's Statues of Abraham Lincoln* (Newark, 1998). But aside from the volumes here cited, few scholars have dealt with the subject of modern public monuments—and none has attempted to treat the subject definitively after the beginning of the twentieth century.

Studies of modern Lincoln painting are even scarcer. The scholar and student owe a tremendous debt for the context provided in Merrill Peterson, *Lincoln in American Memory* (New York, 1994). His chapter, "Shapings in the Postwar Years," introduces Lincoln as the apotheosized myth, destined for generations of iconic treatment in art and statuary, and subsequent chapters usefully illustrate later Lincoln portrayals in several media.

Similarly, one cannot begin to consider "modern" history paintings without first consulting William Ayres, ed., *Picturing History: American History Painting 1770–1930*, particularly Bruce W. Chambers's chapter, "Painting the Civil War as History," and Barry Schwartz's "Picturing Lincoln." We have also benefited from the opportunity to read advance proofs of Schwartz' *Lincoln in Collective Memory* (Chicago, 2000).

Nor can the historian explore the intersecting images of Lincoln and African Americans without first consulting Albert Boime, *The Art of Exclusion: Representing Blacks in the Nineteenth Century* (Washington, 1990); Guy C. McElroy, *Facing History: The Black Image in American Art, 1710–1940* (San Francisco, 1990); and Hugh Honour, *The Image of the Black in Western Art IV: From the American Revolution to World War I* (Cambridge, Mass., 1989).

Individual African-American artists are considered in: Ellen Harkins Wheat, *Jacob Lawrence: American Painter* (Seattle, 1986); Judith E. Stein, *I Tell My Heart: The Art of Horace Pippin* (Philadelphia, 1993); Adelyn D. Breeskin, *William H. Johnson, 1901–1970* (Washington, 1971); and Richard J. Powell, *Homecoming: The Art and Life of William H. Johnson* (Washington, 1992). The standard reference work for the 1990s is Romare Bearden and Harry Henderson, *A History of African-American Artists From 1792 to the Present* (New York, 1993). For Native American artists see William L. Paul, Sr., "The Real Story of the Lincoln Totem," *The Alaska Journal* 1 (1971), 2–16; and Amelia M. Trevelyan, "Seeing A New World: The Works of Carl Beam and Frederick Remington." Gallery Notes, Gettysburg College, 1993.

A superb study of the ways that modern painters have been influenced by period photography is to be found in Van Deren Coke, *The Painter and the Photograph: From Delacroix to Warhol* (Albuquerque, 1964), a book notable for its incisive look at artist Marsden Hartley's Lincoln interpretations.

The ongoing, dramatic reappraisal of the works of another modern painter, Norman Rockwell, is explored in such volumes as Donald Stolz and Marshall Stolz, *The Advertising World of Norman Rockwell* (New York, 1985), and Maureen Hart Hennesey and Anne Knutson, *Norman Rockwell: Pictures for the American People* (New York, 1999).

Thomas Hart Benton told his life story in *An American in Art: A Professional and Technical Autobiography,* which included his personal history of the "American regionalism movement" (Lawrence, 1969). Marsden Hartley is analyzed in Townsend Luddington, *Marsden Hartley: The Biography of an American Artist* (Boston, 1922). See also Randall Griffey. The crucial biographies of two other artists who have portrayed Lincoln are Robert Descharnes and Gilles Néret, *Salvador Dali, 1904–1989: The Paintings* (2 vols., Cologne, 1994) and David Michaelis, *N. C. Wyeth: A Biography* (New York, 1998).

The long tradition and opinion-making influence of cartoon art is ably considered in a number of recent books, among them Roger A. Fischer, *Them Damned Pictures: Explorations in American Political Cartoon Art* (North Haven, Conn., 1996). See also, for example, Bill Mauldin, *Up Front* (1945); John Updike, *Pens and Needles: Literary Caricatures by David Levine* (New York, 1969) and *Caricatures and Watercolors by David Levine* (Oxford: Ashmolean Musem, 1987); Gahan Wilson, *Is Nothing Sacred* (New York, 1982); and Saul Steinberg, *The Discovery of America* (New York, 1992).

Something of a renaissance in the art of Lincoln illustration can be charted in such books as Milton Meltzer (with illustrations by Stephen Alcorn), *A. Lincoln in His Own Words* (New York, 1993), and Sam Fink, *The Illustrated Gettysburg Address* (New York, 1994). Particular acknowledgment is due illustrator-collector Lloyd Ostendorf, whose cover art has adorned the quarterly journal *Lincoln Herald* for decades, and whose works were gathered in 1962 for a young readers' book, *Abraham Lincoln: The Boy, the Man* (rev. ed., Springfield, Ill., 1996). Gabor S. Boritt has written on the subject previously with "The Art of Rea Redifer," *Blue and Gray* (October 1992), 55–57, and "Sam Fink of the Gettysburg Address," *Gallery Notes,* Gettysburg College, November 1999–2000.

Comprehensive surveys of Lincoln in philately and American currency are still needed, but Lincoln's image on American coins was tentatively explored in Robert P. King, *Lincoln in Numismatics* (rev. ed., 1966), and the supplement, Edgar Heyl, *A Comprehensive Index to King's Lincoln in Numismatics* (1967). There is still need for a definitive study of Lincoln postcards; James L. Lowe's 1967 *Lincoln Postcard Catalog: A Checklist of Postcards, Old and New* (rev. ed., Folsom, Penn., 1973), might have benefited from the rigorous imposition of a comprehensible system of dating.

Finally, the impact of the Lincoln image on the most elusive—but perhaps the most influential—of all the visual arts, motion pictures, is only now beginning to inspire scholarship. Two illustrated critical analyses recently appeared: Mark S. Reinhart, *Abraham Lincoln on Screen* (Jefferson, N.C., 1999), and Frank Thompson, *Abraham Lincoln: Twentieth-Century Portrayals* (Dallas, 1999). Each traces and appraises the many "Lincolns" of film and television in the past 96 years.

It is interesting—perhaps ironic, too—to note that the latter book, notwithstanding its broad title, in fact covers only the "moving" images of Lincoln (film, television, theater, even robots). Yet by century's end, the appearance of Marsden Hartley's "Young Worshipper of the Truth" in the provocative and widely attended exhibition *The American Century* at the Whitney Museum of American Art in New York, and his "The Great Good Man" on the set of the C-SPAN marathon devoted to presidents, confirmed anew that the ability of art to attract, involve, and excite the modern viewer remains undiminished. (See Barbara Haskell, *The American Century: Art and Culture, 1900–1950* [New York, 1999].) Indeed, as moving pictures flicker across our lives with increasingly breathtaking speed—on the Internet on video games and on satellite and cable television's countless stations—the arresting, incomparable power of the "static" portrait and the statue remains quite alive.

# Contributors

JEAN HARVEY BAKER is Elizabeth Todd Professor of History at Goucher College in Baltimore. Her books include *Affairs of Party: The Political Culture of Northern Democrats* (1984); *Mary Todd Lincoln: A Biography* (1987); and *The Stevensons: Biography of an American Family* (1994).

ROBERT V. BRUCE is Professor of History Emeritus at Boston University. His books include *Lincoln and the Tools of War* (1956); *1877: Year of Violence* (1959); *Bell: Alexander Graham Bell and the Conquest of Solitude* (1973); and *The Launching of Modern American Science, 1846–1876* (1987) which won the Pulitzer Prize in History for 1988.

DAVID HERBERT DONALD is the Charles Warren Professor of American History Emeritus at Harvard University, twice the winner of the Pulitzer Prize, for *Charles Sumner and the Coming of the Civil War* (1960) and *Look Homeward: A Life of Thomas Wolfe* (1987), and the winner of the Lincoln Prize for his best-selling biography, *Lincoln* (1995).

ALLEN C. GUELZO is the Dean of the Templeton Honors College at Eastern College, in St. Davids, Pennsylvania, where he is also Grace F. Kea Professor of American History. His books include *Edwards On The Will: A Century of American Philosophical Debate* (1989); *For the Union of Evangelical Christendom: The Irony of the Reformed Episcopalians* (1994); *The Crisis of the American Republic: A History of the Civil War and Reconstruction* (1995); and *Abraham Lincoln Redeemer President* (1999), which won the Lincoln Prize in 2000.

WILLIAM C. HARRIS, Professor of History, North Carolina State University, is the author of eight books and numerous articles on the Civil War and Reconstruction. His most recent book, *With Charity for All: Lincoln and the Restoration of the Union* (1997), received the Lincoln Prize, Second Place, in 1998.

HAROLD HOLZER serves as Vice President for Communications, The Metropolitan Museum of Art, New York. His books include, with Mark Neely and

Gabor Boritt, *The Lincoln Image* (1984); with Mario Cuomo, *Lincoln on Democracy* (1990); *Dear Mr. Lincoln* (1993); and *The Lincoln Mailbag* (1998). He served in 1999 as guest curator of the art exhibit "Lincoln from Life" at the Lincoln Museum, Fort Wayne, Indiana.

GERALD J. PROKOPOWICZ is Director of Public Programs at The Lincoln Museum in Fort Wayne, Indiana, where he edits *Lincoln Lore* and has co-authored the Museum's permanent exhibit, "Abraham Lincoln and the American Experiment." He is the author of *All for the Regiment: The Army of the Ohio, 1861–1862* (Chapel Hill, University of North Carolina Press, 2001 forthcoming).

DOUGLAS L. WILSON is George A. Lawrence Distinguished Service Professor Emeritus and Co-director of the Lincoln Studies Center at Knox College, Galesburg, Illinois. His Lincoln essays have been published as *Lincoln Before Washington: New Perspective on the Illinois Years* (1997). With Rodney O. Davis, he edited *Herndon's Informants: Letters, Interviews, and Statements about Abraham Lincoln* (1998). His *Honor's Voice: The Transformation of Abraham* Lincoln (1998) won the 1998 Lincoln Prize.

GABOR BORITT serves as Director of the Civil War Institute and Robert C. Fluhrer Professor of Civil War Studies at Gettysburg College. His books include *Lincoln and the Economics of the American Dream* (1978, 1994) and *The Gettysburg Nobody Knows* (1997).

# Index

The artists whose works appear in the portfolio, 154–277, as well as the titles of their works, are excluded from the index.